RODALE'S
COMPLETE
HOME
PRODUCTS
M A N U A L

RODALE'S COMPLETE HOME PRODUCTS MANUAL

THE BEST GUIDE FOR USING AND MAINTAINING YOUR APPLIANCES, TOOLS, FURNISHINGS—AND MORE!

By the Editors of Rodale Press

Produced by The Philip Lief Group, Inc.

Rodale Press
Emmaus, Pennsylvania

Disclaimer:
The information in this book has been carefully researched, and all efforts have been made to insure accuracy and safety. However, due to the variability of local conditions, materials, and personal skills, Rodale Press, Inc., and The Philip Lief Group, Inc., assume no responsibility for any injuries suffered or damages or losses incurred during or as a result of following this information. All manufacturers' instructions should be carefully studied and clearly understood before taking any action based on the information and advice presented in this book.

Copyright © 1989 by The Philip Lief Group, Inc.

Printed in the United States of America

Produced by The Philip Lief Group, Inc., 6 West 20th Street, New York, NY 10011
Project Editorial Director: Nancy Kalish
Design: The Sarabande Press

Library of Congress Cataloging-in-Publication Data

Rodale's complete home products manual: the best guide for using and maintaining your appliances, tools, furnishings and more! / by the editors of Rodale Press; produced by the Philip Lief Group, Inc.
    p. cm.
  ISBN 0–87857–797–1 hardcover—ISBN 0–87857–798–X paperback
   1. Home economics—Equipment and supplies. 2. Home economics—
Equipment and supplies—Maintenance and repair. 3. Domestic
engineering. I. Rodale Press. II. Philip Lief Group. III. Title:
Complete home products manual.
TX298.R63   1989
683'.8—dc19   88-36990
                                                                   CIP

Distributed in the book trade by St. Martin's Press

2 4 6 8 10 9 7 5 3 1 hardcover
2 4 6 8 10 9 7 5 3 1 paperback

Contents

A

Air Cleaners

Air Conditioners

Audio Equipment

AIR CLEANERS

Safety Notes

Know When to Turn It Off

• Always turn off the air cleaner and unplug it before cleaning it or the filter.
• To reduce the risk of fire or electrical shock, do not use an air cleaner fan with any solid-state fan speed control device.

Getting the Most from Your Product

Ion Generators Remove Smoke

Do you want to remove smoke from the air? Air cleaners based on the principle of negative ionization appear to be most effective in getting rid of this pollutant. The negative ion generator cleans the air through a process known as electrostatic precipitation. If you have another type of air cleaner and smoke removal is of paramount concern, purchase an ion generator for the room in which people smoke.

Smart Shopping Tip

Choosing a new tabletop air cleaner is simpler now than ever. The Association of Home Appliance Manufacturers certification program requires that manufacturers provide you with the "clean air delivery rate." The ratings appear on a seal on the machine or carton and allow you to compare its ability to remove dust, pollen, and tobacco smoke particles from the air in a 120-square-foot room.

Troubleshooting Chart

Problem	Cause	Solution
Air cleaner doesn't seem to be working effectively.	Air intakes may be obstructed.	Place machine where air can circulate freely and do not run it on the highest setting unless absolutely necessary.
Indicator light is off.	Power is off.	Check plug, wiring, and on/off switch.
	Cover is not on securely.	Check cover.
	Electronic cells are wet from washing (some models only).	Allow the cells to dry before using.
Crackling noise is heard.	Air cleaner is dirty or wet.	Clean the air cleaner and allow to dry before using.
	Collector plates or other parts are broken or bent.	Call service person.

Cleaning and Maintenance

Cleaning Foam Filters

Clean foam filters regularly—about once a week—to maintain your air cleaner's effectiveness. Wash the filter in a mild detergent, rinse, and squeeze dry with a towel or cloth. To avoid damaging the filter while cleaning it, treat it as you would fine woolens. Squeeze, rather than twist, out the water after washing the filter. Allow it to dry before putting it back in place. Between washings, you can vacuum the foam filter in place in most models.

Filter Lifespan

Your air cleaner's filter will last three to six months before it needs to be replaced. But that can vary with the amount of time you use the appliance and the kinds and quantities of impurities it has to deal with. Examining the filter won't necessarily tell you much, since it will naturally get dirty with use. If you've had lots of company who smoked, if the pollen count was high, or if you've experienced any other conditions that would have made the filter work overtime, count on replacing it after three months. Even if you rarely use the cleaner, replace the filter once a year.

Cleaning the Housing

Treat the air cleaner's housing carefully, making sure you don't inadvertently damage the ion emitting needle or other important parts when you clean it. With a soft brush or cloth, gently wipe dust from inside the housing, the access panels, and the air exit grill. If the housing's exterior gets dirty, clean it with a damp cloth and mild, nonabrasive detergent, but be sure you don't let any excess water drip into the air cleaner.

Cleaning an Ion Generator

If you have an ion generator air cleaner, cleaning the essential part—the little ion emitter pin—is a simple matter. Turn the unit off and unplug it. Then just dip a cotton swab in alcohol and wipe the dirt from the pin. Even with the machine turned off you may feel a slight static shock. This is normal and presents no danger.

The main filter should not be washed. It will need to be replaced every three to six months.

Cleaning an Electronic C Cell and Prefilter

Clean the prefilter first by shaking or vacuuming out the accumulated dirt. If it still appears dirty, soak it in an alkaline—not acid—detergent solution.

To clean the cell, mix 4 ounces of alkaline detergent with a gallon of hot water (150°F to 170°F). Immerse the cell in the solution and soak for about fifteen minutes, stirring the solution intermittently. Rinse the cell in a clean container of hot water by letting it soak for five to ten minutes. Let the cell drain and air dry before energizing.

Be Careful When You Clean

When you're ready to clean an electronic cell, follow these safety precautions:

• Read the safety instructions on the label of the alkaline detergent you'll use.
• Clean with hot water. Wear protective gloves or allow the cell to cool after washing and before handling.
• Be gentle with the collector plates and ionizing wires—they can be damaged easily. Rinse away any detergent residue on the plates after cleaning them. Tip the cell so the tubes supporting the plates can drain properly.

What Your Product Won't Do

It Can't Cope with Smoke

A roomful of smokers could temporarily overwhelm even the best air cleaner. If your guests love to smoke and you or others are sensitive to the fumes, try these extra measures to cope:

• Place a bowl of vinegar near or in each corner of the room to absorb smoke odor. You can hide them behind the furniture or under tables. You can also put dishes of activated charcoal around the room to absorb the odor.
• Light candles. They will remove some smoke, believe it or not, and add a touch of grace to the room.

Pet Hair Is a Problem

Your air cleaner may not alleviate your allergy to your dog or cat, but you can still live with the animal if you ban Fido or Figaro from your bedroom. When it's brushing time, have your pet brushed outside by a friend or family member.

You Still Need to Dust

Air cleaners remove only airborne dust. That's fine for people who are allergic to this substance, but it doesn't help housekeepers much, since large dust particles will still settle on objects. You have to remove the dust the old-fashioned way: with a mop or rag.

AIR CONDITIONERS

Safety Notes

Use the Right Wire

It's important to make sure you use the right size wire if you have to replace your air conditioner's electrical cord. Just take a piece of the old cord with you to the store and match it to the new cord you plan to purchase. You'll need a grounded, three-wire cord and a heavy-duty adaptor with a grounding wire if you're plugging the unit into a standard two-prong outlet. To avoid danger, do not use an extension cord and do not remove the grounding prong from the cord you are using.

Avoid Overloaded Circuits

Avoid plugging any appliance—especially those that require substantial current, such as an iron—into the same circuit as your air conditioner. A good rule of thumb is to install a separate circuit dedicated to the air conditioner and protected by a slow-blow fuse or circuit breaker, especially if the unit bears a rating of more than 7.5 amps. Remember to wait at least three minutes after shutting off the air conditioner before you restart it. Otherwise, you risk tripping a circuit breaker or blowing a fuse.

If you move your air conditioner to another room, examine the circuit breaker or fuse through which your appliance will draw current to make sure that its amp rating is appropriate for your unit.

Use It Wisely

- Don't operate the air conditioner if someone is using a flammable spray (hair spray, lacquer, paint, and so on) nearby.
- If your unit has an air filter, use it and clean it regularly.
- Do not stick anything into the air discharge area while the machine is on, because it may come into contact with the rotating fan, which could be very dangerous. Be especially aware of this problem when children are playing near the air conditioner. Also, don't remove the fan guard, if your unit has one.
- As with all appliances, turn off the unit and unplug it before inspecting or cleaning. And turn off and unplug the unit if you will be away from the house or not using the air conditioner for a long time.
- Make sure you use a new fuse—not a copper or steel wire—to replace a blown fuse.
- The air conditioner can be very dangerous if it operates while it is wet, so be very careful when you are cleaning the unit. Do not spray or spill water directly onto the unit, fan coil unit, or remote control.
- When elderly, infirm, or very young people are in the room, you may want to readjust the temperature control. In general, make sure that the flow of air is not directed at people, plants, or pets for a long period of time; the chill can be counterproductive at close range.
- Be careful not to pull the unit's cord too forcefully, because it may break at the fan coil unit where you can't see the break. Exposed electrical wire will cause shocks!
- If you experience a power outage, turn the air conditioner's control knob to the "off" position. You don't want the unit turning on when all the other household electrical devices go on again; the voltage drops, which can cause fuses to blow.
- Many air-conditioner manufacturers caution not to use their units when the room temperature drops below 70°F.

Getting the Most from Your Product

Bigger Isn't Necessarily Better

An air conditioner that's too large for the room it must cool can do more to make summer's heat uncomfortable than to relieve it. Sure, a big one *will* bring the temperature down—and quickly—but that's the problem. An air conditioner should reduce humidity in a room as well as cool it. If the machine cools the room too quickly and shuts off before it has a chance to bring the humidity to the proper level, it almost defeats the purpose of having the unit in the first place. In order to choose the correct size air conditioner, use this formula: Take the square footage of the room or rooms you wish to cool and multiply that number by 27. This will give you the size air conditioner you need in BTUs.

House Climate Affects Efficiency

Unlike your bedroom, your living room is probably not closed off by a door. So if you have an air conditioner in the living room, the climate in the rest of the house will affect its efficiency. You can make sure that conditions in other areas of the house don't put an extra strain on your air conditioner by taking these steps:

- Keep your attic ventilated with a fan or louvers. This helps keep the overall temperature of the house down as the hot air that rises to the top of the house is allowed to escape.
- Use vent fans in the kitchen, bathrooms, and laundry room to hold down the humidity level.

Setting the Thermostat

If your air conditioner is new, it will take you a while to find the right combination of thermostat setting and fan speed to keep you comfortable. Start by turning the thermostat to its maximum setting and letting the machine run until the temperature and humidity feel just right. Then turn the control back until you hear a click and the machine becomes quieter (that's the compressor shutting down). Wait about an hour. Is it a little too cool? Then turn the controls to a slightly lower setting.

Warming up too much? Turn the thermostat up, but just a little. These fine adjustments should help you zero in on the setting that makes you most comfortable. Keep in mind that your air conditioner must work extra hard to maintain coolness in a room full of people. You'll need to adjust the settings *before* the crowd arrives.

Making the Move

Moving a large air conditioner usually requires the help of one or more people. Is removing your unit for the winter and reinstalling it in the spring a necessary ordeal? If you live in the snowbelt, warm air escaping and cold air seeping in through the unit may increase your heating bill substantially, not to mention the annoying drafts it will create. Before moving the unit, however, first try using a prefabricated air-conditioner cover to cut down on drafts; you can also fashion your own cover with a piece of plastic that is at least 6 mils thick. Keep a close eye on your first few heating bills. If the cover doesn't seem to be helping much, then you'll have to remove the air conditioner.

Keep Your Cool

Even with all the controls set just right, you could be undermining the effectiveness of your air conditioner if you let direct sunlight heat the house while the air conditioner tries to cool it. Close all the drapes or blinds on the sunny side of your house, and check to make sure that no furniture or drapes block the flow of air from the air conditioner. For best results, adjust the louvers on the unit so that air flows toward both sides of the room and slightly upward.

Here are other things you can do to help your air conditioner run more efficiently:

- Use light-colored paint on the exterior of your house to reflect sunlight.
- Be sure your house is sufficiently insulated.
- Install weather stripping on outside windows and doors.
- If you have a fireplace, close the damper when you run the air conditioner.

Plantings for Efficiency

Vegetation can aid—or hinder—your efforts to cool your home. Plant trees near the windows on the west side of your house to shade the windows from the afternoon sun. While you wait for those trees to grow, you may want to put up awnings. Make sure that shrubbery near the air conditioner does not block the flow of air around the unit, and don't plant flowers close by—excess amounts of pollen may be drawn into the unit.

Don't "Choke" Your Air Conditioner

Blocking the flow of air around your air conditioner will prevent it from effectively cooling your room. If the blockage is great enough, cool air coming out of the machine may be directed back into it. If this happens, the thermostat tells the air conditioner that the air temperature is too cool, and the unit shuts down. However, the thermostat quickly senses that the room temperature is too high, and it directs the machine to turn on again. These off-and-on-again cycles could continue until the machine damages itself, so be sure to avoid blocking air flow near the unit.

Come Home to a Cool House

Nobody likes to wait half an hour or more for the house to cool off when coming home from a hard day at work. But running an air conditioner to cool an empty house is expensive and wasteful. Purchase an inexpensive timer, the kind used to turn lights on and off and rated to handle the current drawn by the air conditioner. Set it to turn on the air conditioner about half an hour to 45 minutes before you get home.

Use It as a Fan

Would you like to create just a bit of a breeze on a warm but dry day? Most air conditioners have a setting marked "fan" that will give you a breeze without using excessive electricity. (If your air conditioner doesn't have a fan setting, turn your thermostat to its lowest position.) Use the "exhaust" control in its open position with the fan when you want to clear your house of cooking odors and smoke. Just remember to close the exhaust when you finish airing out the house, since an open exhaust will decrease the air conditioner's efficiency the next time you run it on "cool."

Turn It Off

Do you *really* want to save money? When evening temperatures drop down into the mid-70s, use an exhaust fan instead of your air conditioner. At that temperature, the outside air will be cooler than the air in your house; using a fan to suck in the cool air should be just right for a comfortable night's sleep. It will also cost you about one-tenth the amount to use an exhaust fan rather than your air conditioner—even if you run your air conditioner on its "fan only" setting. When the temperature dips a bit more and you don't need the fan, just open your windows from both top and bottom, and make sure you have at least one window open on each side of your house to create cross-ventilation.

Troubleshooting Chart

Problem	Cause	Solution
Air conditioner is not working.	Electrical plug may be disconnected.	Check to make sure that the plug is firmly pushed into the socket.
	Fuse may be blown or circuit breaker tripped.	Check fuses and circuit breakers.
	Safety device may be activated when outdoor temperature reaches into the 100s (only on some models).	Wait 20 minutes, then reset.
The air does not feel cool enough.	Air filter may be clogged.	Clean air filter.
	Window or door may be open.	Close off the room.
	Unit's air passage may be blocked.	Clear the airway.

(continued)

Troubleshooting Chart—Continued

Problem	Cause	Solution
The air does not feel cool enough	Thermostat may be set too warm.	Put the thermostat on a cooler setting.
	Room temperature may be below 70°F.	Wait until room temperature rises to more than 70°F.
	Louvers not positioned for good air circulation.	Move louvers for better air circulation.
Ice forms on the cooling coil.	Outdoor temperature may have fallen to below 70°F or thermostat may be set too cool.	Defrost by putting the unit to its "fan" setting (only on some models).
	Filter may be dirty.	Clean air filter.
The unit makes a hissing or shhrr-ing noise.	The refrigerant is circulating. This is not a problem.	
The unit makes a pinging noise.	Water is dripping from the unit. This is not a problem when the weather is humid.	
	If the weather is *not* humid and water is dripping from the unit.	Check with your installer.
The unit makes a ticking noise.	The thermostat is operating. This is not a problem.	

Cleaning and Maintenance

Cleaning the Filter

Yes, you can wash your air conditioner's filter with mild soap and warm water. But you will do a neater—and just as effective—job with your vacuum cleaner. Check your filter at least once a week to be sure it's clean enough to do an efficient job.

If you'd rather stick to the traditional soap-and-water method, washing the filter at least twice a month should do the trick. Make sure you rinse the filter thoroughly after cleaning. On some models you just gently shake the water from the filter and air dry it in the shade if necessary. Other models use filters that can be wrung gently; these filters will spring back to shape.

Keep the Cabinet Clean

Cleaning the outside of the air conditioner is a simple task—just use a dust rag or, if the cabinet is very dirty, a cloth dampened in a solution of warm water and mild detergent. Never pour water onto the cabinet, and never use more powerful cleaners such as benzine, gasoline, polishing powder, or thinner.

Early Dust Warning

You should periodically vacuum the evaporator fins (just behind the filter) to keep them free of dust. Even if you don't notice any dust, a torn filter means that household dust has had a chance to get through, reducing the efficiency of the machine. If you spot a tear when cleaning the filter, change it—and vacuum the fins before you use the air conditioner again.

Cleaning the Drain Pan

Some models of air conditioners, especially split-system units, have a drain pan that needs to be cleaned occasionally. You may have to remove a few screws or screw bolts first (after the unit is unplugged), but once that's done, just pour a stream of water from a tea kettle into the drain pan to remove the accumulated dust. Plan to clean the pan when you shut the machine off for the year.

When Your Air Conditioner Sits Idle

Each time you turn your unit off—and on—for the season, there are a few extra steps you should take. *Before* a period of prolonged idleness:

1. Allow the unit to dry out by running the fan for half a day on a sunny day.

2. Turn the air conditioner off and unplug it.
3. Clean the drain pan, the air filter, and the exterior of the unit.

After a period of prolonged idleness:

1. Check the unit for any obstructions, looking at the air inlets and outlets or the condensing unit and fan unit.
2. Check to make sure that the ground wire is still connected.
3. Clean the exterior of the unit, and the drain pan if it's dirty.
4. Plug in the unit and turn it on.

AUDIO EQUIPMENT

Safety Notes

Avoid Audio Injuries

Don't ruin the enjoyment of your audio equipment by becoming the victim of a preventable accident. Follow these precautions:

Antennae: Unless you really know what you're doing, have a professional install your television and FM antenna. If you do it yourself, check to make sure that you've grounded the antenna and that it's well away from power lines.

While it is uncommon, lightning storms can damage your audio equipment and cause electrical shock—even when you have your stereo turned off! If you know a storm is approaching, or if you're going away on vacation, disconnect your FM antenna and unplug your equipment.

Headphones: You can suffer hearing loss from listening to excessively loud music over headphones. You know you've overdone it if you hear a ringing in your ears or can't hear the phone ring even when you listen with an open-air design headset. Before you put on the headphones, set the volume level to zero and then turn it up gradually. Even at reasonable sound levels, take a break after about an hour.

Whether or not you play music loudly, never use headphones while driving. With the soundproofing in most cars, it's hard enough as it is to hear sirens and other danger signals. In addition, wearing headphones while driving is illegal in many states.

Let It Breathe

Your stereo equipment will overheat if it can't breathe. This could lead to equipment failure and could start a fire. Common causes of air-vent blockage include placing units on soft surfaces, such as carpeting; stacking components in a way that covers their air vents (follow the manufacturer's suggestions about what can go on top of what); custom-building enclosures without allowing for enough ventilation; and covering the air holes with decorative objects.

Getting the Most from Your Product

Changing the Acoustics

Were you disappointed with the sound of your stereo speakers when you got them home? Did they sound less impressive in your den or living room than they did at the store? How you place the speakers can alter the acoustics and have an effect on the sound quality your stereo produces. For example, heavy drapes, thick carpeting, and plush furniture will absorb a good deal of sound, making the music sound thin and dull, possibly even muffled. Try opening the drapes when you play the stereo. If you have your speakers on the rug, buy or make stands that raise the speakers to a seated person's ear level. Remove any soft wall decorations (needlepoint, velvet-backed plaques, and so on) from the area near the speakers.

Can the Volume Damage Your Speakers?

Have you heard about the possibility of compact discs damaging your speakers at high-volume levels? It could happen— especially if you have inexpensive speakers with low power-handling capabilities. You shouldn't have any problem, however, unless you like to play the sound of a cymbal at glass-shattering levels or you have a teenager in the house who is enamored of heavy metal.

Whether you're playing compact discs, cassettes, or records, your speakers can be damaged by playing them too loudly only if the number of watts per channel that your power amp or receiver can deliver exceeds your speakers' capabilities.

Out-of-Phase Speakers

You may not be getting all the sound you paid for when you bought your speakers if you didn't hook them up correctly. In fact, if you didn't read the directions when you attached them to your receiver, you may have connected them out of phase. When the wires from the receiver to the speakers are not connected correctly, part of the sound from one speaker will cancel sound from the other, making them out of phase. You'll know if you've done this if the low notes are diminished consistently when you play music.

To avoid out-of-phase speakers, some manufacturers color-code or otherwise identify the two strands of speaker wire to make it easy to attach all the positive and negative wires at exactly the right place at the receiver and at the speakers. But if your equipment isn't identified clearly or if you think you might have crossed a wire somewhere, there's a simple way to check your speakers. Listen to music with a high bass content (lots of low notes). Now reverse the wires at one of your speakers and listen again. The connection that produces the deeper, richer sound is the one to use.

Try Different Brands of Audio Cassettes

If you have a cassette deck, especially one costing less than about $150, it's a good idea to experiment with different brands of tape before picking one you'll stick with. All cassette decks apply a signal called the "bias" to the tape when recording. Every deck has a control that allows you to set the correct bias for a tape within a broad range. There are usually three settings: "normal," "chrome," and "metal." However, variations between the magnetic characteristics of different brands within these types may cause a mismatch with your deck's electronics, producing dull-sounding tapes even when you've chosen the correct setting.

Music lovers with decks that have bias fine-tuning—a feature often found in more expensive equipment—need not worry about this problem, since they can vary the bias current by small degrees to match their deck exactly to a particular brand of tape. The rest of us have to play it by ear—literally. Buy samples of a few brands of tape, then make recordings from a record or compact disc—be sure to select the correct general setting for the type of tape you're using. Then compare your tape recording to the original. Listen especially for accurate reproduction of high notes, such as those from a flute or trumpet. The tape that sounds best is the one you should buy from now on.

Dolby B or C: Does It Make a Difference?

If you bought your cassette deck after 1980, you probably have two types of noise reduction: Dolby B and Dolby C. Dolby C is newer and better, since it reduces background hiss on your recordings to an inaudible level. Dolby B is included so that you may play tapes made with Dolby B and record tapes for play-back on decks that have only Dolby B noise reduction.

What happens if you select the wrong noise reduction method when you play back a tape? You will hear sound that is either too bright or too dull, depending on which kind of Dolby you have mismatched (you will not, however, harm the record-ing). In fact, should the highs on a recording sound too accentu-ated or dulled, the first thing you should check is whether you set the noise reduction control for the Dolby type used in making the recording. Because of the potential for mismatching this setting, whenever you make a tape recording, note on the label which type of noise reduction system you used.

Preventing Cassette Erasure

As with videocassettes, it's very easy to accidentally erase a valuable recording on an audiocassette. All it takes is mislabel-ing the cassette, or not labeling it at all, so that you think it's blank. That can't happen, however, if you use a knife or screw-driver to knock out the flaps on the back of the cassette shell. By doing so, you'll prevent accidentally erasing or recording over your tape. Should you later decide to reuse the cassette, you can put some transparent tape over the openings where the flaps were and record on it again.

Push "Stop" Before Turning Off the Power

Common sense might dictate that if you're playing an audiocassette and you want to stop it in the middle, you can just turn off your stereo and resume listening at any time. Depending on how your cassette deck was made, that might be true. In many decks, however, cutting the power does not disengage the tape-playing mechanism. This leaves the rubber pinch roller, an important component that helps guide the tape and maintain it at the proper tension, pressed against another component called the capstan. Leaving the pinch roller in this position for too long could deform the rubber, giving your tape a bumpy ride when you next play it. The result will not sound pleasant. So if you're in the middle of a tape, push the "stop" button *before* you shut off the equipment.

Doubling Up Your Television and Stereo Antennae

If you already have a rooftop television antenna, you can use it to hook up the FM tuner on your stereo receiver. A device called a signal splitter allows you to do this; it costs only a few dollars, and you can get it at most television or electronics stores. The splitter takes the signal from the antenna and divides it into VHF and UHF, and FM. Once you attach it to the wire from the antenna, all you have to do is hook up the wire from the splitter carrying the FM signal to the antenna screws on the back of your receiver.

Cleaning and Maintenance

Keep Moisture at Bay

Humidity will inevitably harm your audio equipment. Beware especially of putting audio components on the back porch (as some people do with their speakers in the summer) or too near a window. When you clean your components, use a *dry*, lint-free cloth.

Record Care

Notwithstanding the advent of the digital era, most people who listen to music still have LPs. LP (long-playing) records have been sold since 1948, but if you want to enjoy them for many more years, they do need pampering. Avoid touching anything but their outer edge and label. Keep them free of dust: Clean records each time before playing them. You can buy a good commercial cleaner for less than $15 (Discwasher® is probably the most widely available). These cleaners usually consist of a brush and a liquid and are easy to use. Avoid cleaning records with silicone-impregnated cloths, which leave a residue.

Clean the Stylus, Too

Many people (even some audiophiles) think they have problems with their stereo equipment when their records sound noisy and the stereo begins distorting the high notes. In fact, the problem is probably just a dirty stylus (the phonograph "needle"). To clean the stylus, use a commercial cleaning fluid and brush—not your finger. You can check for dust accumulation with a small mirror (often supplied with the cleaner), but you should clean the stylus periodically even if you don't spot dust.

Demagnetize Your Deck

Cleaning and demagnetizing your tape deck should be a monthly task. While the task is very simple, it requires some diligence on your part, since you won't notice any major problems that will remind you that it's time to clean. Demagnetizing assures that no buildup of oxide particles will occur on your tapes, a process that is subtle and easy to miss. The difference this buildup makes in most average systems is negligible—many people probably wouldn't notice the difference in sound until the high notes start sounding a little dull. Nonetheless, most manufacturers suggest that you clean and demagnetize the heads regularly.

You can buy head-cleaning and demagnetizing cassettes for under $20 at audio stores. To use them, pop them in the machine and "play" them as if they were regular cassettes.

CD Care

Your compact discs will probably last longer than you will. (In fact, the Library of Congress is preserving both audio and video archival material by transferring them to this medium.) On the other hand, the care you used to lavish on records will still be necessary with these new marvels. Dust, fingerprints, and dirt will do in your compact discs. Mistreatment won't produce the pops and clicks you hear on records, but it will bring about something much worse: Whole sections of music can be lost where the compact disc's surface has been marred. When your player's laser beam encounters these areas on the disc, it won't be able to read them.

To protect your investment in compact discs, handle them by touching only their edges, and keep them in the containers in which they came when you're not playing them. If you have a portable or automobile player, keep your discs out of the sun—they'll melt. If you smudge a compact disc's surface, wipe it off with a clean cloth—from the center toward the outer edge of the disc, *not* in a circular pattern. Or get one of the commercial disc cleaners that sells for about $20. Although your player can cope with minor scratches, anything more serious may cause permanent loss of some or all of the information on the disc. The industry is developing new products that may be able to help with such disasters. If you end up with a severely scratched disc, ask at your audio store about such "fixer-uppers."

Troubleshooting Chart

Problem	Cause	Solution
Sound is coming out of only one side of headphones.	Loose connection.	Make sure you have the headphone plugged all the way into the jack on the receiver. If this doesn't work, take the headphones in for repair.

Troubleshooting Chart—Continued

Problem	*Cause*	*Solution*
Loud, squeaking sound (feedback) coming from speakers.	Record player is too close to speakers	Move the components farther apart.
Sound is coming from only one speaker, or is distorted in one speaker.	Loose connection to receiver; speaker control switch on amplifier or receiver is not set to transmit sound to both speakers; or the balance control on the receiver is turned all the way in one direction.	Tighten the connections to the receiver and check the speaker control switch and balance control knob and correct if necessary. If the problem still remains, take speaker in for repairs.
Tone arm doesn't track across record.	Defective record.	Check with a new one.
	Dirt on stylus.	Clean off stylus.
	Worn stylus.	Use magnifying glass to check stylus for worn or cracked point. Replace if necessary.
	Record changer not level.	Level the changer.
	Wrong anti-skate setting.	Reduce anti-skate setting.
FM stereo broadcasts are garbled.	Multipath distortion caused by living near tall buildings or mountains.	Replace the simple dipole (crossed wire) antenna that came with your receiver with an indoor TV (rabbit ear) antenna with a directional dial. Tune the station in and turn the dial until the distortion disappears.

(continued)

Troubleshooting Chart—Continued

Problem	Cause	Solution
Radio interference in the kitchen.	Radio may be too close to your microwave oven.	Move radio away from microwave. If you still get static, plug it into an outlet that is on a separate circuit from the microwave.

B

Bicycles

Blankets, Electric

Blenders

Blow Dryers

Books

Bug Killers, Electric

BICYCLES

Safety Notes

Ride Carefully

- Always wear a helmet.
- Wear reflective clothing or strips of reflective tape on your clothing and bicycle when riding at night. Keep your light on after dark.
- Always ride *with* the traffic and observe traffic rules.
- Use hand signals when turning. Extend your left arm straight out for a left turn, bend it at the elbow for a right turn, and point diagonally downward for a stop. To make a left turn in city traffic, proceed straight through the intersection, pull over to the right and dismount, and wait for the traffic light to change so you can cross the street.
- When riding with another person or in a group, ride single file in traffic. Riding two abreast is okay on quiet roads, but it's a safety hazard in traffic-dense areas.
- On a hot day, fill your tires with air at a pressure four or five pounds less than you would ordinarily use. Otherwise, the air in your tires could be heated to the point where a blowout will occur.
- When riding on a street where cars are parked, always be alert to the possibility that a car door will be opened suddenly. Also watch for children playing near the side of the road and animals roaming nearby so you will be ready to brake if they should dart into your path.
- Watch for gravel, debris, sewer grates, potholes, bridge-expansion joints, and similar hazards.
- Stop at all intersections—drivers often ignore stop signs.
- Do not use personal stereos with headphones while riding. You need the use of all your senses to know what's going on around you. Also, they're illegal in some states.
- The horns and bells that most people buy for their bikes aren't loud enough to be heard over the sound of traffic. To be heard in a crowd, buy a Freon-powered or compressed-air-powered horn, available at most bike stores.

Watch Out for Railroad Tracks . . .

Crossing railroad tracks improperly can do some serious damage to your bike and to you. Your bike can suffer a dented rim and or ruined tire, while you could go flying. Slow down, get up off your seat, and cross the tracks at a right angle. Slow is best because crossing too fast can cause your wheel to bottom out on the track. Distribute your weight equally between your feet on the pedals and your hands on the handlebars; this gives you a softer crossing. Crossing at a right angle (perpendicular to the tracks) avoids getting your front wheel caught in the track groove.

. . . and Dogs

If you frequently ride along roads where dogs run free, there are several things you can do to ensure your safety:

- Yell. Sometimes all it takes to discourage a growling dog is a firm "No" or "Stay." Just say it like you mean it, and the animal will probably obey.
- Use a repellent. A well-aimed squirt from your water bottle should do the trick.
- Ride faster. Usually, the dog is merely trying to chase you away from its "territory." The faster you get out of there, the happier the dog will be.

One thing you *shouldn't* do is try to physically harm the dog by kicking or hitting it. The dog may very well give you a nasty bite in retaliation.

Getting the Most from Your Product

Opt for a Comfortable Seat

A comfortable seat (or saddle) is key to a comfortable ride, especially a *long* ride. So make sure your riding position is correct. Start by adjusting the seat to the height that's best for you. To determine that height, straddle the bike and rotate the pedal to its lowest position. Now sit down. Your heel should just touch the pedal when you extend your leg. If it doesn't, adjust the seat by loosening the bolt that holds it to the seat bar. A saddle that's too high will make you rock as you pedal, and a saddle with its nose slanting down will make you slide forward. If you still feel uncomfortable after making some seat adjustments, you probably need a different saddle style—one that's slightly narrower or wider may be a better fit for you.

Don't Hunch Over the Handlebars

If you have a 10-speed bicycle, you shouldn't be hunched over the handlebars when you ride. As you bend to grip the handlebars, your spine should be straight. Adjust the handlebars so that, initially, they are about the same height as your saddle. Then, with experience, you may want to move them down to the position that best suits you. If you have dropped handlebars, keep them either level or slanted downward by a few degrees.

Handy Handlebar Tips

There is no "correct" position for your hands on the handlebars. But when you're riding at a fast clip downhill, it's a good idea to keep your hands close to the brakes. Position your brake levers on the handlebars so that it never takes you more than a second to reach them.

Many cyclists find that wrapping the handlebars with tape keeps their hands from slipping, and thus can help prevent accidents. There are several types of bar tape available. Adhesive-backed cotton is the most common. It gives you a good grip, but doesn't take long to become tattered and dirty. Brightly colored plastic tape is fashionable and stays clean, but lacks padding and is slippery when wet. Padded tape is comfortable but is twice as expensive as the cloth or plastic tapes. Some riders combine different tapes to get a comfortable grip. There's an art to applying bar tape—ask for a demonstration at your local bike shop.

Use Caution with Caliper Brakes

If you're new to the world of multi-speed biking, you may need some riding time to get used to the powerful caliper brakes. If you decide to add caliper brakes to your old bike, test them out in an area that has little or no traffic and start out by biking and braking slowly. Braking too suddenly could send you flying over the handlebars.

Always work caliper brakes with a gentle squeeze. Keep in mind that the brake that controls the front wheel is the brake that has the greater control over reducing your speed. This is because applying the brakes puts extra weight on the front wheel. When you brake, start first with the rear brake, then gently squeeze the front brake. Practice this maneuver at slow speeds first to get the hang of it. If you have to make a quick stop, push your weight back on the seat as you apply the brakes.

When you're not braking, the brake shoes should be $\frac{1}{16}$ to $\frac{1}{8}$ of an inch from the wheel rim. Check the brake shoes frequently and replace them as soon as they become worn.

Get in Gear

The derailleur gears on your bike may be even less familiar to you than the caliper brakes. They work by moving the chain between the sprockets. Always continue to pedal when changing gears. When you shift into a new gear, you may hear some disturbing noises, even after you think you've completed the shift. This just means that you now need to fine-tune the shift. Move the gear levers slightly, either forward or backward, until the noise stops and the ride feels smooth.

The proper gear ratio to use on any type of terrain is that which enables you to continue pedaling at a steady pace. Most people find it comfortable to turn the pedals about 60 to 80 revolutions per minute.

Toe Clips: Do You Need Them?

Toe clips aid riding efficiency by keeping your feet on or close to the pedal throughout the full revolution. They also help by allowing one foot to pull the pedal up while the other foot pushes down.

You will get the most out of toe clips when riding long distances. If you use them while riding on short trips in your neighborhood or in city traffic, keep the straps loose so you can pull your foot out quickly in case you must make an emergency stop.

Cleaning and Maintenance

Keep It Oiled and Clean

Three or four times a year, more often if you do a lot of biking, use a petroleum-base lubricant on:

- Brake levers and mechanisms (*not* on the brake shoes themselves)
- Cables
- Derailleurs
- Drive Chain
- Pedals

You can clean every part of your bike except the chain with a damp cloth. Clean the chain with a solvent-soaked rag. Oil the chain only after it dries.

Unless you're a knowledgeable do-it-yourselfer, have your bike inspected by a bike mechanic at least once a year. This is a good time for minor repairs, replacement of worn parts, wheel adjustment, and lubrication.

Full Tires Ride Best

To get the best ride from your bike, be sure to maintain the proper tire pressure. You can find the recommended tire pressure printed on the sidewall. If not, call your local bike shop for recommendations. Don't use a gas station air pump to inflate your bike tires. These types of pumps quickly deliver a large volume of air, which can blow out your bike tire.

Cosmetic Surgery

To preserve your bike frame's integrity, it's essential that bare metal spots be covered. You can do it yourself, but be prepared for a touch-up job that leaves noticeable results.

First, be aware that you probably won't get an exact match of your original paint. Check out the model paints in your local hobby shop and choose the closest color you can find. Then follow these steps to repair a fresh, small nick or gouge:

1. Clean the area to be painted with rubbing alcohol. Let dry for 10 minutes.
2. Position the bike with the nick facing up.
3. Use a toothpick or tiny brush to carefully apply the paint. Don't get any paint on the edges of the crack.
4. If needed, repeat the above steps on successive days until the nick is evenly filled in.
5. Let the paint cure for two weeks, then rub the area with fine compound and a soft cloth. Then apply auto or bike wax.

For large chips and scratches, you basically follow the same procedure, but start by feathering the edges of the chip by wet sanding with 600-grit paper. Clean and then apply paint as outlined above, but wet sand again after each application of paint.

BLANKETS, ELECTRIC

Safety Notes

Make a Good Connection

Make a special effort to ensure that you firmly connect the electrical control to the blanket. Once you plug the controls into the wall socket, part of the connector that attaches the control to the blanket is electrically live. So if this part protrudes from the blanket instead of being firmly in place, you risk electric shock or a fire.

Keep the Cord out of Harm's Way

It can be especially hard to avoid damaging the cord of an electric blanket since its path may take it between the mattress and box spring, through bed slats, and around and under foot-boards and headboards. Running it past and through these obstacles can wrinkle, pinch, and fray the cord. If you notice this happening to the cord on your electric blanket, try rear-ranging its path so that it runs under the bed instead of the mattress. If that doesn't work, keep the electric cord out of harm's way by installing hooks out of view on the footboard or headboard.

Be Careful of Faulty Heating Elements

Do not attempt to repair a shorted, open or frayed heating element that is sewn inside your electric blanket. Chances are, a worn wire will have little or no insulation left, and if you touch one, the result will be a severe electrical shock. If your heating element is malfunctioning, and it is sewn in and not a separate unit, discard the blanket.

Did You Pick Up a "Bargain"?

If you bought an off-brand electric blanket at a way-off price, watch out! While these appliances have a solid safety record, remember that they're generating heat electrically while you sleep, and you need to be sure that you bought a safe product. A good indication that your electric blanket was made with safety in mind is the "UL" symbol—the Underwriters Laboratories mark of approval. If your blanket is not so marked, consider getting rid of it and buying one that does come with this seal.

No Pets Allowed

If your pet usually sleeps on your bed, you'll have to change its habits when you buy an electric blanket. Pets can cause the blanket to overheat where they sleep, and they can also damage the wires inside the blanket with their claws.

Other Prudent Precautions

• Don't use an electric blanket on a child's bed unless he or she understands the instructions and can operate the controls easily.

- Don't use the blanket on a waterbed, sofa, bunkbed or mechanically adjustable bed.
- Don't dry clean or use bleach when washing your electric blanket. The chemicals can destroy the insulation on the wires.
- Don't use safety pins to secure the blanket or clothespins when drying it; they can damage the wiring.
- Use only one electric blanket per bed, and never use it with an electric heating pad or mattress pad.
- Don't place other blankets on top of an electric blanket, or it will overheat.
- Never iron an electric blanket.
- Avoid using mothballs or moth-repellent sprays.
- Do not dry your electric blanket in commercial or laundromat dryers.
- Make sure the blanket is completely dry before turning it on.
- When storing an electric blanket, fold it end to end or side to side to avoid creasing the internal thermostats.

Getting the Most from Your Product

Keep the Control Clear

You could inadvertently fool the thermostat control on your electric blanket. Its job is to monitor the room temperature and turn the appliance on or off to maintain the right amount of warmth under the blanket. If you place the control near anything that radiates heat—for example, a radiator—or accidentally cover it—say, with a pillow—it will misread the room temperature and your blanket won't work the way you want it to. So make sure you put the control in a place where room-temperature air can circulate around it. If your unit did not come with a plastic control hanger to attach to the bed frame, ask for one at your appliance dealer or write to the manufacturer. This simple little device holds the control in a place where you can easily find it. It's up to you to put it where it can take a correct reading.

Even if your electric blanket's control dial doesn't light up, you can still find the right setting in the dark. Simply put some tape at the settings you most commonly use so that you can feel for the correct one.

Cleaning

Time to Clean It

When washing your electric blanket, avoid twisting and wringing it. Presoak the blanket in a solution of gentle soap and tepid water for fifteen minutes. Rinse. Then either machine wash in warm water on the delicate or gentle cycle for two minutes or hand wash in warm water. Spin dry the blanket in the washer.

How do you avoid twisting and wringing the blanket when you have to dry it completely? Try this trick: Line dry it by hanging it over parallel lines set a foot or two apart. Not only will it dry wrinkle-free, it should also dry quickly, since air can freely circulate around the entire blanket. If you can't rig up two parallel clotheslines, use your shower rod. Once the blanket is dry, gently stretch it back to its original size.

Troubleshooting Chart

Problem	Cause	Solution
Blanket is not heating properly.	Outlet may not be functioning; blanket connections may not be secure.	Check outlet and connection to blanket. Secure connections or plug in.
	Room may be too warm.	Lower heat to 72°F. or below. Raise blanket temperature setting.
	Control is near heat source.	Move control to a cooler area.
Control is making a "clicking" sound.	This is normal. Thermostat makes clicking sound when it goes on or off.	
One side of blanket is not responding to control.	Dual controls may have been switched.	Switch the controls back to their original places.

Troubleshooting Chart—Continued

Problem	Cause	Solution
Blanket shocks the user.	Cord may be frayed.	Replace cord. Blanket should be safety-checked by manufacturer's authorized repair shop before using it again.
	A metal object may be stuck in blanket.	Check for pins, clips, or other metal objects. Blanket should be safety-checked by manufacturer's authorized repair shop before using it again.
	Plugs in a dual-control blanket may be in wrong sockets.	Reverse the plugs.

BLENDERS

Safety Notes

Blender Musts

Follow these simple precautions when you use your blender:

- Do not place hands in the blender container while blades are spinning.
- When cleaning your blender, handle the blades carefully; they are very sharp.
- Do not put the blender base in water or other liquid.
- When reassembling the unit after cleaning it, always be sure to insert the blades in the blending container before placing it on the base.

- Do not turn on the blender until the container is securely attached to the base so vibrations won't shake it off.
- Use rubber spatulas exclusively—and only with the machine turned off and unplugged. Scrape down the sides of the container, moving thick foods toward the blades.
- Turn the motor off before you remove the container from the base.
- If the food container turns while the motor is on, switch it off immediately and tighten the cutting assembly.
- Always cover the container before turning on the blender. Hold the cover lightly when starting the motor and while it is running.
- If your blender cover has a special opening for adding ingredients while operating the blender, always use it rather than lifting off the cover to insert something.
- Replace a food container that's chipped or cracked.
- Keep the countertop on which you're using the blender dry and clean. Otherwise, small food scraps or water could be drawn into the motor.
- Try the next higher speed if the motor sounds like it's straining.
- When blending hot liquids, do not fill the food container to the top. Keep your hands away from the cover opening.
- Do not leave the blender unattended while it is in use.

Getting the Most from Your Product

Don't Dull the Blades

Do you want to make sure those cold drinks are really cold? Then by all means, add ice when you blend them. But never process ice in a blender without putting in the liquid first, or you will dull the blades.

Blender Leaving Footprints?

If your machine didn't come with padding for its feet—or if that padding has worn off—get some felt and glue it to the parts of the blender that will touch the surface of your counter.

Multispeeds: What They Mean

The key to using machines with ten or more speeds is to remember that there is little difference between one speed and the next higher or lower speed. So don't worry if you forgot exactly which speed you used in your recipe the last time you used the blender. Approximate speed is close enough.

Telling One Button from Another

On some blenders, the first few buttons work only when you hold them down—for pulse-type blending—while the others provide continuous operation. If these buttons are not clearly marked, you may wish to do so yourself. This prevents over-blending something that just needs a few short bursts from the machine. One way to differentiate the buttons is by dabbing fingernail polish or paint on or just above them. Alternately, glue something with a recognizable texture (such as a small scrap of felt or piece of sandpaper) to the first few buttons.

Avoiding Spillovers

Adding ingredients to a blender already in motion can result in a mess, with liquid splashing over the top. In some models, this can occur even when the container is only half filled. Use a lower speed if you have to add ingredients while the blades turn.

Don't Burn Out Your Blender

Avoid overtaxing the motor by blending large quantities of foods in small batches. This also helps you get uniform results. With too much food in the container, the portion on the bottom, closest to the blades, gets overblended while the portion on top is underblended.

Adapting Recipes

Occasionally, you may have to be a little creative with recipes that call for blending. For harder foods, slightly increase the amount of blending time. And to produce uniformly blended food, cut all the ingredients to the same size before you blend them.

Your blender can be a helpful tool for quickly blending pancake batter. But be sure not to overblend. Use low speed to mix the batter just until the dry ingredients are moistened. For most other recipes, you can blend the liquid ingredients in the blender, then combine them with the dry ingredients.

Great Ways to Use Your Blender

- Smooth lumpy gravies or sauces. Blending on low speed is all that's needed.
- Make bread crumbs from stale bread. Break the bread into uniform pieces before processing.
- Chop nuts for baking. Use on/off pulses to quickly chop nuts to desired size.
- Grate Parmesan cheese. If you cut the cheese into equal-sized pieces, you will get a finer, more evenly grated cheese than if you use a food processor.
- Make homemade baby foods. Puree cooked fresh fruits and vegetables to desired consistency.

Troubleshooting Chart

Problem	Cause	Solution
Blender is blending too slowly.	Too much food is in the blender.	Process less food in each batch.
	Food is stuck in the operating parts.	Clean the blender thoroughly after each use.
Machine is turned on and humming, but blades won't turn.	Motor may be broken.	Turn blender off immediately and bring in for professional repairs.
Blades are secured tightly to container but liquid leaks out.	Seal is worn.	Turn blender off, unscrew blades, and replace seal.

Cleaning, Maintenance, and Storage

Quick Cleaning

To get years of service from your blender, wash it after each use. Besides keeping the appliance clean, this will ensure that you don't leave anything in the blender that could damage it. For example, inadvertently leaving liquids in the machine for more than about four hours could damage the gaskets.

To clean, fill the container halfway with warm water and a few drops of detergent; with the cover on, run the mixture on low speed for a few seconds, then rinse. Turn the container over and let dry completely before storing. For stuck-on food, put some water and ice in the machine and run it awhile, then follow your usual cleaning routine.

Depending on how often you use it, take apart the basic components of the blender—the blades and gasket that unscrew from the bottom of the container—and wash them every month or two. (A bottle brush works well here.) Wash the outside of the blender housing with a damp cloth, when the machine is unplugged.

Clean Storage

When your blender is not in use, protect it from dust and scratches with a blender cover.

What Your Product Won't Do

Some Foods Just Don't Cut It

While your blender can do a few things very well—especially pureeing soups, chopping apples, making milkshakes, mayonnaise, salad dressings and dips, or anything involving liquids— it is less useful for making cracker crumbs and peanut butter. It is not at all good for whipping cream or egg whites, grinding meat, juicing, crushing ice, or mincing vegetables. Save those tougher jobs for your food processor, or do them by hand.

Dried, sticky fruit, such as dates, are very hard on blenders. If you do use them in your blender, chop the fruit with short on/off bursts.

BLOW DRYERS

Safety Notes

Pull the Plug

Unplug your blow dryer and put it away after you turn it off, *especially* if you use it in the bathroom. The point at which the appliance's cord couples to the switch is live even when the switch is in the "off" position. A plugged-in but turned-off dryer accidentally knocked into a bathtub full of water can deliver a severe and possibly lethal shock to the tub's occupant. You can also get quite a shock if you bend over the sink while drying your hair and get the blow dryer wet, or if you touch the unit after dropping it near any water.

If your blow dryer does fall into water (whether the unit is on or off), always unplug it immediately, with *dry* hands. *Do not reach into water or any other liquid to retrieve it*. After unplugging the unit, carefully draw the dryer out of the water by its cord. Do not plug it in again until it has been serviced.

Recently built houses have ground fault circuit interrupters (GFCI) built into bathroom outlets. These circuits cut down on the possibility of electrocution from an appliance touching water. If your house doesn't have them, contact an electrician to have them installed.

Getting the Most from Your Product

Lightweight Drying

Even though most blow dryers weigh less than a pound, on some days yours can feel like it weighs a ton, especially if you have a large unit and thick hair that takes a lot of time to dry. But if you think that a lighter model might suit you better, consider this: such a unit would weigh less but would also probably be less powerful. Thus, you would have to use it for a longer period of time to dry your hair, possibly making your arm just as tired. If your blow dryer feels heavy, try holding it differently. For example, you could keep your arm closer to your body, bracing your elbow against your side for support. Or you could use both hands. Another alternative is to sit down while you dry your hair.

Preventing Hair Damage

What's the best way to blow dry your hair? The technique depends on the look you want, although control settings of "slow" and "cool" are best for most kinds of styling. To make sure the process doesn't harm your hair:

- Avoid concentrating on one spot for more than a few seconds at any time. Move the dryer before you feel a burning sensation on your scalp.
- Keep the dryer in constant motion. This provides the most effective drying action without drying out your hair.
- Hold the dryer 6 to 12 inches away from your hair.
- Don't overdry your hair—use the dryer until your hair is just slightly damp.

Cleaning, Maintenance, and Storage

Keep On Blowing

Follow these steps to maintain your blow dryer in top shape for a long time:

- Keep the air intake area clear of hair and lint by cleaning it out with a small brush—a toothbrush will do the job. The more blocked this part becomes, the harder the motor in your unit has to work.
- Turn off the unit if you have to put it down—say, when the phone rings. This is especially important if you place the dryer on a soft surface, such as a mattress. Not only will you prevent a fire, you will also keep the intake area from being "smothered" by the soft surface, which could result in motor burnout.
- Store your dryer only after it has cooled.
- Coil the cord loosely rather than tightly wrapping it around the dryer, and don't hang the dryer from its cord.

Troubleshooting Chart

Problem	Cause	Solution
Blow dryer shuts off in the middle of drying.	Dryer has overheated and automatic shutoff feature has been activated.	Turn the dryer off, unplug it, and allow it to cool completely before reusing.
	Hair or dirt may be obstructing air intake.	Check the air intake areas for any obstructions.
The motor runs but there is no air flow.	Air intake may be blocked.	Inspect and clear the air intake.
Blow dryer rattles and whines.	Impeller may be broken or bent.	Have impeller replaced if it can be removed separately from motor.

BOOKS

Cleaning, Maintenance, and Storage

Keeping Books Clean

Your books should be cleaned at least once a year. Pull them from the shelf by the middle of the spine, dust each individually, and dust off the shelf. While a clean cloth is the traditional tool for dusting books, you can avoid accidentally pushing dirt down between the pages by using a vacuum. Or hold the book shut and use a small, soft artist's paintbrush to brush away dust.

Fighting Mildew

High heat and humidity constitute ideal growing conditions for mildew, which, if given enough time, will eat your books. Remove the powderlike spores from your books with the round dusting brush of your vacuum cleaner. When vacuuming old or very worn books, cover the vacuum cleaner pipe opening with cheesecloth before placing the brush on it. This will lower the suction, preventing the cleaner from pulling up loose parts of the paper or binding.

Expose mildewed pages to the open air, but not in the sunlight. If they're damp, dust some cornstarch on them and remove it after an hour or two. Using a sponge or cloth, gently wipe mildew off leather bindings with saddle soap.

Before putting these books back on the shelf, wash the shelves with a mixture of a gallon of water and a cup of chlorine bleach and let them dry thoroughly. To keep mildew at bay, place a piece of charcoal in the bookcase to absorb dampness.

Flatten Folds and Creases

Page creases and folded corners can be sponged flat with a damp sponge or ironed with a warm iron through clean paper. Protect the underlying pages with a piece of cloth or towel. Don't allow coated or treated paper to be dampened. If the page is dirty, clean it with a rubber eraser before applying heat or moisture.

Blot Your Books

If you accidentally spill water on a book page, place a blotter on either side of the page, then press with a medium-hot iron until the page is smooth and dry.

Store Them with Care

Books are made of organic substances, and need tender loving care. If possible, keep them in a room lit by incandescent bulbs, with a temperature of 60°F and 50 percent humidity. If you use fluorescent lighting, either buy the tubes with built-in ultraviolet light filters or purchase filters and install them. Do not cram books into tight spaces or jam them against walls or ceilings, because friction and high pressure can harm and weaken the covers. Avoid leaving newspaper clippings in them, since the acid in newsprint will ruin the paper in your books.

For More Information . . .

If you have a large library of old or valuable books, you might want to know about the various products available to aid in their preservation. You can write to these library supply houses for information about preservation products:

Talas
213 West 35th St.
New York, NY 10001

University Products, Inc.
P.O. Box 101
Holyoke, MA 01014

BUG KILLERS, ELECTRIC

Safety Notes

Zap Bugs Safely

- Always use the cord provided with the unit or a three-wire extension cord made for outdoor use.
- Plug the cord only into a grounded outlet. Make sure it doesn't sit in a puddle of water or damp area. Never place the cord where anyone could trip over it. To avoid accidents, you may want to consider burying an electric cable underground.
- Make sure the unit is placed out of the reach of children and pets.
- Always use the screen if one comes with your electronic model.

When Sparks Fly

Test your electric bug killer before you install it. You will notice a few sparks when you first plug it in, which is normal. However, if the bug killer continues to give off sparks, it may be because the vertical grid wires have been forced too close together during shipping. Unplug the unit and use an insulated screwdriver to separate the wires where you saw sparks. You may have to do this a few times before the sparking stops.

Getting the Most from Your Product

Pick the Best Spot

Never put a bug killer near the patio, pool or any other place in the yard where everyone gathers. A unit here only attracts bugs to the very spot you want to keep bug free! For best results, place bug killers at least 30 to 50 feet from the locations in the yard your family uses. For extra effectiveness, put the bug zapper between the area you want to protect and bushy or swampy spots where the pesky bugs congregate and breed.

'Round-the-Clock Zapping

Should you keep your electric bug killer turned on day and night? For the first few weeks, it's a good idea to keep the unit running all the time. This 'round-the-clock zapping interferes with the bugs' breeding cycle and makes a significant dent in the insect population. After that you can run the unit just at night or whenever bugs are making a nuisance of themselves.

Keep It Dry

Operating a bug killer while it's raining takes years off its life. If you're home when it rains, unplug the unit and reconnect it only after it has dried out.

Death by Drowning

If you have a silent unit that kills insects by blowing them into a water-filled tray, be sure to replace the water regularly. At each water change add at least a teaspoon of liquid soap or detergent. The soap disrupts the surface tension of the water, causing the bugs to go under when they are blown into the water. Mount the unit no more than six feet above the ground and point it in the direction of the area you want to clear.

Cleaning, Maintenance, and Storage

Clear Away the Bugs

You should clean your bug killer frequently to remove dead insects. It might seem logical and effective, but vacuum cleaning is not recommended for electric bug killers. For thorough cleaning, most models have a slide-out collecting tray that you can empty and wash in mild soap and water.

If your bug killer has an outer cage, don't use a water spray to clean it. Instead, unplug the appliance and brush the cage grid lightly to remove the insects.

In addition, make sure you hold the bug killer securely when you take it down to clean it; many bug killers are top-heavy and easy to drop.

Replacing the Bulb

The black light bulbs used in most bug killers begin to lose their power before they burn out. To get maximum service from your unit, change the bulb every summer, even if the manufacturer says it has a life of two or more seasons.

Off-Season Storage

Since any kind of moisture can seriously damage your bug killer, it's imperative that you store it inside during the winter in a dry location that's also out of children's reach.

C

CABINETS AND COUNTERTOPS

Getting the Most from Your Product

Which Material Is Best?

Cabinets: The most common materials for kitchen or bathroom cabinets are wood, plastic laminates, and metal. Glass-faced cabinets, found in Victorian-era homes, are also becoming more popular.

Wooden cabinets, available in solid wood or veneers, can be painted or stained, oiled or varnished—depending on your budget or taste.

Laminates are easy to maintain. More durable than wood cabinets, they resist nicks, scratches, and stains and clean very easily.

To preserve the luster of your cabinets for many years, no matter what their composition:

- Keep cabinets free of grease and dust buildup.
- Wipe up splashes immediately.
- In the bathroom, wipe off condensation after you shower or bathe.

Countertops: There are many kinds of countertops—laminates, such as Formica, Corian or 2000X—butcher block, ceramic tile, cultured marble, and natural marble. Today, the majority of kitchen and bath countertops are made from some kind of laminate because this good-looking and durable material lasts for years with very little care.

However, even laminates are not invincible. They can stand up to temperatures as high as 275°F, but not for long. In fact, leave anything at 140°F on your countertop for a while and you may find your laminate separating from its core material. To prevent this, use a trivet or hot pad between your pot and the countertop.

Here are some additional tips for getting the most out of your laminate countertops:

- In the kitchen, always use a cutting board when preparing foods. And don't drag things with sharp edges across the surface. Laminate countertops can be permanently scratched or chipped by knives and other sharp utensils.
- In the bathroom or in the kitchen, do not let water pool on laminate surfaces for long periods, especially near seams or corners or where the sink is joined to the countertop. Because laminate is glued to the wood underneath, it can loosen and raise up with repeated soakings.
- Never scour the surfaces with abrasive powders or materials.
- If you have a laminate countertop next to your stove and the laminate bubbles from the heat, replace the countertop with a butcher block or ceramic surface.
- Scratches, stains, and small scorch marks on Corian or 2000X countertops can be sanded out. Just be sure to use only a fine-grade sandpaper.

Cleaning, Maintenance, and Storage

Cabinets: Replace or Reface?

If you're unhappy with your cabinets, updating rather than replacing them may be the answer. After years of use, the surfaces may become worn and a bit shabby, or the cabinets may be dated. After all, tastes and styles do change. The basic cabinetry, however, may be sturdy, with a lot of good years left. So why replace them when you can reface or refinish them for a fraction of the cost? Here are some ways to give your cabinets a new look:

- The easiest way to renew painted metal or wooden cabinets is to repaint them. Or you can refinish wooden cabinets by stripping and sanding them and then applying stain and a coat or two of polyurethane.
- If you're tired of the style but the cabinet space is adequate for your needs, you can redecorate a kitchen or bath simply by changing the doors and drawer fronts and gluing laminates or veneer to other exposed areas. Even cabinet interiors can be

redesigned or rearranged to afford more convenient storage space.

• Sometimes just changing the hardware can be a quick, effective, and inexpensive way to update your kitchen or bath. You can choose from a variety of styles, shapes, and sizes. Just be sure your new hardware is the same size as that which you're replacing.

Cabinet Care

Protect the fine finish of your wood cabinets by keeping them clean and polished. When you work on the wood, always use a clean, soft cloth—never a dish cloth that could contain detergent or grease residues. An old cloth diaper makes a perfect cleaning cloth. Wipe all surfaces with a damp cloth; then promptly dry with another cloth. Apply a light coat of paste or liquid furniture wax (without a cleaner), rubbing it into the wood in the direction of the grain before the wax can set; then buff with a soft, clean cloth. It's a good idea to clean and wax your cabinets at least twice a year.

To clean painted metal and painted wood cabinets, use an all-purpose household cleaner. Clean glass-faced cabinet doors with a glass cleaner or wash with a weak solution of ammonia and water, then wipe dry. For plastic laminates, clean as you would laminated countertops (see the next section).

Cleaning Laminate Countertops

Plastic laminates are remarkably stain-resistant. However, they are not stain-proof. The ink from supermarket price stickers can leave its mark, as can bluing, laundry bleaches, oven cleaners, hair rinses, and dyes. Your first line of defense is to wipe up the stain as quickly as possible. For stubborn spots, try dipping a cloth in chlorine bleach and blotting the stain for no longer than a minute. An alternative method is to put a few drops of lemon juice on the stain and let it set for about 30 minutes. Then sprinkle some baking soda on the juice and wipe it all up with a terrycloth towel.

A nonabrasive, all-purpose household cleaner applied with a nylon bristle brush should do for ordinary cleaning. Occasionally use a cleaner wax to protect the surface against stains.

Never use abrasive cleaners or pads, strong acid, ammonia, or other solvents for cleaning countertops of any material. You may damage the surface.

Shiny Formica is easier to keep in top shape than the duller laminate. If your Formica is the matte finish and the grease stains are getting out of hand, try rubbing the spots with club soda.

Ceramic Tile Tips

Ceramic tile is a good choice for countertops because it is so durable. It resists scratching, scorching, and fading. The surface can handle small cutting or slicing jobs without fear of damage, but heavy chopping is not recommended. Keep a cutting board handy to protect your good knives.

Ceramic countertops *must* be sealed after installation to make them waterproof and keep them sanitary. This prevents the tile from absorbing grease, dirt, mildew, and bacteria.

One of the greatest advantages of tile countertops is that they are very easy to clean. Simply use a clean cloth or sponge and all-purpose household cleaner or a mild detergent and water. Rinse well and dry.

Butcher Block Can Take the Heat

Butcher block is an excellent surface to have next to the stove because it can take considerable heat. It requires periodic sealing with vegetable or mineral oil. Vegetable oil is also an excellent cleaner, but for ordinary cleanups, wipe with a damp cloth and dry immediately.

Recent stains can be lifted out with lemon juice. Simply pour some on the area and let it soak in. After half an hour, you should be able to just wipe up the spot. To get rid of stubborn stains and the crosshatching indents that come from using a knife on the surface, lightly sand the area with a fine-grain sandpaper.

Treat Marble with Care

A piece of marble set into your counter is a wonderful surface for making pastry and some kinds of candy. It's not as durable as it looks, however, and can chip or scratch quite easily. As a result, it should not be used as a cutting surface. If you must cut unbaked pastry into different shapes or smaller pieces, first transfer it to a floured cutting board. Also, be careful when working with high-acid foods such as lemon juice—they will etch the surface.

Once installed, marble should be sealed. If used as a surface for food preparation, seal with vegetable oil. For areas other than the kitchen, a commercial sealer can be used. Cleaning marble is easy—use soapy water and rinse, or simply wipe with a damp sponge. Never use an abrasive cleaner.

Always remember to keep appliances and dishes away from marble because they can scratch it. It is much easier to use preventive measures than to try to fix scratches after they have been made. The only way to completely remove scratches is to have the marble polished by a professional.

CAN OPENERS

Safety Notes

Hands Off!

- Keep your hands away from the moving parts of an electric can opener.
- Do not use your can opener to open pressurized cans, aerosol cans, or cans containing flammable liquids such as lighter fluids.

Getting the Most from Your Product

Running on Empty

If your electric can opener suddenly starts running by itself when you haven't even touched it, don't panic. The mechanism that supports the handle and keeps it from contacting the switch that turns on the motor has simply worn out. What to do? You have two options (aside from paying for repairs or getting a new opener):

- Keep the can opener unplugged when not in use.
- Get an on/off switch from the hardware store and wire it into the power cord. This will enable you to cut the current flow to the appliance without having to unplug it.

Pliers—A Useful Accessory

You can avoid getting cut by the sharp edge of open can lids by keeping a small pair of pliers handy. After you've opened the can, simply grasp the lid edge with the pliers and drop the lid into the trash. This also eliminates the mess of getting food from the lid on your hands or clothes.

Watch Where You Hang Your Opener

Before you install an under-the-cabinet electric can opener, consider that you may be bending over when you use it. Obviously, you wouldn't install the opener over the stove, but have you thought about electrical appliances that give off heat? For example, will you use the countertop space under the opener for a toaster oven or similar appliance? Place the unit at the various locations you've considered and simulate reaching over and using it. If you notice any problems, find another site.

Keep Frozen Juice Cans Frozen

Frozen juice often comes in cardboard cans, which seem designed to give electric can openers trouble. The trick is to open these cans when they are hard, so open them as soon as you remove them from the freezer. If the concentrate is too hard to mix and you don't want to use your blender, cover the top of the can with plastic wrap and place it in a pan of warm water for a few minutes to help soften the concentrate.

Work around Bumps and Dents

Manufacturing methods often leave burrs, dips, dents, and bumps on the tops of the cans. As effective as modern electric can openers have become, they can't always handle these aberrations, so take a detour. If you notice the problem beforehand, start your opener just after the glitch and end the opening process when you come around to it again. But if your opener notices it before you do and protests by coming to a halt, remove the can and start the opener again just after the problem.

Give Your Opener a Helping Hand

When you open a can with an imposing-looking rim, or one that's dented, be prepared to assist your can opener. If the appliance is struggling, gently turn the can counterclockwise to supplement the motor's efforts.

Reverse a Troublesome Can

There's no law that says you can't take a can that's hard to open and turn it upside down. The other end may prove less troublesome. (If you've already broken the seal, however, be sure to cover the half-opened end to avoid leaks.) It helps to open both ends if you recycle your cans—the can is easier to flatten for storage.

Move the Opener for Tall Cans

To open a can that's too tall to fit between your can opener's cutting tool and the countertop, move the opener to the edge of the counter or table, permitting the can to hang over the edge. Keep the palm of your hand under the can to support and steady it as it is opened.

Troubleshooting Chart

Problem	Cause	Solution
Electric can opener shuts off suddenly in the middle of operation.	Overheating caused opener to shut off automatically.	Turn off can opener and let cool for at least 15 minutes before turning it on again.
Cutter blade doesn't pierce can lid.	Cutter is bent or dull.	Check cutter, replace if necessary.

*Troubleshooting Chart—*Continued

Problem	Cause	Solution
	Cutter assembly is bound.	Inspect and clear away food or paper particles; lubricate.

Cleaning, Maintenance, and Storage

Don't Scrub a Manual Opener

Don't scrub your manual can openers. Old openers can be cleaned with a paper towel you've dipped in soap and hot water. Use another paper towel to rinse it. Newer manual can openers have a protective silicone coating on the gears. If you wash these with water, the gears will rust and freeze up. If you have an opener with this silicone coating, or if you're unsure, simply wipe the gears clean with a dry paper towel. The same cleaning rules hold true for the cutting tool on your electric can opener.

Handy Maintenance Tools

Use an old toothbrush to get your can opener free of tiny food scraps. Pipe cleaners also make good can opener cleaning tools, and a cotton swab soaked in a little cooking oil will lubricate the mechanism that turns the blades.

What Your Product Won't Do

It Can't Open Rimless Cans

Don't even try to open a rimless can (such as those that evaporated milk comes in) with your electric or manual can opener. These cans are meant to be opened with the pointed end of a bottle opener.

CARPETS AND RUGS

Getting the Most from Your Product

Removing Furniture Indentations

Leave a piece of heavy furniture in one place long enough and it will make its mark on your carpet or rug. However, there's an easy way to get rid of such indentations. Hold a steam iron over the area—not touching it—long enough for the steam to get into the pile. (If you only have a dry iron, put a wet cloth on the carpet and hold the heated iron over it.) Then brush the pile with a clean whisk broom and watch the indentation disappear.

Rotate Your Rugs

Floor coverings probably receive more wear than anything else in your house. You can add years of life to your carpets and rugs by taking a few preventive steps. Start by installing runners at heavy traffic locations, and be sure to have door mats at all exits and entrances. Protect your rugs from wear by turning them from time to time and by moving the furniture to create new traffic and wear patterns. (Moving the furniture also helps prolong the life of your wall-to-wall carpeting.)

Discourage Fading

A faded carpet or rug often has a sad and forlorn look. While all color fades with age, there are two things you can do to delay the inevitable. First, vacuum the carpet or rug regularly. Second, since sunlight is a prominent culprit in the fading process, keep the blinds drawn or the curtains closed to prevent sunlight from shining directly on your floor covering.

Cleaning and Maintenance

A Word from the Carpet-Wise

Just how important is regular vacuuming? According to one leading carpet manufacturer, frequent vacuuming is a must because dust particles act like sandpaper on the carpet pile. Make at least five passes over each area of carpet when you vacuum, to get it as clean as possible. Vacuum in every direction, but for your last pass, vacuum in the direction of the pile. And always vacuum *before* the carpet looks dirty.

Removing Carpet Stains

No matter what the stain, for good results with minimal carpet damage, follow these steps:

1. Begin the stain removal process as soon as possible—ideally, before the stain has a chance to dry and set.
2. Start cleaning from the outside of the stain, working in toward the middle. (Never use any cleaner on your carpet that you haven't tested first, to be sure it won't damage the color or the fibers. Test on an inconspicuous area, or on a carpet scrap, if you have one.)
3. Use a dull, flat blade, such as a putty knife or the blunt side of a spoon, to remove solid particles.
4. Always *blot* rather than rub wet stains. Use a white paper towel without a printed design. Place the towel on the stain and press down on it—don't rub. Be careful not to wet the stain too much; the water or cleaning liquid should *not* go through to the backing.
5. When applying a stain removal agent, use a dry cloth and a minimum of the cleaning substance.
6. Pick up the stain remover by blotting with another clean cloth. To make sure you get all the liquid, place a wad of white paper toweling about a half-inch thick on the spot and put a book on top of it to press it down. Leave it there overnight.
7. Brush your carpet's pile with a whisk broom after it drys.

Watch Out for Bowl Cleanser

If you have carpeting in the bathroom, beware of a prime source of carpet stains: toilet bowl cleanser. It's easy to drip this substance on the carpet while moving the brush from the bowl to its storage place. Keep something under the brush to catch the drips when you move it; stains from toilet bowl cleanser are permanent.

Put Chewing Gum on Ice

Here's an easy way to deal with a gummed-up carpet. Use ice cubes to chill and solidify the gum, then scrape it off. Ice or ice water makes a good first line of defense any time you spill a liquid on the carpet. It may loosen the stain sufficiently for you to pick it up by blotting it with a white paper towel.

Fluff Your Throw Rugs

If your throw rug needs brightening up but you don't want to go to the fuss and bother of putting it through an entire washing, just throw it in the dryer along with a wet towel and set the machine for fluffing. Wipe out the dryer afterwards, however, to avoid inadvertantly soiling your next load of clothing.

Brush Away Pet Hair

Pet hair always seems to accumulate at the baseboards and stick to the carpet. An easy way to remove it is with a toilet brush. Buy a new brush for just this purpose. Run the brush along the carpet—the bristles will pick up hair more effectively than any vacuum.

Carpet Deodorizers

Use baking soda to deodorize your carpet. Spread about one cup of baking soda evenly over the dry carpet (use one cup for each room). Vacuum after thirty minutes. For heavy odors, such as from pet stains, try undiluted white vinegar or a diluted disinfectant on the spot. Blot it well and then wipe dry.

Cut Down on "Sprouts" . . .

Did you ever notice carpet yarn that seems to be sprouting above the rest of the carpet? Those tufts may have been pulled up by a pet's claw, a child's toy, or some other passing object. Simply cut them down to size with a sharp pair of scissors or a nail clipper.

. . . and Pilling, Too

Treat pilling—attached fuzz balls—the same way as you would sprouting. Pilling is natural for some carpeting when you first buy it. But if it persists, you either are using a vacuum cleaner with a comb mechanism—suitable *only* for cut-pile carpets—or a vacuum cleaner that's defective and needs servicing.

Repairing Cigarette Burns

Use the fuzz you remove from pilling to repair cigarette burns. Cut away burned carpeting and glue the pilling (or carpet sprouts, if you have any) to the bald spot. Cover with paper toweling, press down with a few books, and a day later you will find little evidence that any disaster had struck.

CLOCKS

Getting the Most from Your Product

Pendulum Clock Care

A fine pendulum clock adds a touch of elegance to your home. Give the mechanism and its case the care it requires, and the clock will run accurately and look good for generations. Bear in mind these precautions:

• To avoid tarnish, handle brass parts only with a soft cloth.

- If you move, take out the weights, pendulum, and finial, secure the chains, and keep the chime rods from banging into each other by inserting tissue paper between them.
- Stop the pendulum if you take a trip lasting longer than a week.
- Keep the clock away from moist air sources, including vents and outside walls.

Stand It on Its Head

If you have an old electric clock that seems to have given up the ghost, try turning it upside down for a few days. This may redistribute the clock's oil throughout the mechanism, lubricating the parts that have quit on you.

All Wound Up

Your wind-up clock will last longer if you go easy during your daily winding. To keep the mechanism operating smoothly, wind with short turns of the key, and don't turn it until it won't turn any more. Give the spring a little leeway so it won't become overtaut.

Cleaning and Maintenance

When You Need a Professional

You can oil the clock yourself and polish the case—if it's wood or brass—just as you would any other piece of fine furniture, but leave the cleaning of the inner mechanisms to a professional. This should be done about every five years in order to keep the clock running perfectly. If you live in a particularly dusty or moist environment, or the clock is placed in the kitchen when grease can invade it, you may want to have it professionally cleaned more often.

Older Clocks Sound Off

If you have an older clock that has developed a whirring noise in addition to ticking, don't worry. Nothing is wrong. As a clock ages, its sounds change.

CLOTHES DRYERS

These Don't Belong in Your Dryer

Your dryer can damage rubber, foam rubber, and plastic garments—or garments with decorative trims made of these materials. More serious, however, is the fire hazard that these articles present; they can ignite or cause spontaneous combustion when dried with heat. If you have any doubts about an item, don't put it in your dryer.

Garments to keep out of a clothes dryer include:

- Fiberglass articles, such as curtains
- Galoshes
- Materials that have been saturated or dampened with cleaning solvents, flammable liquids, or flammable solids
- Articles containing Kapok, such as certain pillows and life jackets

Items you may want to dry on a rack or in the dryer on the air setting include:

- Bath mats
- Bibs
- Padded bras
- Plastic baby pants
- Rugs with rubber backings
- Stuffed toys or pillows
- Tennis shoes
- Woolens and silks (because they'll shrink if exposed to heat)

Keep Sharp Objects Out

Sharp objects can damage the inside of your dryer, so be sure to empty pockets of pins, ballpoint pens, and the like before tossing in the clothes. And don't forget to zip up zippers, clasp clasps, and hook hooks.

General Precautions

- Never plug the dryer into an outlet that has not been well grounded.
- Make sure that children never play in, with, or around a dryer. When it is time to retire your dryer, remove the door of the drying compartment; like refrigerators, discarded dryers become a tempting play area for children.
- Never reach into the dryer while the drum is in motion.
- If you plan to be away on a long vacation, unplug the power cord, turn off the machine, close the gas valve (for gas dryers), and clean the lint screen.
- Run the dryer only if the lint screen is clean, in good condition, and in place. A loose, damaged, or blocked lint screen can lead to overheating and fire.
- Never run the dryer where there are explosive fumes. Do not store gasoline or other flammable substances near the dryer or other appliances.
- If you smell gas, extinguish any open flame, open the windows, and call your gas company immediately. Don't touch any electrical switches, because the switching action could produce a spark.
- Keep the area around the dryer clean and free from rags, paper, lint, and chemicals.

Getting the Most from Your Product

Hot Enough for You, Hot Enough for It

Don't place your dryer in a room that's uncomfortably cool for you—or for it. To make sure your dryer runs at peak efficiency, use it in a room where the temperature is at least 50°F, preferably a bit warmer. Make sure, too, that the dryer is not blocked by curtains or drapes.

Use Your Dryer Efficiently

You can save electricity by not overdrying clothes and by running several loads consecutively. Each of the loads after the first one will start with a dryer that's already warmed up; therefore the dryer doesn't need to use as much energy to reach the appropriate temperature. And, if you run your load through an extra spin cycle in the washing machine, you'll save money by lessening the time the clothes will have to tumble in the dryer. (Washing machines cost less to run than dryers.)

Is It Done Yet?

The length of time it takes to get your wash dry depends on several variables. Your load of wash will take longer to dry if:

- It is very large (especially if it's a large load of heavyweight fabrics).
- The lint screen is dirty.
- The temperature is set on "air dry" or "low."
- The temperature of the room in which the dryer is located is below 50°F (the cooler the room, the harder your dryer has to work).
- You rinsed the wash in cold water.

Shake 'n' Bake

Your clothes tumble around a lot from the time they enter the washing machine until they complete the dryer's last cycle. So when transferring them from your washing machine to your dryer, shake them out. This will not only help cut down on wrinkling, but it will also separate sheets and shirt sleeves that have twisted around other garments. You want to expose as much of the garment's surface to air for the best drying.

Avoid Wrinkles

Are your permanent-press clothes coming out of the dryer full of wrinkles? Use this checklist of possible causes to help you correct your wrinkling problem:

- Too much or too little water in the washing machine.
- Not enough or too many clothes in the washing machine and dryer. Keep the load half full for permanent-press fabrics.
- Clothes left in the dryer too long after the cycle is over.
- Garments washed too often in hot water (an improper water setting for permanent-press material).

Get Rid of Wrinkles

Now you know how to avoid wrinkling permanent-press clothes, but what do you do with your current load of wrinkled garments? Here's how to smooth out the wrinkles:

1. Put the items back through the dryer's cycle with the setting at "permanent press."
2. Now rinse them again and rerun them through the dryer, again at "permanent press." If this doesn't work, try drying them at a high-heat level for 10 minutes or so. Remove the clothes immediately and hang them up. Or soak a towel in water and wring it out. Add it to your load in the dryer and run it through another cycle.

Use Softener Sheets with Care

If you notice oily stains on your clothes when they come out of the dryer, it's possible you used your fabric softener sheets improperly. To avoid this:

- Add the softener sheet before starting the machine.
- Avoid overloading the dryer. This prevents the softener sheet from mixing with your entire wash. If you pack the load too tightly, chances are the softener sheet will become entangled in one item for the entire drying cycle.
- If you're drying synthetic or permanent-press fabrics, be especially careful not to use excessively high heat.
- Some manufacturers recommend that you stay away from these softener sheets altogether, suggesting that such products can block the lint filter, cause a lint buildup in the dryer's duct system, and coat the mechanism in the dryer that signals when to turn the heat on and off. You may want to use a fabric softener in the wash cycle instead. If you do use a softener sheet, make sure it's guaranteed safe for your dryer.

Drying Mixed Loads

When drying a load of clothes with different weights and textures, set the dryer for the lighter-weight fabrics. If time is critical, stop the machine every 10 minutes and remove the clothes that have already dried.

Dry These Only Until Damp

Certain fabrics and clothes should be removed from the dryer while they are still damp. These include:

- Delicate fabrics such as silk and wool (many of these should not be machine-dried at all; check the garment labels).
- Garments with plastic buttons that warp if heated for too long.
- Items you plan to starch.
- Knits of cotton or cotton blends.
- Table linens that will be ironed immediately.
- Synthetic fabrics (overdrying generates static electricity).

Buffer Large Items

Laundering large items such as blankets, drapes, curtains, or slipcovers? When it comes time to put them in the clothes dryer, dry one item at a time and add a few towels as buffers against the tumbling action of the dryer.

Build a Handy Hanging Rack

If you want to avoid touch-up ironing, place permanent-press garments on hangers as soon as you remove them from your dryer. You can build a rack for the hangers right next to the dryer. Install it on hinges attached to the wall so you can swing it out of the way when you're finished using it.

Check for Leaky Door Seals

If, after going through the troubleshooting chart that follows, your dryer still doesn't seem to be working as efficiently as it should be, check to make sure that the door seals are tight and that cool air is not leaking from the room into the dryer while it is running. To test for leakage, while the dryer is on, hold a tissue against the seam where the door and the cabinet meet. If the tissue gets drawn in toward the appliance, you need to get a replacement seal from your dealer.

You can remove a glued-on door seal by gently pulling it from the door jamb or door of the dryer. Some door seals are attached with tabs. Provided you have the right replacement door seal, it won't be difficult for you to install it. If your seal was glued on, you should use a special nonflammable glue, which you can purchase from your dealer or a hardware store, to install the new seal. If you have any questions, ask your dealer.

Troubleshooting Chart

Problem	Cause	Solution
Dryer won't start.	Power is interrupted.	Make sure that dryer is plugged in, fuses are not blown, and circuits are not tripped.
	Door is open.	Close door.
	Start switch has not been pressed.	Press start switch.
Dryer turns on but does not heat.	Fuses or circuit breaker is blown.	Check and replace if necessary.
	Gas supply valve and/ or burner valve is not open (for gas dryers).	Check valves.
	Gas supply tank is empty (for gas dryers).	Refill tank.
Clothing takes too long to dry.	Controls are not set properly.	Check controls.
	Lint filter is clogged.	Clean lint filter.
	Exhaust duct is clogged.	Clean duct area.
	Dryer is overloaded.	Dry fewer articles next time.
	Dryer has too few clothes.	Add one or two similar items, even if dry, to ensure proper tumbling.

Troubleshooting Chart—Continued

Problem	Cause	Solution
	Clothes were not sorted properly.	Dry heavy garments separately from lighter garments.
Dryer makes a clanking noise.	Buttons, zippers, etc. make noises.	Close zippers, check pockets before drying.
Dryer makes a thumping noise.	If dryer has not been used for a while, it may make a noise.	Noise will disappear soon.
	Dryer may not be level.	Use a level to check side to side and back to front. Adjust legs if necessary.

Cleaning and Maintenance

Keep the Hot Air Flowing

Dryers thrive on a continuous flow of hot air. A buildup of lint, however, cuts off the hot air supply. Keeping the lint screen clear will increase your dryer's efficiency. Clean it both before and after you use it by simply rolling the lint off with your fingers.

Don't overlook the exhaust duct, which can clog in time. Clean this vent semiannually with a soft brush or vacuum cleaner. This job is important both for cleanliness and safety. The lint buildup in the exhaust system could eventually cause a fire. Make sure you turn the dryer off and *unplug* it before attempting to clean lint from the duct area.

Remove Dryer Stains

Dyes that run off bright or noncolorfast clothing can stain the inside of your dryer. If the drum is already stained, make a paste of some detergent and warm water. Use a soft cloth to rub the paste into the stain. Wipe off the moist residue with another damp cloth; then throw some clean rags in the machine and run it through a cycle. You can also use a liquid spray cleaner instead of the detergent paste. Do not pour water into the drum.

Drum Care

Your dryer's drum needs some special attention. When you finish drying a load, leave the door ajar to air out the drum and prevent condensation from forming on it. And if you have been drying garments that are heavily starched (some starch remains in the fabric even after the wash), wipe the drum with a damp cloth. If you've been drying noncolorfast fabrics or those recently dyed, wipe the drum using warm soapy water and then wipe it again with a plain damp cloth.

One word of caution: If you leave your dryer door open between loads, be sure to check the dryer before closing the door. It's the perfect hiding place for cats and kids.

COFFEE GRINDERS

Safety Notes

Grind Safely

Follow these steps for operating your coffee grinder safely:

- Never interfere with the lid lock on your grinder.
- Keep your fingers away from all moving parts.
- Never immerse the grinder in water or any other liquid.
- Wait for the blades to stop rotating before you remove the cover.
- Always unplug the grinder before wiping it out.
- Store the grinder with its cover in place.

Getting the Most from Your Product

Stretch Those Beans

Most people who grind their own coffee use the drip method of brewing. This method requires a fine grind, which is ideal both for flavor and economy. (The finer the grind, the less coffee you need for rich flavor.) Just remember that if you make certain specialty drinks, such as Irish coffee, you will have to use a bit more coffee.

Maximum Storage

Some coffee grinders offer you space to store coffee beans. While this is convenient, it doesn't help to maintain the freshness of the beans. Instead, freeze or refrigerate the beans in an airtight container for maximum freshness, and dip into your store each time you brew.

Staccato Grinding

To keep your small coffee grinder operating at peak efficiency, run it in short, even bursts of power. The motors in these small machines can easily overheat if allowed to run for too long.

Cleaning and Maintenance

Crucial Cleaning

Coffee grinders need frequent cleaning because oil from the beans remains in the machine after you use it, and the oil can turn rancid in just a few days. All it takes is a wipe with a damp cloth after each use. Remember to unplug the appliance first.

COFFEE MAKERS

Safety Notes

Perk with Care

When using your percolator, follow these precautions:

- Make sure the lid is securely in place before brewing and serving.
- Do not remove the cover while the coffee is brewing.
- Unplug the percolator and allow it to cool completely before cleaning it by hand.
- Do not immerse the base in water.

Don't Share the Outlet

Even though drip coffee makers may seem like small items, they do draw quite a bit of electricity. Take care not to plug other appliances into the same outlet as the coffee maker, or you may blow a fuse.

Drip Safely

Follow these precautions when using your drip coffee maker:
- Do not use the carafe of a drip coffee maker on a gas or electric range or in a microwave.
- Place the coffee maker only on a flat, dry surface.
- Keep the lid on when brewing and pouring.
- Unplug the coffee maker and allow it to cool completely before cleaning.
- Be sure not to boil the carafe dry. This can eventually cause a fire.

Getting the Most from Your Product

Brew It Right

To make a really good pot of coffee, follow these easy steps for percolating:

1. Moisten the basket before you add the coffee and be sure to use a coarse enough grind—both reduce the chance of grinds getting into your brew.
2. As soon as the coffee is ready, unplug the unit.
3. Remove the basket of grinds. (Invert the lid of your coffee maker and use it as a receptacle for the basket when discarding the grinds.)
4. Reconnect the coffee maker to reheat the coffee.

5. For a second batch of coffee that's as good as the first, always rinse out the pot with cold water before brewing more.

It's All in the Water

Use cold, distilled water—not tap water—in your percolator to cut down on the need for extensive pot cleaning. You will avoid mineral buildup and, according to many coffee lovers, brew a tastier cup of coffee.

How Long Does It Take?

Several factors influence how long it takes to brew coffee in a percolator:

The number of cups you brew: the more cups, the less time it will take.

The relative cleanliness of your unit: if it wasn't cleaned properly the last time it was used, your percolator may be a bit sluggish, lengthening the brewing time.

Make Sure You Have Liquid in the Pot

Believe it or not, many people forget to add water before plugging in their percolator. To avoid damaging the coffee maker by plugging it in dry, try placing a strip of colored tape—to remind you to add water—on the plastic plug that goes into the outlet. If you stop noticing the tape, attach a warning note for yourself next to the outlet.

Percolation Woes

If the water in your coffee maker heats up but won't percolate, it may have a defective thermostat. But before you take it to an authorized technician for repair, try cleaning the percolator tube. (If you've lost the cleaning brush supplied by the manufacturer, use a pipe cleaner.) If grinds are imbedded in the valve at the end of your percolator tube, try using a toothpick to dislodge them. You can also use a toothpick to clean the basket. To prevent grinds from getting into the percolator tube, cover the top of the tube with your finger when you put the coffee in the basket.

How to Unstick the Percolator Tube

Remove a stuck percolator tube by running the unit, without water, for no more than 30 seconds. Then, unplug the appliance, grip the tube with a pot holder, and pull gently to get the tube out of the heating well. As soon as you have it out, cool the appliance with tap water.

Help Your Carafe Live Longer

Before you place the hot carafe of your drip coffee maker on a table or countertop to serve guests, be sure the surface is not cold or wet. And remember that your carafe should never be placed on any warming element other than its own.

Cleaning and Maintenance

Percolate It Clean

To get rid of discolorations, oils, and mineral buildups in your coffeepot, fill it with water and add ¼ cup of cream of tartar or 2 teaspoons of baking soda. Then insert the tube and the empty basket into the pot, put the lid on the unit, and run the appliance until the water stops percolating. (If you have hard water, follow this procedure, but with a mixture of water and white vinegar.) When finished, run the appliance through its full cycle with plain water to make sure you've removed all traces of the solution, then wash the pot. Follow this cleaning regimen about every two or three weeks if you use the unit daily. For mineral deposits that won't come off with cleaning solutions, try steel wool and elbow grease.

Don't Forget the Faucet

Disassemble the faucet on a large, multicup coffee maker, then clean it with warm, soapy water and a soft bottle brush. (Forcing a brush into the assembled faucet will damage the mechanism.) For daily maintenance, clean the faucet by pouring hot water into the coffee maker and letting it run through the faucet. If the faucet drips, check to make sure that it is firmly in place.

Scour the Heating Well

Use an abrasive soap pad to scour the heating well, the cavity into which you insert the percolator tube. A vinegar solution also works well as a cleanser.

Keep Your Drip Coffee Maker Clean

While you should periodically wash the carafe and filter unit of a drip coffee maker in soap and water, the rest of the unit needs attention, too. To keep it clean, mix 1 cup of plain white vinegar for each 5 cups of cold water. Adjust the mixture to suit the capacity of your coffee maker. Pour the solution into the reservoir and turn on the coffee maker for 1 minute. Wait 30 minutes, then turn it on again and let it run as if you were making coffee. When it has finished its brewing cycle, turn off the machine, empty the carafe, and rinse it thoroughly. Then repeat the process, but this time with cold tap water only. You may want to run a second carafe of cold water through to be sure you've gotten every last bit of grime. When finished, wash the carafe and filter basket before using the coffee maker again.

COOKWARE

Safety Notes

Tips for All Types of Cookware

- Never leave an empty piece of cookware—or one that has boiled dry—on a hot gas or electric burner. The cookware may discolor, or even melt! If melting occurs, turn off the flame immediately. Do not attempt to move the cookware until it has cooled completely.

- Make sure you know just how much heat your cookware can withstand. Many pieces that can be used over high heat on top of the stove cannot be used safely under a broiler or in an oven heated to over 425°F. At the very least, such overly high temperatures will discolor your cookware, and possibly melt the handles.
- If possible, always turn pan handles to one side when cooking on top of the stove to avoid knocking over pans filled with hot food, which can cause serious burns.
- Do not allow gas flames to extend up the side of your cookware. Keep flames low enough so that they only touch the bottoms of your pots and pans.

Getting the Most from Your Product

Eliminate Burn Spots

Use a little baking soda and vinegar on your cookware's burn spots. Just moisten the pot, dust baking soda on the burn, then sprinkle with vinegar. After about half an hour the pot will be ready to wash with the rest of the dishes.

Unstick Covers

You're almost ready to bring the meal to the table when you discover that the cover on the pot you had allowed to cool has become stuck. This results from the formation of a partial vacuum. Don't try to remove the cover by force, since you could hurt yourself. Instead, put the pot back on the warm burner for a few minutes and then take the cover off as soon as you remove the pot from the stove.

Keep Aluminum Stain-Free

You can avoid discoloration of your aluminum cookware by not letting it soak in soapy water for too long and by not covering pots when you store them, since you may be sealing in moisture.

Cast Iron Must Be Seasoned

Although new cast-iron cookware is often seasoned at the factory before shipping, it's a good idea to reseason it before use. Start by scouring the cold, dry pot or pan with a stiff brush and soapy water. Rinse well and pat dry. Then pour about a tablespoon of salad oil or unsalted fat into the pan and coat all the surfaces, using a paper towel. Next, add enough oil to cover the bottom of the pan and heat the pan until the oil is hot, but not smoking. Swirl the pan to coat the oil over the bottom and sides, then place it in an oven (200°F to 250°F) for an hour. Turn off the oven, but leave the pan in place overnight. Remove the pan the next day and wipe off the excess oil with a paper towel. The pan is now ready to use.

If you receive an old cast-iron pot or pan that hasn't been used for a while, if your pan gets rusty, or if food burns onto it, you'll have to reseason it. First, get the rust off with soap and water and a stiff brush. Next, coat the lid and the inside surface with suet or vegetable oil. Bake the pot in the oven at the lowest heat setting for two hours. After the cast iron has cooled, wipe out the oil with a dry paper towel to clean it; washing it in water will destroy the seasoning.

To prevent rusting, remove food from your cast-iron pots or skillets immediately after cooking and never let them soak in soapy water.

Keep Copper Looking Good

Not only is copper elegant, it's also wonderful for cooking. With a little extra care, your pots can give you many years of fine service. Here are some tips for keeping your copper in tip-top shape:

- Never use metal utensils in a lined copper pot because you risk the chance of scratching the lining. Always use wooden spoons or plastic stirrers.
- Never whip or beat food in your lined copper pans.
- Avoid browning or sauteing foods in copper pans or skillets. The high temperatures needed for both methods of cooking could cause the lining to blister.
- Never put an empty copper pan over a hot burner.

- Never soak copper vessels and never store food in them.
- Never clean copper with an abrasive cleanser or scouring pad.

Made for Microwave

Cookware made especially for microwave ovens will add to the effectiveness of your appliance if you take a few simple precautions:

- Use this cookware only for its intended purposes. For example, do not place it in a toaster oven, put it on a range top, or run it under a broiler. Some cookware comes with special covers for storage; these should not be used for cooking.
- Mix food with rubber spatulas or wooden spoons rather than with anything sharp. This protects your cookware as well as prevents any unpleasant tastes from getting into your food that can result from using steel utensils.

Use Microwave Shelves Wisely

Cooking shelves make microwave meal preparation a breeze, doubling your cooking space and allowing you to cook more than one dish at a time. However, if you place a large dish on the shelf, it may prevent a substantial amount of microwave energy from reaching the item below it. That's fine if you want to warm bread and rolls below the shelf, but if the food on the bottom needs longer cooking, place only small dishes on the top shelf, with space between them to allow energy to get through, or rotate the top and bottom dishes.

When Nonstick Coatings Peel . . .

What can you do with a pan in which the nonstick coating has finally started to chip or peel off? We recommend that you stop using the pan. Some people may try to remove the remnants of the nonstick coating, but this is no easy task. Those that are left are likely to mix in with the food and be ingested. To minimize damage to a nonstick surface in the future, take special care not to use sharp utensils on it. When storing your pan, it's a good idea to line the inside with a paper towel to keep other pots and pans from scratching it.

Keep Stainless Steel out of the Heat

When cooking, use low to moderate heat to keep your stainless steel cookware in top condition. Start at a medium setting and lower it when you notice steam rising from the pot. If you're in a hurry and want to start with a pot you've just taken from the refrigerator, begin with low heat and increase it only when the pot has reached room temperature.

Cleaning and Maintenance

Stain Removal Tips for Aluminum

If your aluminum cookware is stained, here's an easy way to clean it. Fill the pot with water and add 2 tablespoons of cream of tartar; then boil the solution for 25 minutes. After the water has cooled, empty the pot and give it a new sheen with steel wool. Use cream of tartar to make aluminum surfaces shine, too.

If you don't have cream of tartar, try soapy steel wool, which should give you as much cleaning and shining power as a commercial aluminum cleaner. Be sure to rub against the "grain," not with it. Another trick for discolored pans is to fill them with enough vinegar to cover the discoloration and then bring to a boil. Simmer for 5 to 10 minutes, remove from the heat, and let cool for at least an hour. Then wash as you would normally.

Boil Away Stubborn, Sticky Food

Sometimes stuck-on food particles in cookware won't come off no matter what you do. Before you give up, fill the pot or pan about halfway with water and add ¼ cup of baking soda. Bring to a boil and then let cool for an hour. A little scrubbing should then do the trick.

Keep Cast Iron Dry

The key to caring for cast-iron cookware is to never put it away with any moisture on it. That means drying it thoroughly after washing in warm water—no soap and no detergent—and then storing it in a dry place. An easy way to get cast iron completely dry is to place it on the stove over low heat for a few minutes. When cool, coat the pan lightly with vegetable oil.

Shine Those Copper Bottoms

Don't let stained copper discourage you. You can remove the discoloration and restore the original luster of the metal either with a commercial cleaner or by dipping a cloth in white vinegar, sprinkling it with salt, and rubbing the offending spot. Or try a paste of salt, flour, and lemon juice to clean the copper.

Reline Copper Pots

Eventually, the lining of your copper pot will get worn to the point where it needs relining. You'll know that this time has come when you notice a worn spot at least the size of a quarter on the outside of the pot's bottom.

If it's not convenient to have the pot relined immediately, wash it thoroughly before each use to avoid leached copper in your food. Food cooked with a worn copper pot may be unappealing, distasteful, and, eaten often enough, poisonous.

Avoid Abrasives on Microwave Cookware

Avoid using steel wool or other abrasive cleaners on microwave cookware. Instead, clean it with plastic scrubbing pads. For hard-to-remove stains, try a commercial coffee-maker cleaner or soak the cookware in a mixture of one part liquid chlorine bleach to four parts hot water. A paste of baking soda and lemon juice works well on plastic cookware. Just rub it over the stain and let it stand for a while before washing.

Clean Nonstick Cookware Gently

To loosen food or stains on nonstick surfaces, use about a capful of your dishwashing soap and just enough water to cover the food. Then put the pot or pan on the stove and bring the water to a boil. Turn down the heat and simmer for about 10 minutes. Wash the pan as you would normally and recondition with a coating of vegetable oil.

Stainless Steel Cleaning Tips

Even if your stainless cookware has the following problems, you can still make it as attractive as the day you bought it:

- To remove *white spots* (caused by cooking with salt or storing foods containing salt in a pot overnight) pour some white vinegar directly on the discoloration and wipe it off with a paper towel. To prevent these spots while cooking, add salt after the water has come to a boil.
- To remove *stuck-on food* fill the pot with water, enough to cover the food scraps. Heat to boiling and then simmer for about 10 minutes. Let the water cool and then remove the food with a rubber spatula. If you experience this problem often, you could be using a heat setting that's too high. Try lowering it and lengthening cooking times.
- To remove *stubborn stains*, rub them with a plastic scouring pad. You also might try rubbing the stainless steel with a cotton ball soaked in rubbing alcohol. For a bright shine, use ammonia and water.
- To remove *"heat tinting"* caused by overheating, use a commercial stainless steel cleaner. Simply follow the directions on the container.

CORN POPPERS

Safety Notes

No Butter in the Popper

Never put butter directly into the corn popper because the butter will burn and smoke. Always use the butter dispenser. Better yet, melt the butter in a saucepan, then drizzle it over the popcorn in the serving bowl.

What Kind of Bowl?

If you use a metal bowl to catch the popcorn from your hot-air popper, the hot popcorn will heat the bowl. Be sure to place a potholder or trivet under the bowl to protect your counter or tabletop and use a potholder to pick up the full bowl. On the other hand, if you opt for a plastic bowl, make sure it can stand up to the heat from the corn popper—some types of plastic tend to melt.

Good to the Last Pop

Even after you turn the corn popper off and unplug it, a few kernels still may pop. Do not peek into the chute to see if any pieces are still there; hot kernels can jump in your face, causing injury. It's much safer to hold the machine with pot holders, then tip it over and gently·shake out any remaining kernels.

Popping Precautions

When operating your popper, a few simple rules should be followed:

- Keep children away from the popping chute of a hot-air popper. The chute is a potential danger zone during and shortly after popping because of the high temperatures reached by the unit.
- If you have a hot-air popper, make sure that all vents are clear of obstruction.
- Never immerse the base of a popper in water.
- Allow poppers to cool before cleaning, and with hot-air poppers, let the cover cool before removing.

Getting the Most from Your Product

Preheat before Popping

For best results, always remember to preheat your hot-air popper for 2 to 3 minutes before adding the popcorn. It takes a little more time, but it's worth the effort.

Cut the Butter

To be sure that your butter is ready at precisely the right time for your popcorn, it's a good idea to cut the butter into small pieces before adding it to the butter dispenser. If you're making two or more batches of buttered popcorn, wait a bit between batches to let the popper cool. Otherwise, the butter will melt as soon as you put it into the hot dispenser.

Keep Kernels Fresh

Corn kernels without the proper level of moisture will produce a disappointing batch of popcorn. To get larger and fluffier popcorn, store the kernels in an airtight container either in the refrigerator or at room temperature. The idea is to keep the moisture constant. If the kernels haven't been stored properly, here's how to refresh them: Put the corn in an airtight jar. Don't fill it all the way. You will need room to add water—1 teaspoon per cup of popcorn—and to shake the contents several times a day for two or three consecutive days. Between shakings and afterward, keep the container in the refrigerator.

Getting the Salt to Stick

Many corn poppers work without oil. The result is crispy popcorn that is reminiscent of corn popped over an open fire. However, it's difficult to get salt to stick to corn popped without oil. If you want to add salt, put 1 or 2 teaspoons of vegetable oil over the corn first.

Quick Troubleshooting

A popper can and does overheat, causing the thermostat to turn the appliance off. When this happens, unplug the popper from the wall outlet, remove the cover, and the chute—if it's separate from the chamber. Use hot pads, if necessary. Empty out all the popped corn and unpopped kernels from the chamber. Let the popper cool for 10 to 15 minutes before using again.

Microwave Popcorn

Popping corn in a microwave should not present any major problems. Start by sticking to the minimum amount of time called for in the instructions that come with the corn. You can always increase the cooking time, if necessary, the next time you cook up a batch. If the popping stops before the time recommended, remove the popcorn from the microwave. Waiting too long for a few more pops results in burned popcorn. It's best to throw out the kernels that don't pop rather than risk scorching.

Cleaning and Maintenance

Clean Gently

To clean hot-air poppers, unplug the unit from the outlet and popping chamber, allow to cool, and wipe the base with a soft, dry cloth. Wash the cover and butter melter in warm, soapy water.

To clean a popper that uses oil, wipe the nonstick surfaces with a soapy sponge or dampened cloth. Rinse by wiping with a moistened towel, then dry. Use a nonabrasive cleaner every once in a while to get rid of oil buildup. To clean the cover, wash in hot, soapy water.

No matter what type of popper you have, don't use steel wool and abrasive cleaners.

Banish Popper Stains

Use a commercial coffeepot destainer to remove discolorations from the nonstick surfaces of your corn popper. Then wash with soap and water and recondition the surface with a teaspoon of vegetable oil. Or try removing stains with lemon juice or vinegar and a soft cloth.

Keep Corn from Sticking

Want to avoid having particles of corn stick to the nonstick surface of your popper? Simply recondition it periodically by rubbing a teaspoon of vegetable oil over the surface with a paper towel.

CURLING IRONS

Safety Notes

Don't Curl in the Bathroom

It's dangerous to use a curling iron in the bathroom, where there are too many chances for water to come in contact with the appliance. Don't use or store the curling iron where it can fall into a tub or sink, and *never* use it while bathing. If the curling iron should fall into water or other liquid, unplug it immediately—do not reach into the water to retrieve it.

Curl with Common Sense

As with other electrical appliances, curling irons carry the risk of burns, electrocution, fire, and personal injury if not used with common sense. Keep these points in mind when using your curling iron:

- Never leave the curling iron unattended while it is plugged in.
- Do not use attachments that are not recommended by the manufacturer of your appliance. Attachments from other manufacturers may look similar, but may damage your curling iron.
- Never use the curling iron if it has a damaged cord or plug or if it has been dropped in water. Instead, take it to a service center for repair.
- Never block the air openings of the curling iron and don't leave the appliance on a soft surface, such as a bed or couch, which can block the air openings and possibly cause a fire. Keep the air openings free of lint and hair.
- Curling irons are very hot when in use. Take care not to let the

curler touch bare skin. Be especially careful if you are using the appliance on a child or an elderly person.
- Always unplug mist curling irons before filling with water. And keep in mind that while emitting steam, this type of curler may cause burns if it is used too close to the skin, scalp, or eyes.
- If your curling iron has a brush attachment, never wrap the cord around the brush. This could cause the cord to wear prematurely and break.

Getting the Most from Your Product

Dry Your Hair First

Want to get the most from your curling iron? You'll get the best results if you dry your hair first, before you start to curl it. Another point to remember: Don't use your curling iron in a bathroom or other humid area—the humidity can, depending on your hair type, take the curl right out of your hair or, conversely, leave you with a frizzy mess.

Wait for the Light

Some curling irons can be filled with water to create steam during the curling process, but be sure to wait until the indicator light comes on before working on your hair. If the water inside hasn't yet reached the right temperature, the unit's operation is likely to be uneven. At worst, hot water (instead of steam) could come sputtering out of the vents.

Don't Use Hair Spray First

Curling irons and hair sprays don't mix—the spray can clog the curler's steam vents. Only use hair spray after you curl.

Curling Wigs

You can use your curling iron on wigs made from human hair but not on those made of synthetics. Use the curling iron on natural wigs the same way you would if it were your own hair, taking care not to keep the unit on any section for too long.

Cleaning and Maintenance

Keep the Dust Out

Keep all air and steam vents clear of dirt, hair, and dust. To clean, be sure the curling iron is unplugged and cool, then clear out the vents with a damp cotton swab or toothpick. (If they're really gummed up, you may need to use something more firm, such as a needle or straight pin.) To clean the exterior of the curling iron, wipe with a damp cloth.

Keep the Cord Tidy

Does the cord on your curling iron (or other appliances) resist all your efforts to store it neatly? If you no longer have the wrapper that held the cord together in a tidy bunch, try using a cardboard toilet paper roll as a substitute. Just loop the cord until you can slide it into the roll.

Troubleshooting Chart

Problem	Cause	Solution
Not enough steam.	Mineral deposits clogging vents.	Unplug the iron and let it cool completely. Use a needle or toothpick to unclog the vents.
Unit doesn't heat.	No power at outlet.	Replace fuse or reset circuit breaker.
	Cord may be damaged.	Check cord for wear. Have it replaced if damaged.
	Heating element may be defective.	Have element replaced.
Unit blows fuse when used.	Circuit overloaded.	Reduce number of appliances on circuit.
	Cord or plug short-circuited.	Inspect for breaks and have repaired if necessary.

(continued)

Troubleshooting Chart—Continued

Problem	Cause	Solution
Unit blows fuse when used.	There's moisture in the wiring.	If unit has gotten wet wait 24 hours before turning it on. If it still causes problems, have repaired.

D

Deep-Fat Fryers

Dehumidifiers

Dishwashers

DEEP-FAT FRYERS

Smoke Signals

Achieving and maintaining the right oil temperature for successful deep-fat frying is critical. If the oil in your deep-fat fryer starts smoking, you probably exceeded the safe temperature level, which is around 380°F. When that happens, immediately turn down the temperature control setting.

Know When Your Oil Has Had It

Oil for deep-fat frying can and should be recycled. To store your oil for reuse, strain it through cheesecloth and place it in an airtight container. For best results, keep it in a cool spot. How long can you continue to recycle your frying oil? Look for these signs that your oil is no longer usable:
• The oil thickens and its color darkens.
• The oil foams when cooking.
• Foods don't seem to brown the way they used to.
• The oil smells rancid.

Keep Fishy Oil Separate

If you deep-fry fish or seafood, save that oil separately from your other frying oil and use it only for more seafood. Otherwise, you'll impart a definite "fishy" taste to blander foods, such as french fries.

Minimize the Mess

Deep-fat frying can make any kitchen messy. But taking two easy precautions will keep the situation from getting out of hand. First, use paper toweling to blot-dry foods before frying them—water in any quantity causes cooking oil to spatter. Second, use a reliable brand of vegetable shortening or cooking oil. Avoid using margarine, butter, or olive oil because these fats burn or smoke at lower temperatures.

DEHUMIDIFIERS

Safety Notes

Keep It Dry

Although the dehumidifier's job is to combat moisture, it is still an electrical appliance that has the potential to cause damage if it becomes wet.

- Never attempt to empty the drip pan or collector bucket while the unit is running. If the water spills, you could be in for a nasty shock.
- If you use your dehumidifier to dry a wet floor, be sure the unit is sitting on a dry surface before you turn it on.
- Don't let the dehumidifier's power cord sit in or near liquid.

Getting the Most from Your Product

Time to Turn It Off

Most manufacturers warn that running your dehumidifier when the room temperature dips below 65°F can damage the compressor. To play it safe, you should probably turn the unit off when the temperature is a few degrees warmer. If you run your dehumidifier at night, listen to the weather forecast. Lower nighttime temperatures will probably bring the relative humidity to a bearable level by the time you fall asleep and this makes it unnecessary to run the unit.

Let the Air Flow

In order to extract the maximum moisture from the air, a dehumidifier must have air circulating freely around it—but this doesn't mean fresh, outdoor air. Close all doors and windows before turning on the unit. And don't hide the dehumidifier behind furniture or in a corner—keep it several inches away from walls or other barriers so air movement in and out of the unit isn't restricted.

Give Your Dehumidifier a Litter Box

If you do not have a hose connected to your dehumidifier to drain away water, the drip pan or collector bucket may overflow. Some units have automatic shutoff devices that sense when the collector is getting full, but if your unit is new, watch it carefully at first to be sure it shuts off in time to prevent an overflow. To play it safe, place the dehumidifier inside a large plastic litter box to collect any errant water.

Bigger Is Better

If you find that you have to run your small, low-capacity unit continuously, and you still can't get rid of all the humidity in the room, you may need a new and bigger unit. To dehumidify a large area, or one in which humidity runs consistently high, a bigger, higher-capacity model is more efficient. While a large model will probably cost more initially, over time you'll save on your electric bill because the unit will run less frequently.

Troubleshooting Chart

Problem	Cause	Solution
High humidity remains after several days of use at maximum setting.	Built-up humidity not released from furniture and other room contents.	Let the machine continue to run at maximum setting. It may take weeks to remove all moisture.

Troubleshooting Chart—Continued

Problem	Cause	Solution
Dehumidifier does not run.	Fuse is blown or circuit tripped.	Check fuses, circuit breakers; make sure plug is connected to outlet.
	Appliance has reached the level of dryness you set.	Some units turn off when selected dryness level is reached; turn to the maximum level, then reset.
	Drip pan or collector bucket is full (on models with automatic shutoff).	Empty water from unit.
Dehumidifier runs too much.	Windows or doors near the unit are creating an environmental imbalance.	Close windows and doors.
	Grille or dehumidifying coil is dirty.	Clean grille and/or coil.
Dehumidifier is on but not working properly.	Room temperature is too low.	Do not run unit when temperature is below 65°F.
Frost appears on coils.	Room temperature is too low.	Do not run unit when temperature is below 65°F.

Cleaning, Maintenance, and Storage

Keep It Clean

Before you use your dehumidifier for the season, vacuum the air passages, the coils, and the fan blades to remove dust. At the end of the season, before storing the unit, wash the coils and fan blades with a household cleaner or diluted bleach to discourage mildew growth.

Halt Algae Growth

The easiest way to head off algae is to wash out the drip pan or collector bucket every month. If the algae builds up, clean and then place a few teaspoons of ammonia in the collector to kill off the spores.

Take a Break

Whenever you turn off your humidifier to empty the collector, take a break before turning the unit back on. The compressor needs about five minutes of rest so that it isn't damaged by a quick off/on action.

Eliminate Odor Problems

If your dehumidifier smells musty, unplug the unit, and then open it and remove water that has collected in the base under the compressor and fan. If you smell tobacco when you run the dehumidifier, vacuum the condenser fins. If that doesn't work, spray some air freshener on the condenser.

Do without Drip Pans

If you have a dehumidifier in your basement and your basement has a floor drain, make life easier on yourself by placing the unit directly over the drain. You can also run a hose from the unit to the floor drain. Either way eliminates the bother of emptying the drip pan.

What Your Product Won't Do

It Can't Cool the Air

Did you ever run your dehumidifier on a hot day and discover that you were feeling even less comfortable than before you turned it on? A dehumidifier produces heat when it condenses water vapor—the air that comes out of the unit is *dryer* than the air that went in, but not any cooler. If you're feeling uncomfortable, it's best to turn off the unit and open the windows and doors.

DISHWASHERS

Safety Notes

Get the Point?

Improperly loading knives and other sharp utensils into your dishwasher could cause injury to you and could damage your appliance. To ensure safety when handling these items:

- Always place them in the dishwasher with the handles pointed up.
- Keep all sharp objects away from the door gasket, since they can easily puncture the seal.

Disconnect the Spray Hose

Before you run your portable dishwasher, check to be sure you've disconnected the sink spray hose, if you have one. It's not a good idea to have a spray hose on the same line with a dishwasher—the spray hose may burst when the dishwasher is running.

Getting the Most from Your Product

Tips for Energy and Washing Efficiency

To save energy and still get the most from your dishwasher, follow these suggestions:

- Operate the machine only when it is fully loaded.
- Don't use a "rinse and hold" cycle.
- Don't use your dishwasher to warm plates.
- In hot weather, run the dishwasher at night to cut air conditioning costs. You may save energy dollars all year long by running your dishwasher (and other large appliances) at night. Some electric companies charge lower rates for energy consumed after midnight. Check with your local utility for information about these "off-peak" rates.

- Turn off your dishwasher before it starts its drying cycle. This saves about one-third of the energy cost. Open the door after the final rinse and let the dishes air dry.
- Scrape plates well before washing.
- Use only fresh detergent.
- Don't block spray arms or detergent cups when loading dishes, and leave space between dishes for circulation.
- Clean the drains regularly.
- Be sure the dishwasher sits level and doesn't wobble.

Choose the Right Wash Cycle

Though there are differences in wash cycles on various makes of dishwashers, use these guidelines to choosing the right cycle setting:

Short or Quick Wash. Use this setting for small loads and lightly soiled dishes.

Normal or Full Wash. Use this setting for everyday dishes. Usually the machine goes through two wash and rinse cycles followed by a dry heat cycle.

Soak and Scrub. Use this setting for soaking and washing hard-to-clean dishes.

Rinse and Hold. Some dishwashers feature this as a special setting for rinsing a partial load. By using this cycle, you can keep dishes moist until you're ready to wash a full load. Do not use soap with this cycle.

Match Detergent to Water

Get maximum performance from your dishwasher by using a detergent with the right phosphorous content for the hardness of your water and by choosing the right cycle. If your city water department doesn't have information on the hardness measurement for your water supply (expressed in grains per gallon), you may have to pay to have a private company determine it. If your water hardness exceeds 4 grains per gallon, you need a detergent with a phosphorous content above 8.7 percent. You'll find the detergent's phosphorous content printed on the package.

How Much Detergent?

Let the hardness of your water determine the amount of detergent you use in your dishwasher. For water hardness up to 4 grains (soft), use one tablespoon of detergent. For 5 to 8 grains (medium), use 2 to 3 tablespoons of detergent. Hard water—9 to 12 grains—requires 3 to 4 tablespoons. For water hardness of more than 12 grains, you can try adding an extra teaspoon of detergent for each grain over 12. (Add the detergent to the bottom of the tub when the main wash cycle begins.) But with water this hard, you may need a water softener.

How to Deal with Hard-Water Film

Have your drinking glasses ever emerged from the dishwasher covered with a film? If you rub one of the glasses with vinegar and the film lifts, the cause is water hardness. You can remove the film by adding vinegar to your next load of dishes. Be sure, however, to keep all metal objects out of this load. Use a two-wash cycle, and after the second fill, stop the dishwasher and add 2 cups of vinegar to the wash water.

There are several things you can do—short of installing a water softener—to get around this problem in the future:

- Make sure you're using a detergent that matches the hardness of your water, and keep the soap dry. If you've had the detergent for more than a few weeks, throw it out and try a new batch.
- Use water that's at least 140°F.
- Check to be sure that you're loading the dishwasher so the water sprays over the surface of every dish and utensil.
- Use the heat dry feature instead of economizing with air drying.
- Add a rinse agent to cut down on filming.

Keep Glasses Sparkling

If rubbing vinegar on a filmed-over drinking glass does not remove the film, the coating is "etched on;" unfortunately, a permanent condition. Steps you can take to prevent this in the future include:

- Use less detergent (because the problem here could be water softness).
- Use another detergent if your current soap was designed for water harder than yours.
- Avoid water softeners.
- Make sure the water temperature does not exceed 140°F.
- Do not use water for other purposes, such as baths or showers, while using the dishwasher.

Make Sure the Water's Hot

If your water heater is far from your dishwasher, the hot water may not reach its maximum temperature when you first draw it from the tap. (Fill a cup of hot water when you first turn on the faucet and measure its temperature with a candy or meat thermometer.) If the temperature is below 140°F, let the hot water run until it reaches 140°F before you turn on the dishwasher. If the water doesn't reach that temperature after a few minutes, raise the setting on your water heater. Cooler water won't get your dishes clean.

Detergent: Help or Hindrance?

If your dishes are no longer coming out clean and you've accounted for the water hardness and checked your water temperature, the problem could be with your detergent. Pour some of your detergent into a glass of hot water. Does it dissolve quickly and completely, or does it leave a residue? If it does leave a residue, either your detergent has been around too long and needs to be replaced, or you should try another brand. Also consider switching brands if you discover lumps of detergent in the dispenser after you've washed a load of dishes. At the store, shake the detergent box before you buy it. If the contents sound and feel lumpy rather than powdery, the detergent has been on the shelf too long.

Once you bring it home, keep your detergent fresh by storing it in a moisture-free container in a cool, dry place—*not* under the sink.

Rinse Flatware First

You don't have to rinse dishes before placing them in your dishwasher, but it is a good idea to run some water over flatware, especially if you're not going to run the dishwasher right away. Food containing salts and acids can tarnish silver and stainless steel if left on too long. In fact, it's not a good idea to wash silver in the dishwasher, because the detergent may remove the silver plating. But if you do wash silver, be sure you don't wash stainless steel flatware and silverware in the same load, because silver can pit and tarnish stainless steel.

Neatness Doesn't Always Count

To get your silverware really clean, don't neatly place forks with forks and nestle spoons together. Instead, load unlike pieces of silverware together (say, knives and forks) and like pieces alternately head to handle. This method exposes the maximum surface of each piece to the spraying water.

Take the Water Pressure Test

To work effectively, your dishwasher—depending on its size—requires water pressure between 15 and 120 pounds per square inch. To test your water pressure, turn off all your other faucets, place a ½-gallon container under the hot water faucet of your kitchen sink, and open up the hot water faucet all the way. The container should fill within 14 seconds.

If your water pressure is low, it's possible that the trouble is only temporary, perhaps caused by a break in your city or town's water system. Try the test again in a day or two. If the pressure still isn't high enough, the problem could be with the pipes and plumbing in your home or in the main water supply to the house. But before you begin to replace pipes in your house, call in a professional to check out the problem.

Keep Aluminum Away from Soap

Your detergent's alkalinity could discolor aluminum pots and pans if undissolved pieces of soap strike their surfaces. Prevent this by keeping aluminum away from the detergent dispenser.

Troubleshooting Chart

Problem	Cause	Solution
Leftover detergent in dispenser after machine has completed all cycles.	Detergent is old or damp; dishes are blocking flow of water to detergent cup.	Get new detergent or rearrange dishes.
Small food particles still sticking to dishes after washing.	Spray arms are clogged with tiny food particles.	Remove spray arms from machine, run tap water through them. Use a stiff brush to clean the strainer and remove any particles in the holes.
Dishwasher does not turn on.	Fuse has blown or circuit breaker tripped.	Check fuses and circuit breakers.
	Door isn't closed or not latched.	Close door, latch securely.
	Water supply to dishwasher is not on.	Check water supply.
	Overflow protection float is not in place.	Some dishwashers have an overflow protection float that must be in place for operation.
Dishes are not clean.	Water temperature is too low.	Most manufacturers recommend that water temperature entering the dishwasher be between 120°F and 140°F.
	Racks are not loaded properly.	Load racks so that dirty surfaces face the spray. Dishes should not touch each other. Make sure nothing stops rotation of the spray arm.

Troubleshooting Chart—Continued

Problem	*Cause*	*Solution*
	Detergent dispenser is overfilled.	Too much detergent can cause the dispenser to stay closed.
	Too little detergent is used.	Use at least 2 tablespoons of detergent in each detergent cup.
	Detergent is too old.	Use fresh detergent.
Dishes are not drying properly.	Racks are not loaded properly.	Dishes must be placed so they drain. Some water on dishes is normal. Open door once cycle has ended and allow dishes to air dry, or use a commercial rinse aid.
Dishwasher is leaving spots or film on dishes.	You have hard water or water with a high mineral content.	Use a commercial liquid rinse aid.
	Water temperature is too low.	Increase water temperature to between 120°F and 140°F.
	Detergent is not fresh or incorrect amount has been used.	Use fresh detergent and fill dispenser properly.
Dishes have black or gray marks on them.	Dishes rubbed against aluminum pieces.	Scrub dishes with a mild abrasive cleaner. Next time, load dishwasher so aluminum pieces do not rub against dishes.
Nonstick cookware has white marks on it.	Some nonstick surface has been removed by dishwasher detergent.	Reseason the cookware and wash by hand next time.
Dishwasher does not drain properly.	Food is clogging drain screen.	Clean the drain screen.

(continued)

Troubleshooting Chart—Continued

Problem	Cause	Solution
Dishwasher makes a rattling noise.	Dishes are not loaded properly.	Make sure dishes are loaded so they don't touch.

Cleaning and Maintenance

Banish Lime Deposits

If you live in an area where the water is hard, you may notice lime deposits building up inside your dishwasher. Unfortunately, they won't go away through the self-cleaning action that takes care of other dirt. One way to eliminate lime deposits is to put 2 cups of vinegar in the soap dispenser and run it through a full wash cycle with the dishwasher empty (do not add detergent). Or, you can wet the deposits and sprinkle a powdered, citrus-flavored breakfast beverage (such as Tang) on them. After about an hour, wash a load of dishes as you would normally and the stains should wash away. The citric acid in the powder gets rid of the buildup.

Check the Air Gap

In some areas, plumbing codes require that you have an air gap for your dishwasher—a plumbing device that prevents water from backing up into the dishwasher if a drain clogs. If you have this feature, be sure to check it at least once a month. An air gap can easily become clogged with crumbs and grit. To clean it, make sure the dishwasher is off and cool, unscrew the plastic cap on the air gap, and clean out any dirt with a toothpick.

Winterize Your Dishwasher

If you have a dishwasher in your vacation home, take these precautions before closing the house for the winter to make sure that you will have a working dishwasher when you return next season:

1. Cut off water and electricity.
2. Drain the water line by disconnecting it from each side of the inlet valve.
3. Reconnect the line.
4. Pour a quart of nontoxic propylene glycol antifreeze (the kind that's used in sanitary water systems in recreational vehicles) into the dishwasher's tub.

When you are ready to use your dishwasher again, fill the detergent cups and run the empty dishwasher through a full cycle before loading it with dirty dishes.

What Your Product Won't Do

Items for the Sink

Since the following materials do not do well in dishwashers, it's best to wash them by hand:

• Anodized aluminum and lacquered colorware may change color.
• Bone china and china with a gold or silver rim may crack or chip, and the gold or silver finish may wash off.
• Cast iron will rust.
• Crystal may break or crack.
• Dirilyte, the material in gold-colored flatware, will discolor.
• Gold-plated flatware may lose its finish.
• Knives with hollow handles may come apart; your dishwasher's cleaning action could loosen the glue that attaches the handles to the knives.
• Pewter will not hold up under high water temperatures and will discolor, or the finish will pit.
• Plastic objects not marked "dishwasher-safe" will melt in hot water.
• Silver may lose its finish.
• Tin may rust.
• Wooden dishware may warp, crack, or lose its finish.

F

Fans, Electric

Fire Extinguishers

Flooring

Food Mixers

Food Processors

Freezers

Furnaces

Furniture, Indoor

Furniture, Outdoor

FANS, ELECTRIC

Fan Fundamentals

- Be very careful not to touch any moving parts on the fan.
- Never let the fan come into contact with water or other liquid.
- Always unplug the fan from the wall outlet when it's not in use and before you clean it.
- Make sure you place the fan on a level, stable surface where it cannot tip or fall easily.
- Keep children and pets away from fans.

A Higher Alternative

Do you worry about the safety of window or floor fans when small children are in the house? Consider buying a ceiling fan. Not only is it safe because it's out of reach, but it moves a lot of air with very little noise.

Provide Plenty of Head Room

It's never a good idea to install a ceiling fan in a room with ceilings less than eight feet high. Besides the obvious potential for head injuries to tall people, a ceiling fan will also get in the way of raised arms, such as when getting dressed or when doing stretching exercises.

Getting the Most from Your Product

Turn It Off and Save

Fans equipped with thermostats can save you money on your electric bill. If you're not careful, however, the fan can run while you're not home, wasting a lot of electricity. If the fan is not operating when you leave the house in the morning, you may just think that it's turned off; more likely, though, the thermostat has shut the fan down in the cool, early morning hours. But as the day heats up, on goes your faithful fan, serving no purpose other than to use electricity. So make it part of your morning routine to hit that "off" switch.

Twice As Cool

If you have both a fan and a window air conditioner, use them in tandem to make your house comfortable on the warmest days. If your air conditioner is powerful enough, direct its cool air to other rooms with the help of a floor fan. For example, place a floor fan in a hallway outside the air-conditioned room. Use the fan to draw cool air to other rooms. A hassock-style floor fan is ideal for this cooling technique, because you can point it at almost any angle you wish. Just be sure to keep children away from the floor fan—some units have enough space between the blade guards for an inquisitive child's fingers to reach dangerously close to the blades.

Round-the-Clock Duty

In the daytime, the air in your house is likely to be cooler than the outside air. Shut all the windows before the sun hits your house, thereby trapping the cool air inside. Then turn on a floor fan to circulate the air. At night, when the outside temperature drops faster than the inside, open a window and place your fan in it to draw in the cooler outdoor air.

The Pause That Refreshes

Even at the beginning of the hottest days, your house is likely to be quite cool if you've had your fan on all night. Take advantage of this and save electricity by turning off your fan for a while. With the windows closed and the drapes and shades drawn, you should be able to stay cool for quite a while before your house starts to feel stuffy.

Bring In Outside Air

It makes sense to pull cool air in and through the house from outside by using a window fan on its exhaust setting. But you can defeat the purpose by leaving windows or doors open near the fan, causing a substantial amount of air to be pulled in at these locations, and not from other places in the house. To use an exhaust fan efficiently and to create a flow of air throughout the house, open only those windows and doors that are farthest away from the fan. If you will operate this fan only in its exhaust setting, install panels around it to prevent it from drawing air in at its sides.

Cooling One Room

When you want to cool only one room, even if it has only one window, use a window fan on its exhaust setting. Simply open the window at both the top and the bottom, then place the fan in the bottom. The fan will draw air in through the top, circulate it throughout the room, and then blow it out through the bottom of the window.

Eliminate Those Bad Vibes

Ceiling fans have a good track record with noise because they are installed with a rubber block or grommets to prevent noise from vibration. This hardware is very flexible, however, and will make an unbalanced fan shimmy from side to side. To eliminate vibrations, be sure the fan's blades aren't warped, and install the fan with hardware that can support at least 50 pounds.

Troubleshooting Chart

Problem	Cause	Solution
Fan doesn't start.	Fuse or circuit breaker is blown.	Replace fuse or reset circuit breaker.
	Cord is defective.	Check cord for breaks. Replace if necessary.
Fan vibrates or is very noisy.	Fan is resting on or against an uneven surface.	Place an oscillating fan on a cushioned surface; place a cardboard shim between a window fan and the window frame.

Troubleshooting Chart—Continued

Problem	Cause	Solution
	Blades are defective.	Check for bent blades, broken parts, or loose hub. Repair or replace.
	Fan guards are loose.	Tighten or replace.
	Blades are striking the frame.	Straighten blades.

Cleaning and Maintenance

Dust Your Blades

Disassembling a box fan to clean the blades is quite a chore. You can free yourself from this bothersome task by using your vacuum cleaner to get the dust off your fan. An alternative is to use your hair dryer to blow the dust off. By tackling the dust regularly, you'll eliminate the need to get in there and scrub.

Keep Kitchen Fans Clean

An accumulation of grime and grease can throw fan blades off balance, eventually causing the bearings to wear down un-evenly. The most likely environment to produce grease is, of course, the kitchen. So if you keep a fan in the kitchen window, be sure to regularly clean the blades with a dilute ammonia mix to cut through the grease. (This is a good habit to follow for cleaning kitchen exhaust fans, as well.)

Safe Attic Fan Repairs

Your attic fan is likely to have an overload protector. If the fan has shut down and you're tinkering with it to see what's wrong, the fan could start going again—with disastrous consequences. You can circumvent potential accidents by putting in an "off" switch near the fan. A better alternative is to cut off electricity to the fan at the circuit breaker or fuse box before you approach the fan.

FIRE EXTINGUISHERS

Safety Notes

When a Fire Starts . . .

Follow these steps if a fire breaks out in your house:

1. Get everyone else out of the house quickly.
2. Call the fire department.
3. Determine whether you can get out safely.
4. If your escape route is clear, next decide if the fire is small enough to be put out or slowed down by the use of your fire extinguisher.
5. Use the extinguisher, then get out.

Use It Right

Stay at least six feet from the fire and near an exit when using your extinguisher. Point the nozzle at the base of the fire rather than at the smoke or flames. As you spray the chemical from your fire extinguisher, sweep it back and forth rapidly along the base of the fire. At first the flames will shoot up, then die out. Once the extinguisher is used up, and if the fire is still burning, get out quickly.

Get the Whole Family Involved

At least once a year, review fire safety and fire extinguisher use with your family. Make sure everyone knows how to get out of the house quickly, and make sure that all but the youngest members of the family know how to operate the extinguisher. This means you must locate the extinguisher in an easily accessible place, and within reach of the smallest family member who will use it (but beyond the reach of small children).

Cleaning, Maintenance, and Storage

Monthly Inspections Are a Must

Keep your extinguisher where it won't experience extremes of heat or cold, and inspect it monthly. During the monthly inspection, examine the nozzle for clogging and check the pressure gauge. If the pressure is too high or too low, have the extinguisher serviced. Make sure it's free from any corrosion. If it has been dropped or has sustained damage of any kind—even a dent—take it out of service and have it checked by your dealer. Refill the unit with a fresh batch of chemical mixture every six months, or immediately if someone partially discharges it. If you have a dry chemical extinguisher, turn it upside down once a year and tap it with a rubber mallet to keep the chemical from caking.

Keep It Handy

To be sure that your fire extinguisher is there when you need it, place it:

- Near an exit, but not in a drawer or on a shelf.
- In a spot that is easy to reach.
- Well away from potential fire starters, such as stoves or cans of flammable material.

FLOORING

Getting the Most from Your Product

You Have to Wax Linoleum

If you have a linoleum floor, you know that it's durable and easy to clean. Unfortunately, cleaning just isn't enough. Because moisture will damage a linoleum floor, the floor must be periodically waxed. A self-polishing wax (liquid) will last about two months, while a polishing wax (either liquid or paste that must be buffed) should last about twice as long.

Keep Linoleum Dry

Whether you're wiping up a spill or actually cleaning the floor, don't let water or any liquid sit on linoleum. Liquid can seep through seams, destroying the adhesive that holds it in place.

Don't Dent the Floor

Always use plastic or rubber coasters under chair and table legs to protect your resilient (vinyl) or wood flooring from dents and gauges. If you have to move something heavy (such as a refrigerator) across the floor, slide it on pieces of heavy cardboard to minimize floor damage.

Cleaning and Maintenance

Less Is Best

When it comes to cleaning resilient (vinyl) flooring, a damp mop, mild detergent, and a bit of elbow grease is all you should need. If you have a linoleum floor, every few months you'll need to apply a coat of wax to help bring up the shine and protect the surface.

Protect a No-Wax Finish

No-wax floors require a different approach to maintenance than floors that demand waxing or polishing to add a shine. Begin by removing loose dirt by sweeping or vacuuming as often as necessary. Because no-wax floors have no protective polish, you must take extra measures to protect the surface from gritty dirt that could be easily ground in.

A mat by the door can do wonders to reduce the amount of dirt tracked inside. You should avoid using mats with a rubber backing, however, since they can leave stains where they have come into contact with your no-wax floor.

At least once every two weeks you should thoroughly clean

the floor to prevent a waxy film building up on it. Use a general-purpose detergent recommended for floors, dilute it with water according to the directions, and use it with a sponge mop. Do not use it in greater strength. In addition, stay away from soap-based products; they can leave behind the dulling film you're trying so hard to get rid of.

For stubborn dirt, use a nylon scrubbing pad. Do not use steel wool or an abrasive cleanser meant for scouring. Rinse the floor completely with a large amount of clean, warm water. Mop up your rinse water, being sure to remove it from all indentations on the floor, and then let the floor dry thoroughly before anyone walks on it.

Poly Your Wood Floors

Since wood can be easily marred, it's a good idea to finish it with polyurethane. Pad chair legs with heavy-duty felt or use plastic casters since it's easy to scratch the polyurethane. Wipe up spills promptly.

Bring Back the Gloss

When normal foot traffic begins to reduce the gloss of your no-wax floor, restore it with the application of a special no-wax floor finish available at floor retailers and your hardware store.

For best results, and to avoid trapping dirt, make sure you thoroughly vacuum, wash, and rinse the floor before applying the finish.

Solve the Stain Problem

Your detergent may have a hard time getting rid of certain stains—such as ink, lipstick, mustard, iodine, paint, varnish, tar, and asphalt—from your resilient (vinyl) flooring. If the spill has dried, remove the excess with a plastic spatula or other tool that will not scratch the surface. Then wet a cloth with liquid detergent and wipe the stained area. If the stain still shows, use rubbing alcohol to remove ink, lipstick, mustard, and iodine. If it still doesn't come off, follow up with a wipe of chlorine bleach as well.

Use turpentine to remove paint and varnish, nail polish

remover to remove nail polish, and lighter fluid to remove tar or asphalt. Try to use as small an amount as possible of these products and a clean white cloth when removing stains.

When using any of the above products on your floor, don't walk on the area until at least 30 minutes after it's been treated. Then rinse with water and let the floor dry. Keep in mind that rubbing alcohol, turpentine, nail polish remover, and lighter fluid all produce fumes and are all highly flammable, so use caution. Always use these products in a well-ventilated room and try not to breathe in the fumes.

Banish Tile Streaks Forever

The best way to avoid streaks on your tile floor is to first wash it with soap and water and then rinse it thoroughly with *clear* water. Otherwise, if you use the same water to rinse that you washed with, the dirt particles suspended in it will cause streaking.

Get at the Grout

To clean the grouted valleys between tiles, use a grout cleaner. Apply it with a stiff toothbrush, rinse with clear water, and watch the dirt disappear. Use a scouring-powder paste *only* for very stained grout.

Put Down Curled Edges

Besides being unsightly, curled floor edges can be a safety hazard. Put down curled edges with linoleum cement (available from hardware stores). Apply the cement with a putty knife, and then weight down the floor for twenty-four hours.

Make Filler for Holes

You can make a paste filler to fill small holes in your vinyl, provided you have a spare piece of flooring. Fold the spare piece with the surface on the outside and scrape along the fold with a utility knife. Catch the flakes in a bowl. Continue to fold and scrape along the length of the flooring piece until you have more than enough flakes to fill the hole. Add a few drops of clear nail polish and stir until the mixture has the consistency of putty.

Surround the hole you wish to patch with masking tape to protect the rest of the flooring, then force the paste filler into the hole with a putty knife. Scrape off the excess and smooth the filler with the knife. After the filler has set (about 30 minutes) buff the patch with 00-grade steel wool.

FOOD MIXERS

Safety Notes

Mix Safely

- Keep your fingers, hair, and utensils away from the beaters while the mixer is operating.
- Unless you have a cordless rechargeable hand mixer, always unplug the mixer when you're finished with it.
- If you allow children to use the mixer, supervise them as they use it.
- Make sure you remove the beaters from the mixer before washing.
- Do not immerse the mixer—except the removable beaters and dough hooks—in water.

Getting the Most from Your Product

Keep Your Mixer in Optimum Condition

- Don't overtax the motor by mixing anything too thick. If the beaters slow down and the motor sounds like it's straining, stop the mixer immediately and either add more liquid to the batter or finish mixing by hand.
- Always wipe up food spills immediately with a damp sponge and then dry with a soft cloth. Cleanup is easier when food has

not had a chance to harden. For stubborn spots, full-strength liquid detergent works best.

• When cleaning beaters of excess batter, never bang them against the mixing bowl or sink. Bent beaters lose their efficiency.

The Best Way to Use a Hand-Held Mixer

The key to success when using a hand-held mixer is to guide it through your food correctly. Move the mixer slowly along the sides and through the center of your mixing bowl, always in the same direction.

Stabilize the Bowl in Your Stationary Mixer

Want to stop your bowl from "slippin' 'n' slidin'?" You can cure its wanderlust by putting it on a damp towel before you begin mixing. Some bowl movement, however, is normal when the beaters are whirling away.

Hands-On Kneading

Kneading dough for bread with a stationary mixer is a little like letting a bucking bronco loose on your countertop. If the mixture tries to jump the edge of your counter, simply guide the bowl lightly with your hands. Be sure to stay well clear of the churning dough hooks.

Mix Dry and Wet Ingredients Neatly

If you want to mix dry and wet foods smoothly, without making a mess, try processing them briefly at one of the slow speeds to moisten the dry food. Then gradually work up to the speed the recipe calls for.

Start at Room Temperature

Unless your recipe specifies otherwise, all ingredients you mix should go in at room temperature. So take food out of the refrigerator far enough in advance to allow it to warm sufficiently by the time you're ready to begin mixing.

Tips for Beating Eggs

Eggs need special attention when they are to be added to your mixer. Here are two suggestions for handling this ingredient:

- You don't want egg shells in your mixture, nor do you want to discover that an egg is bad as you break it into the bowl; it's best to break the eggs into a separate bowl before you add them to your mixture.
- When beating egg whites, be sure to remove any oil that may be on the beaters or on the surface of the bowl. Even a little oil can keep the egg whites from aerating properly.

Keep Your Cordless Mixer Operating at Its Peak

To keep your cordless mixer running at top efficiency:

- Keep in mind that most cordless mixers require a full sixteen consecutive hours to become recharged.
- Use the mixer regularly and use it until it is discharged, and then recharge it.
- Use the mixer at normal household temperature.
- Take the mixer to a service professional when it comes time to replace the battery pack.

Troubleshooting Chart

Problem	Cause	Solution
Motor overheats.	Bearings are out of alignment.	Gently tap sides of the base while the motor is running at its highest speed.
Motor runs but beaters won't move.	Beaters are bent.	Replace beaters.
Motor doesn't run.	Fuse may be blown.	Replace if necessary.
	Cord is defective.	Check cord for breaks. Replace if necessary.

Cleaning, Maintenance, and Storage

Getting into Hot Water

Use hot soapy water to wash the beaters, dough hooks, and bowls of your mixer. With the appliance disconnected, clean the mixer head with a damp cloth. (Note: abrasive cleaners may mar your mixer's finish.) Always dry the beaters, dough hooks, and mixer head as soon as you've washed them.

Use a twist fastener to secure the cord in a coil; you can damage the cord if you wind it around the machine. Store a hand mixer on its heel rest, clipping the beaters to the side if the machine has clips for this purpose. Keep all mixers in a clean, dry location. A cordless model should always be stored on its storage/recharging base.

FOOD PROCESSORS

Safety Notes

Cutting Blade Safety

The cutting blades and disks of a food processor are very sharp and can cause serious injury if misused. For safe handling:

- Always put the work bowl or disk attachment in place before putting the blade or disk over the motor shaft and make sure it is down as far as it will go.
- Check to make sure that the cover is locked in place before running the food processor.
- Never put your fingers or utensils into the feed tube while the machine is on.
- Never leave the processor unattended while it is in operation.
- Always wait for the blade or disk to come to a complete stop before removing the cover from the work bowl.

- Always remove the work bowl from the base before removing the blade.
- Remove the blade before emptying the work bowl, or hold it in place with a spatula to prevent it from falling out when the bowl is tilted.
- Wash the blades immediately after each use, and wash them separately from the rest of the dishes. If left unnoticed in a sink of sudsy water, the hidden blades could cause a nasty cut.
- Store these blades apart from other household utensils in order to prevent injury. Special storage containers for the cutting blades are available from the manufacturers.

Be Careful with Hot Food

Do you want to process hot foods? Keep in mind that the food processor does not work at its best with a mixture heated to boiling. Moreover, working with hot food can cause serious burns. It's safer to let the food cool a bit before processing and reheat before serving.

Getting the Most from Your Product

Adapt Your Own Recipes

Want to adapt your own recipes for use with a food processor? Use the following guide to help you choose the best order for processing your ingredients:

- Always process dry ingredients that are to be used as garnishes first, when the bowl and blade are dry. No need to wash the bowl; simply wipe it out before proceeding to the next step.
- When chopping, it's best to process small, hard ingredients first; then chop the larger, firmer ones.
- Always start with the hardest ingredients, and then progress to the softer foods, and lastly the liquid ones.
- When mixing batters, add the dry ingredients last. For best results, blend them in with short on/off bursts until they are just mixed through.

Use Short Bursts

The key to getting the right consistency of your processed food lies in processing the ingredients in steps and watching the food carefully. After a while you'll know in advance how long each kind of food is likely to take. But when you start, use very short bursts of power—a second or two at a time. The machine will work faster than you expect, and once you've gone too far with the processing, there's no turning back. What should have been coarsely chopped may end up finely minced. With a little practice, you will discover that the pulse lever allows you to control the degree of processing you desire.

Process Small Batches

For best results, do not fill your food processor to the brim. It's a good idea to do a few small batches rather than one large one to prevent overflowing. When chopping, especially, you will get a more uniform dice by processing small batches.

Don't Wash the Bowl

Ordinarily, you should wash out the work bowl after each use. But you won't need to do this when chopping, slicing, and shredding ingredients that will be mixed together in the same dish.

For Uniform Size . . .

If you want chopped foods to come *out* of your processor in uniform pieces, the food must go *into* the processor in chunks of approximately the same size rather than assorted sizes.

The Key to Cutting Rounds

If you'd like to slice fruits or vegetables into even rounds, such as limes or cucumbers, first trim one end with a knife. Then place the food, flat side down, into the feed tube. Apply slight pressure on the food pusher and process.

Variable-Speed Savvy

If your machine has a variable-speed control, use the slower speeds for soft foods. For kneading dough, it's easier to switch back and forth between slow and fast speeds.

Layer Those Hard-to-Handle Foods

Mushrooms, radishes, and strawberries are all round, small, and difficult to slice uniformly in a food processor. The best way to handle them is to follow this procedure: Trim both ends with a knife. Then place as many as will fit in a single layer in the feed tube, flat sides down, and process. Remember to process only one layer at a time for perfect slices.

Freeze Soft Cheese . . .

Shredding cheese can create problems for your machine. Soft cheeses, such as mozzarella, can become very sticky and clog the feeder if they are at room temperature. Try freezing soft and semi-soft cheese for 30 minutes before shredding. Your food processor should have no problem with hard cheeses, such as Romano and Parmesan, when they're at room temperature. When shredding cheese, be sure not to apply too much pressure on the food pusher. The motor may slow down or the cheese may crumble.

. . . and Sticky Fruits

It's much easier to chop sticky fruits like prunes and dates after they've been in the freezer for about 10 minutes. Dust the fruit with some flour before processing.

Pulse Away Stuck-On Foods

To remove stuck-on food particles from the sides of the work bowl, try a few short on/off bursts with the pulse control. If that doesn't work, use a rubber spatula.

Add Liquid Last

Adding a liquid to a mixture in a food processor? Avoid spattering by pouring the liquid in last and through the feed tube while the machine is running.

Troubleshooting Chart

Problem	Cause	Solution
Food is unevenly chopped, minced, or mixed.	Processor is overloaded.	Process food in smaller batches.
Liquid leaks out of the work bowl.	Processor has too much liquid in the bowl.	Reduce liquid; avoid processing beverages.
Food falls over in food tube while slicing.	Food is not cut uniformly or feed tube is not full enough.	Cut food into equal-sized chunks. Use small feed tube for only a few pieces.
Food is unevenly sliced.	Feed tube is not properly packed and/or you are not applying even pressure on the pusher assembly.	Pack foods into the feed tube more snugly and apply even pressure on the food pusher.
Processor is abnormally vibrating or the disk or blades are rattling.	Blade or disk is not seated properly.	Turn off the processor, unplug, and reassemble blade or disk.
Food remains on top of the slicing and shredding disk after processing.	This is normal.	Cut remaining pieces by hand.

Cleaning, Maintenance, and Storage

Cleaning Your Processor

Some foods, such as carrots, may leave stains on your food processor's white plastic parts. Try a mild abrasive cleanser or dishwasher detergent mixed with a little lukewarm water to wash off the stains. Clean all parts in mild soap and water and don't forget to clean inside the shaft of the blades. A small bottle brush and some soap and water should do the trick. The base is easily cleaned with a damp cloth and a mild all-purpose cleaner.

What Your Product Won't Do

When a Blender Is Better

Your food processor can handle many tasks, but there are some that your blender or portable mixer can handle even better. These include:

- Chopping carrots
- Making mayonnaise
- Mashing potatoes
- Mixing cake batter
- Whipping cream
- Beating egg whites

Avoid Dull Blades

While your food processor is capable of cutting up ice—and may be used for processing ice chips in recipes that call for it— avoid using it as an ice chopper. This will only dull your blade. A good rule of thumb is to keep any substance you can't cut with a knife out of your food processor.

FREEZERS

Safety Notes

Use Freezer Gloves

You can get freezer burn if you handle frozen food or touch the interior surfaces of your freezer too much. If your hands are wet, your fingers can stick to frozen surfaces. Play it safe and keep a pair of gloves (oven mittens will do) near the freezer to wear when handling frozen food.

Use Your Freezer Safely

- Always use your freezer's three-pronged plug with a grounding receptacle; and be sure to unplug the freezer before replacing a light bulb or making repairs.
- Do not operate the freezer in an area near explosive fumes.
- If you have a chest freezer and you have small children, put a locking latch on the freezer door. Small children have been known to crawl into freezers looking for food. When the door shuts, they are trapped.
- Remove the door when you discard your freezer to prevent children from trapping themselves and suffocating.

Getting the Most from Your Product

Keep It out of the Heat

To ensure that it runs efficiently, put your freezer in a location where it will not absorb heat from any source, including:

- Direct sunlight
- Furnace
- Gas or electric range
- Radiator
- Water heater
- Wood stove

Fill It Slowly

It's tempting to use any new appliance to its limits once it's delivered. But you have to be patient with a new freezer. It may take the freezer about 24 hours to reach 0°F—the desirable temperature for long-term storage of food. (Use a freezer thermometer to make sure.) So refrain from stuffing the freezer with food, especially if it's your own fresh-cooked food that needs to be brought down to 0°F quickly. Instead, add a moderate amount each day and wait until the food is solidly frozen before adding more. In an upright model, start with no more than a single layer of food on each shelf.

Label and Rotate Frozen Foods

It's important to label food in your freezer, including the name of the item and the date it was frozen. Otherwise, you end up throwing out good food thinking that it may be spoiled, or you waste time defrosting packages that are past their prime. Label *everything* that goes into your freezer, even if you plan to use it within the week. Use a dark crayon to mark information directly on the package or on adhesive labels. If the food is wrapped, include the package's contents on the label.

You can color code your frozen packages, using a different color for each week you add items to the freezer; you can buy colored stick-ons at a stationery store.

Other information you might include on the label is the dish or type of meal for which you intended this food (if it isn't something complete, like a casserole) and a reminder about anything else you have in the freezer that would go nicely with this item.

No matter how you label your packages, put recently added food in the back (uprights) or bottom (chests) of the freezer, so you can reach and use the older food first.

Keep a Checklist

It's a good idea to maintain a freezer inventory. You might find that one of the following methods suits you.

- List the freezer's contents on a piece of paper, place it in a plastic bag, and tape it to a convenient place inside the freezer.
- Use a bulletin board near the freezer.
- Record each item on 3- by 5-inch index cards.
- Enter the inventory on your personal computer, if you have one.

Fill 'Er Up

Freezers run most efficiently when full. But what do you do if you don't have enough food to do the job? Pack the freezer with water-filled milk cartons (leave enough space to allow for expansion when the water freezes).

The Shape of Meals to Come

Do you know that the shape of your freezer containers has a lot to do with how much food your appliance can hold? Rectangular and square containers let you make maximum use of your space. Using these shapes, you can store about 40 pints per cubic foot of space. Cylindrical containers limit your storage capacity to approximately 25 to 30 pints in the same space.

There's also a lot to be said for freezing food in meal-size amounts. Smaller packages freeze faster, thus preserving your food at the peak of freshness. And when mealtime arrives, small packages thaw faster.

Freeze Fresh-Cooked Food After It Cools

You've just cooked something that you want to freeze, but how cool does it have to get before it can go in the freezer? The rule of thumb is that the food should be at least cool enough to touch. You can hurry the process by plunging containers of fresh-cooked food into ice water and dunking vegetables directly in cold water as soon as you blanch them.

Prevent Freezer Burn

Food kept in the freezer can suffer burnout—freezer burn, to be more specific. You can recognize freezer burn if the food has dried out, become tough, has turned white or gray, and its flavor has disappeared. Improper packing causes this problem, when air and water get in and chemically interact with the frozen food. To prevent this, follow good packing procedures. Use packing material suitable for freezer storage and make sure you squeeze the air out of every package you wrap for freezing.

The best freezer storage materials are:

- Freezer bags
- Heavy-duty aluminum foil
- Jars with fitted lids
- Kraft paper with cellophane bonded to it

Organize That Chest Freezer

If you have a chest freezer, you probably are used to food piles inside your freezer that get bigger and bigger. Ultimately they get too big and they topple over. Solve this problem by stacking the food in shopping bags or other heavy-duty bags. The bags will also help you organize your freezer's contents more systematically.

Open Uprights Sparingly

Upright freezers offer you easier access to your food than chest models, but they cost more to run. Cold air tends to drop to the bottom of any space, so your upright unit uses more energy to keep its entire vertical space at the temperature you desire. Also, because the shelves on its door are not near the coils, that space requires even more energy to remain cold. Therefore, if you own an upright, try not to open the door—which causes the unit to work even harder—when you don't have to. Plan your freezer use carefully so you can take out whatever you need in a minimum number of trips to the freezer on any particular day.

Make the Most of Your Freezer

Are you making full use of your freezer? It isn't worth what you paid for it if it's become just an extension of your refrigerator/freezer. To get your money's worth:

- Plan meals well ahead of time. When you cook, prepare more servings than you need and freeze the rest for future dinners.
- Cook when you have extra time on your hands, even if you don't need the food immediately for meals. Freeze the results for use when your schedule is more harried.
- Watch the newspaper carefully for food sales, especially those involving discounts for buying in quantity.

Get Advice from the Professionals

The Department of Agriculture publishes a booklet called "Home Freezing of Fruits and Vegetables," and you can get it and other related material at reasonable prices. Another must is Home and Garden Bulletin No. 162, which describes what foods should be frozen and/or refrozen. For information about current prices and ordering, write to:

Consumer Information Center (P)
P.O. Box 100
Pueblo, CO 81002

For answers to questions about freezing meat and poultry, call or write:

The Meat and Poultry Hotline
USDA-FSIS
Room 1165-S
Washington, DC 20250
(800) 535-4555
(202) 447-3333 in Washington, DC, area

Give It Time to Cool Off

If packages are returned to a just-defrosted freezer, they will stick to the shelves. Simply refrain from replacing them until the temperature in the freezer has had some time to drop. And before you put them back, wipe the packages to rid them of all external moisture.

While You Were Out . . .

Vacation time. You've arranged to have someone water the plants and get the mail. Maybe you even asked the police to keep an eye out for prowlers while you're gone. But did you ask anyone to check your freezer? If you're vacationing in the summer, when much of the country is subject to lightning storms, you could be away during a power outage. Were that to happen, your freezer could be off long enough for some food to spoil. How would you know if your unit had gone out? Simple. Leave a bag of ice cubes in the freezer and examine them when you return. Have the individual cubes turned into an undifferentiated mass of ice? If they have, it means that the cubes melted and refroze, which means that your food did the same and will have to be discarded. If you have a person watching your house while you're away, ask him or her to peek at the freezer at least once or twice—and to notify you (and try to save your food) if there is a blackout in your absence.

In Case of a Blackout

What would you do to preserve the food in your freezer during a power outage? Leaving the freezer door closed will keep most food frozen for about 24 hours, but then what? Your best chance to ward off spoilage over an extended period of time (two to four days) is to pack the food in 2 pounds of dry ice for every cubic foot of freezer space. (Remember to wear protective gloves, so you won't get burned from the dry ice.)

Troubleshooting Chart

Problem	*Cause*	*Solution*
Freezer does not work.	Freezer may be unplugged, a fuse blown, or circuit breaker tripped.	Check plugs, fuses, and circuit breakers.
	Control knob may be set to "off."	Set control to "on" or other operational setting.
Motor is on for a longer time than is normal.	The door may be open slightly.	Close door.
	Temperature control is set too cold.	Change control to a higher temperature setting.
	Gasket is worn or dirty.	Change or clean gasket.
	Condenser and base grill are dirty.	Clean condenser of dust and lint.

(continued)

Troubleshooting Chart—Continued

Problem	Cause	Solution
Water is in the defrosting pan or on the exterior of the freezer.	This is normal when the weather is hot and muggy.	
	Door is being opened for too long or too often.	Plan trips to freezer to keep door closed as much as possible.
Water is on the floor.	Freezer drain may be obstructed.	Clean the drain, removing any ice from the freezer bottom, as necessary.
Dishes vibrate on the freezer shelves.	A slight amount of vibration is normal.	
	Freezer is not level or floor is uneven.	Adjust the freezer.
Freezer makes noises.	Refrigerant is circulating; ice cubes may be dropping; temperature controls click on and off; cooling coils make cracking and popping noises; defrost water is dripping.	
Freezer has an odor.	Freezer interior needs to be cleaned.	Clean interior.
	Strong-smelling foods are not wrapped tightly.	Wrap foods more tightly.

Cleaning and Maintenance

When to Defrost

Chest-type freezer models offer more convenience when it comes time to defrost. You should defrost a chest freezer about every 12 to 18 months, depending on how often you use it and how much frost is visible. An upright requires defrosting about every six months.

Keep It Frost-Free

Between defrostings, it's a good idea to remove frost buildup whenever you notice it. You can do this safely by carefully using a plastic ice scraper. Use the scraper on the side walls only, never on the shelves that contain cooling coils.

When you're ready to defrost, disconnect the freezer and remove the food. If you don't have an insulated food chest to store the food in, you might want to wrap the food in a blanket or in several layers of newspaper, which act as insulators. Keep the freezer door open. Some freezers have a drain plug, which should be removed (and replaced after defrosting, or warm air will enter the freezer). For models without a drain plug, use heavy towels to catch the frost as it falls.

Use the plastic scraper to loosen soft frost. Hard frost can be softened by placing deep pans of hot water on the top freezer shelf, then closing the freezer door for approximately 15 minutes. You can repeat the procedure on other shelves if the frost is particularly bad.

Another trick recommended by some manufacturers is to use an electric fan to circulate warm air around the freezer. This can be dangerous, however, if the fan comes into contact with any water.

Whatever method you use, never use sharp, pointed objects to pry or chip the ice away from the walls and shelves of the freezer, and never use salt or a salt solution; either action could cause irreparable damage to the freezer.

FURNACES

Safety Notes

Check the Flame

The appearance of the flame at the main burner of your gas furnace is a good indication of how your unit is operating. After the furnace has been on for at least 10 minutes, look for the following signs of trouble:

- A rough, unstable, yellow flame
- Flames that curl or seem to lift off from the burner
- Flames that touch the heat exchanger

If you spot any of these problems, call a serviceperson to check the furnace.

Your Furnace Needs to Breathe

Your furnace needs air to do its work. Modern airtight construction and improved insulation have reduced the supply of fresh air entering many homes. Other appliances and home components, such as clothes dryers and fireplaces, add to the demand for air. Obstructed air passages could lead to a buildup of dangerous carbon monoxide in your home, so keep flues and vents clean and clear.

Carbon monoxide is odorless and colorless. If you breathe it in you will experience some or all of the following symptoms: dizziness, nausea, and headaches. Other warning signs of obstructed air passages include fireplace smoke that does not go up the chimney and gasses that won't rise through the flue. Any of these conditions combined with unexpectedly thick frost on your windows signal danger.

You can check each possible culprit in your house, including the furnace, with a simple test. With all windows and doors closed, start the dryer and every vented appliance in your house. After 10 minutes, hold a lighted stick of incense about 2 inches from the draft opening on each appliance. If the smoke does not move toward the draft hood, that appliance is not sufficiently vented. If you can't open its air supply yourself, call a serviceperson. Until you have it repaired, don't use that appliance without first opening a window.

To check exhaust fans, hold a lighted stick of incense nearby while the fan is on. If the smoke is not drawn toward the exhaust opening, don't use the fan until you've cleared its ventilation system.

If you have a fireplace, light a fire in it. If smoke from the fireplace did not draw up the chimney, open a nearby door or window and see if the smoke rises now. If it does, you probably need to have an air duct installed.

Lengthen the Life of Your Furnace

To prevent hazardous conditions—and to lengthen the service life of your furnace—heed these safety tips:

- Keep the area around the furnace—at least 5 feet—clear of any combustible matter, particularly painting and cleaning materials.
- Be sure that air for ventilation and combustion flows freely to the furnace. Keep all air paths, such as vent grilles, clear.
- Make sure that any exposed insulation in the vicinity of the furnace won't be affected by the heat.
- Whenever you have to shut down your furnace for repairs, be sure to cut off both gas and electric power to the unit.

Getting the Most from Your Product

Choosing a New Furnace?

Some of today's furnaces are about twice as fuel-efficient as the old ones. Condensing furnaces, in particular, not only get more from every gallon or cubic foot of fuel, they also don't need a chimney. Pulse-combination furnaces, another new technological development, need soundproofing, but are even more efficient than condensing models. These high-tech heaters cost at least $2,000 and take about eight years to pay back in fuel savings.

Troubleshooting Chart

Problem	Cause	Solution
Oil burner isn't making heat.	Thermostat is set too low.	Turn thermostat up to maximum, wait 30 seconds. If nothing happens check other causes, listed below.
	Furnace switches are not turned on.	Check both switches— one at furnace and one at top of cellar stairs.
	Fuse or circuit breaker has blown.	Check fuses and circuit breaker.
	There's not enough oil in the tank.	Check oil tank.
Rooms aren't warm enough when hot-air furnace is on.	Filters and/or registers are dirty.	Replace filters; clean registers.
	There are air leaks in the ducts.	Seal ducts with duct tape.
	Register is closed, ducts are blocked, or duct damper is not positioned correctly.	Open register; remove obstructions; adjust damper.
Soot collects in the house when hot-air furnace is on.	Filters or ducts are dirty.	Replace filters; have serviceperson clean ducts.
Gas furnace doesn't heat.	Pilot light is out.	Relight the pilot.
	There's no gas.	Call the gas company.
Pilot light won't stay lit.	The pilot port is dirty.	Clean pilot port if you can reach it, or call serviceperson.
	Thermocouple is defective.	Call serviceperson.

Troubleshooting Chart—Continued

Problem	Cause	Solution
You smell gas.	Pilot light is out.	Turn off the gas supply and call the gas company.
	There may be a leak.	Turn off the gas supply, ventilate the room and call the gas company.

Cleaning and Maintenance

Leave Inspection to the Pros

A year after your new gas furnace is installed, have it inspected by a serviceperson. After that, have it inspected every two years. Make sure the pressure regulator, main gas valve, and safety control valve are checked, as well as the primary air supply nozzle. Also have your thermostat checked and make sure your fan belt is operating at the right tension.

Do-It-Yourself Gas Furnace Maintenance

While professional inspections are a must for your gas furnace, there are some regular maintenance chores that you can do yourself, such as:

• Clean or change the air filter every month or two.
• Vacuum dust and lint from the registers regularly.

Check Your Oil Burner

An oil burner requires sensitive adjustments to operate properly and safely, and that should be left to a serviceperson. But you can perform these routine checks on your furnace (call the serviceperson if you find any of these problems):

• Several times during the heating season, turn off the burner and peer into the furnace through the peephole to check the firebox for broken bricks.
• Look for any accumulation of soot around the furnace.

- Check for a persistent smell of oil around the furnace or coming out of the chimney. Have any leaks in the oil line fixed immediately.
- Keep the area around the furnace dry.

Clean Your Electric Furnace

Depending on your electric furnace model, clean or change the filter every month during the winter. You could damage your unit and decrease its heat and cost efficiency if you don't take care of the filter.

In addition, twice each winter clean the registers, grilles, and blower fan blades. Tighten the fan belts once a year and replace them when they show signs of wear. Also check joints in the duct system once a year and seal any leaks with duct tape.

FURNITURE, INDOOR

Getting the Most from Your Product

Furnishing your home is an expensive venture, and it has probably taken you years to accumulate all the furniture you now have. It's not unrealistic to get decades of life from good-quality furniture—some pieces will outlive you! Here's how to make sure you get the most from your furnishings:

- Keep all furniture away from heat sources or direct sunlight. Heat dries out wood, wicker, and leather, and sunlight makes fabrics fade.
- Control the humidity. Extremes of humidity can warp and crack wood, so use dehumidifiers if you live in a humid climate, or humidifiers if you live in a very dry region.
- Wipe up spills immediately. This prevents moisture rings on wood and stains on fabric.

• Clean your furniture frequently: dust and polish wood; vacuum and brush upholstery; clean and condition leather.

Cleaning and Maintenance

Read the Label

Furniture manufacturers have divided their products into four categories according to the kind of cleaning materials you can use on them. Frequent vacuuming and light brushing, your first line of defense, will make professional cleaning only an occasional necessity for any fabric. Although your cushions may have zippers, don't remove the covers for spot cleaning. Fabrics bearing the following codes (on the label) should be cleaned in the following manner:

W–Use the foam from a mild detergent or nonsolvent upholstery shampoo. Work in the foam with a soft brush using a circular motion.

S—W–Clean as for the "W" category; however, you can also use nontoxic dry cleaning products.

S–Use a water-free solvent or dry cleaning product.

X–Vacuum and brush only. Do not use water- or solvent-based cleaning agents.

Flip Your Seats

Many times, one end of a sofa or one chair in a room is sat upon more than the others. Such uneven wear will eventually cause the seat cushion to flatten out or get lumpy. To help your upholstered furniture wear evenly over the years, flip the cushions regularly. Turn them top to bottom for several months, then switch them every once in a while (swap the far-right sofa cushion with the far-left cushion; switch two matching chair cushions).

Lather the Leather

To clean and condition leather furniture, dust it with a soft cloth, then use a damp cloth to work in saddle soap, rubbing it into a lather. Wipe off the excess soap with a second damp cloth, then polish the leather with a soft, dry cloth. This same procedure works well for vinyl furniture, too.

If your leather furniture has dried out, you need to restore it with oil. Pour some lanolin or castor oil into a jar and warm it in a pan of hot water. Wipe the oil on the furniture with a clean, soft cloth and allow it to soak into the leather for 24 hours. Then buff the leather with a clean cloth.

Remove Leather Stains with Care

You can remove stains from leather furniture by rubbing gently with a solution of soap and warm water. Don't apply ammonia or abrasives—you will ruin the leather.

Wicker and Polish Don't Mix

Don't use polishes and furniture waxes on wicker furniture— instead, vacuum it regularly, especially if you live in an area with moderate to heavy air pollution. The tiny amount of iron in household dust acts as a catalyst, helping sulphur and moisture in the air combine to produce sulfuric acid. This chemical weakens the wicker fiber and makes it brittle. To vacuum wicker correctly, use a brush with your vacuum cleaner, brushing the dust toward the nozzle. Hold the nozzle just above the surface of the wicker, being careful not to touch the wicker, especially when cleaning old furniture, because the suction may pull up already loosened fibers.

Once you've cleaned your wicker, don't try to protect the finish with shellac or varnish. These finishes will penetrate the fibers, then dry and harden. The result—brittle wicker that is more susceptible to damage.

Clean Wicker Gently

To clean wicker, use a mild soap solution and wash gently with a soft-bristle brush. (Use a toothbrush for hard-to-reach areas.) If possible, clean the furniture outside on a warm day so that it dries quickly. If soap and water isn't enough to remove embedded dirt, use ethanol (ethyl alcohol) to get it out. This is the denatured "methylated spirits" sold in paint stores, *not* the "ethanol" you can buy at the drugstore. The fumes from this substance can be dangerous, so it's best to use this outside or in a very well ventilated room. Dampen a cotton swab in the ethanol and rub it softly on the dirty spot. Discard each swab as soon as it gets dirty.

Don't Let Wicker Dry Out

Your rustic cane and reed furniture will give you years of use and pleasure in return for a modest amount of care. Most important in caring for wicker furniture is to keep it out of direct sunlight and away from any direct sources of heat. This will prevent the fibers from drying out and warping. Some wicker becomes dry and brittle with age, no matter how well it's been cared for. You can restore its resiliency by taking it outside and hosing it down. The fibers will absorb the water and become more flexible. Do this on a warm, dry day so the furniture dries quickly. Don't use this method on sea grass or twisted paper wicker or they will be ruined.

Make Your Cane Chairs Last Longer

You can add to the longevity of your cane chairs by keeping them away from dry air, never letting anyone stand on them, and always carrying them by the frames and never by the seats. Every once in a while, turn the chairs upside down, dampen the seats and backs with warm water, and allow them to dry. This will tighten up the cane, and help it look better and last longer.

Polish Away Water Rings

Any water left on an unwaxed wood surface will create white water spots or rings. These marks seldom go all the way into the wood, so they can usually be polished away. Use an abrasive such as 0000-grade steel wool or pumice mixed to a paste with turpentine, light oil, or mineral spirits. You may first want to try a paste of kitchen scouring powder and oil or, believe it or not, just some old-fashioned white toothpaste. If you use steel wool, rub gently with the grain of the wood. Apply any paste with your fingertip and rub with the grain.

Once you remove the water mark, you will find that the

cleaned area is now duller than the rest of the surface. It's best to treat the entire surface with the same abrasive, and then wax it for an even finish.

Use Crayons for Scratches and Burns

Most hardware and hobby shops carry wax and shellac sticks for touching up wood furniture. These are perfect for hiding minor scratches and burns—or you can use ordinary crayons if you have a good color match. Just rub the stick or crayon across the scratch, then buff with a soft cloth. For cigarette burns, first scrape out any burnt wood, then use the stick.

For serious marks, you must clean the hole, and then melt the wax stick and dribble it in. Use the dull edge of a table knife or the edge of a plastic credit card to scrape the wax until it is level with the surface. If the repair was done to a little-used area of furniture, you're done. Otherwise, you'll have to coat the repair with thin shellac (you may want to coat the entire surface for an even finish), and then apply a coat of varnish over the entire surface after the shellac has dried.

If You Strip . . .

If you feel that a piece for furniture is too far gone for touchups and must be stripped, follow these precautions:

- Remove all hardware from the piece before beginning. That includes doors or any other components fastened by screws.
- Work in a cool, well-ventilated place—outside in the shade, if you can.
- Protect upholstered fabric with a cotton drop cloth.
- Use a ½-inch scraper and brush. File and sand the edge of the scraper to prevent damaging the wood.
- Delay repairs until after you strip the wood. The stripping chemicals you use could get into recently repaired furniture joints and melt the glue.

WARNING: The chemicals in furniture strippers are potentially very hazardous. Methylene chloride, the main ingredient in many "paste type" furniture strippers, is a suspected carcinogen, and as of late 1988 federal agencies are considering whether it should be banned or restricted from consumer products. The safest approach is to avoid using chemical furniture strippers entirely. Bring your furniture to a refinishing shop, and let them handle the hazardous materials.

FURNITURE, OUTDOOR

Getting the Most from Your Product

Keep It Dry and Clean

Outdoor furniture naturally gets a lot of abuse—it sits through summer rains (and sometimes even early snowfalls before anyone thinks to put it away). It puts up with climbing kids and pets, wet bathing suits and towels—not to mention plenty of spilled drinks and greasy barbecue. To keep your outdoor furniture looking its best:

- Bring it in out of the rain or at least cover it with plastic.
- In winter, store it somewhere dry, if possible. If it has to go into a damp basement or garage, keep it covered, and keep wood legs off the damp floor.
- Wipe up spills as soon as they happen. Repair rips or tears in a timely fashion, as well.

Seal Wood Before You Use It

Wood outdoor furniture is handsome and sturdy, but it is susceptible to rot caused by rain, snow, and ground moisture, so you should seal it with an exterior stain and sealer. Use spar varnish for a colorless sealer, or find a finish that matches the color of the wood. You can also paint the wood with weatherproof paint. No matter what type of sealer you use, be sure to put an extra coat or two on the feet and any other part of the furniture that touches the ground.

Redwood Needs Protection, Too

Many people think that because redwood is naturally weather resistant, there's no need to seal it. But there are redwood sealers on the market that are worth using to help your redwood furniture retain its color over the years and protect it from spills.

Cleaning and Maintenance

Hold a Spring Inspection

Spring is the perfect time to inspect your outdoor furniture to make sure it's ready for summer duty. Here's a rundown of what you should be looking for:

- Tighten the screws or bolts that hold the furniture together. Don't be tempted to use a table or chair with wobbly legs or joints—you'll only put more stress on the joints, increasing the chance that the piece will literally fall apart.
- Check the moving joints on folding furniture. If the joints are stiff or don't move at all, lubricate them with a wax or silicone lubricant that won't leak out and get on people's clothes when they sit on or carry the furniture.
- Repair broken webbing by reweaving the material. You can buy rolls of webbing at hardware and outdoor furniture stores.
- Take care of any pitting or rust spots on aluminum or wrought iron furniture before they face another season (see below).

Get the Rust Out

If aluminum and cast or wrought iron outdoor furniture has been exposed to the elements, it will eventually begin to pit or rust. Aluminum furniture that becomes pitted or oxidized can be easily restored with jelly or liquid aluminum cleaner. If the pitting isn't too bad, first try scrubbing the furniture with steel wool. Whether you use a cleaner or steel wool, keep the finish looking new with a coating of paste wax—car wax is good—and buff until it's shiny.

Cast or wrought iron presents more of a challenge—this

metal will definitely rust and it can take some hard work to get it cleaned up. To eliminate rust, you must sand it away, either with a sanding disk that attaches to a standard electric drill, or if you don't mind more demanding physical labor, with a wire brush. After you've sanded out all the rusty areas, you must prime the bare metal before repainting the entire piece. When you repaint, be sure to use a rust-inhibiting paint, and be sure that both the primer and the finish coat are compatible.

G

Garage Door Openers

Garbage Disposers

Garden Tools

Griddles, Electric

GARAGE DOOR OPENERS

Safety Notes

Keep Kids Away

Children and automatic garage door openers do not mix. According to the Consumer Products Safety Commission, several children have been killed in recent years while playing with automatic garage doors. Kids play a game that involves starting the closing action and then running to get out of the garage before the door comes all the way down. Unfortunately, children end up getting hit by the door. You can prevent this by keeping the control device locked in the glove compartment of your car and by locating the wall-mounted switch high enough so children can't reach it. Be sure to mount it sufficiently high so that even if a child stands on something, he or she can't get at the switch. And for safety's sake, adjust the automatic reverse mechanism to react to the smallest amount of pressure. Usually that means turning the adjustment screws for a ⅛-inch gap in the spring. Adjust the clutch to slip upon encountering any obstruction. Test your settings by putting an empty box under the closing door. The door should reverse directions without crushing the box.

Less dangerous but harmful to the operation of the door opener is the simple game in which a child continuously opens and closes the door. Your unit may have a mechanism that automatically shuts down the opener to prevent the motor from overheating. If this happens, you won't be able to use the opener for as long as 30 minutes; if it doesn't shut down, the game can damage the motor.

Getting the Most from Your Product

Is Your Door in Good Shape?

A garage door opener works best when installed on a garage door that's working smoothly. Use the guidelines below to make sure your garage door isn't hampering the opener:

- Can you move the door with little effort? If not, oil the hinges, pivot points, and roller bearings.
- If your springs are in good shape, the door will not accelerate near the top of its movement when it's almost fully opened nor when it approaches its fully closed position. If it does seem to take off at these points, adjust the springs.
- Remove the lock from the door, since you will no longer need it and it could impede the door's motion when it is under the control of the automatic opener. Similarly, take off handles or anything else sticking out from the door. Such protrusions could cause injury if anyone's clothes get caught on them while the door is being automatically opened or closed.
- Make sure the rear track hangers tilt upward, toward the rear of the garage. This will keep the door from accelerating upward when you open it. Clean the tracks and grease them well.

Cleaning and Maintenance

Blow the Dirt Away

To work well, your garage door opener needs to be free of dirt and dust. Clean the opener's moving parts easily with an air blower—available at most hardware stores. Take special care to clean the motor's housing, since an accumulation of dust here acts as an insulator, which could overheat the motor.

Perform a Monthly Check

Every month, check the safety reverse on your electric door opener. Make any necessary adjustments. Check the manual, disconnect and make sure it's working properly. Be sure that everyone who uses the door opener knows how to manually open the door in the event of a power failure or mechanical problem.

Every six months, be sure the door is operating smoothly and lubricate if necessary.

Troubleshooting Chart

Problem	Cause	Solution
Garage door doesn't respond when manual control is used.	Fuses are blown or circuit tripped.	Check fuses and circuit breakers.
	Motor is overheated.	Wait 5 to 20 minutes then try control switch again.
Door operates by manual control but not by remote control.	Remote control needs new battery.	Replace battery.
	Bad transistor or other component in remote control.	Have professionally serviced.
Remote control has operating range of less than 25 feet.	Remote control needs new battery.	Replace battery.
	Remote control needs to be moved to a different location in the car.	Move the remote control until it works within the full 25-foot range.
Door operates on its own.	Wire to manual control has short circuited.	Check circuit; check wire for breaks.
	Codes need to be changed or secoder needs to be replaced.	Change codes; replace secoder.
Door doesn't open or close completely.	Door is obstructed.	Turn off power and remove obstruction.
Motor turns on but door doesn't move.	Ice buildup on track or door is frozen shut.	Warm garage and clean track. If problem continues, disconnect until weather warms up.

GARBAGE DISPOSERS

Safety Notes

Keep Your Hands Out

• Never put your hand in the garbage disposer unit.
• Turn the power off at the fuse box or circuit breaker before making even the most minor repairs or adjustments.
• Drop your food waste into the disposer—don't try to pack it in, or you may jam the unit.

Flying Debris

Under certain circumstances, your garbage disposer is capable of expelling objects it can't digest. Foods and other substances that pose a danger—and are not fit for feeding to the disposer—are clam and oyster shells, large whole bones, metal (be on the lookout for aluminum foil scraps and bottle caps), glass, china, and plastics. In addition, many disposers cannot handle corn husks or artichokes.

Getting the Most from Your Product

Soften the Load

While your garbage disposer can handle many hard and fibrous materials, it disposes of them best when you mix them with softer garbage. Likewise, most machines can digest grapefruit and melon rinds, but often with some difficulty. Make it easier on your unit by cutting up the rind before grinding it down.

Use the Disposer before and after Meals

You can make the after-dinner grind less of a chore by running the garbage disposer *before* dinner to get rid of the debris from the meal preparation—salad leaves, vegetable peels, and the like. Then put in the table scraps after dinner. Always let the unit run for about fifteen seconds after the shredding sound stops, just to make sure that all the waste is flushed.

Don't Let Wastes Sit Around

Always grind whatever waste is in the disposer and run cold water until it's clear. Letting wastes sit in the disposer can lead to unpleasant odors, a clogged drain, or a jam in the unit.

Save Money and Water

You can flush out your garbage disposer without running up your water bill or wasting water during a shortage with this simple trick—when you pull the stopper out of a sink full of dishwater, flush the disposer at the same time.

Cold Water: The Essential Ingredient

Cold water facilitates the operation of your disposer. It helps harden grease so it can be shredded efficiently. Remember to always run a steady stream of cold water both before and during the garbage disposer's use.

Does your garbage disposer seem to work too slowly? Try increasing the flow of cold water. You may also want to run the cold water at a faster rate when getting rid of meat scraps or other greasy garbage. Continue to run the water for about a minute after the disposer has done the dirty work—this will keep the drain line clear.

Keep the Drain Covered

The drain cover may be the most useful part of your disposer. Be sure the cover is in place whenever the garbage disposer is not being used. It's the best way to prevent knives, forks, and other objects from finding their way into your unit.

Double-Duty Drains

Does your dishwasher drain through your garbage disposer unit? If so, run the disposer for a few seconds both before *and* after you use your dishwasher. This will ensure that you have removed all wastes from the line before you wash your dishes, and that any pieces of food washed out by the dishwasher are cleared from the drain. Keep the drain cover on your disposer while the dishwasher is running to prevent any water from splashing out. Don't operate the disposer and dishwasher at the same time.

Cleaning and Maintenance

Keep It Fresh

You don't need a commercial cleansing product to make your garbage disposer smell fresh. You can banish any unpleasant smells simply by pouring a cup of vinegar into the drain while running the disposer. Follow the vinegar with a cold-water rinse. To give the unit a lemon-fresh scent, grind half a lemon.

Sharpen and Clean in One Step

Vinegar ice cubes will help you keep your garbage disposer blades sharp and clean. Make the cubes with a half cup of vinegar, filling the rest of the ice tray with water. (Buy a separate ice cube tray of a different color or shape than the ones you usually use to avoid accidentally serving the vinegar cubes.) Run a few cubes through the disposer once a week.

Use Drain Cleaners with Care

Should your garbage disposer's drain become clogged, use only drain cleaners marked "enzymatic cleaner" or "safe for disposers." Any other kind could damage your unit.

Don't Worry about Stains

If you peek down into the disposer and notice that the grinding plate is stained brown, don't worry. It's just a surface stain and has nothing to do with how your unit functions.

Troubleshooting Chart

Problem	Cause	Solution
Unit makes rattling sounds.	Object may be stuck inside.	Carefully use a pair of kitchen tongs to remove object; put floral clay on the end of wooden spoon and poke down hole until clay presses against object. Remove clay and object.
	Mounting screws may be loose.	Check flange under sink and tighten screws.
Disposer motor hums but unit doesn't work.	Flywheel is jammed.	Turn off unit. Put broomstick handle into opening until it nudges first barrier. Lightly jab with handle until it turns freely in both directions. Wait at least 15 minutes before turning on unit. Grind ice cubes to remove any traces of sticky substance.
Older unit runs but grinds slowly.	Grind ring is worn.	Have grind ring replaced.
	An impeller blade on the flywheel is loose.	Have flywheel replaced.

GARDEN TOOLS

Safety Notes

Handle Hand Tools with Care

- Avoid nasty surprises by always laying rakes, hoes, and other hand tools with pointed sides facing the ground. Add a bright red or orange stripe to the handles of garden tools so they're easy to spot among the grass; if you can see them you're less likely to trip over them and take a tumble.
- Always hang sharp hand tools up and out of reach of small children when not in use. Even an innocent-looking trowel can do some damage when handled incorrectly by little hands.

Cleaning, Maintenance, and Storage

Get the Rust Off and Keep It Off

Unfortunately, garden tools have a way of being left outside. If it should happen to rain while they're out there, you'll discover how quickly metal parts can rust. Luckily, you can remove rust from your tools with ordinary household supplies. Saturate a new steel wool pad with soap and dunk it in kerosene or turpentine. Rub the rust spots and they should begin to disappear. Finish the job by rubbing again with a crumpled piece of aluminum foil.

To keep rust from forming in the first place, coat the metal parts of tools periodically with a light layer of penetrating oil; you should also oil them just before you store them for the winter. An easy way to oil just about any garden tool is to dip it into a bucket of sand to which you've added oil drained from your car or lawn mower.

In-Season Care

To get the most from your garden tools, follow these care tips:
- When you're done with the day's garden chores, dry off any metal parts that are wet.

- If the blades or tines are caked with soil, pry it off with an old paint stirrer. A wire brush is also handy for whisking off layers of grime.
- Once a month or more often if needed, oil moving parts on pruners and hand trimmers.
- Watch for and tighten any loose screws and nuts. Repair or replace any bent or broken parts.
- Sharpen your spade and hoe several times throughout the season.

To the Point

Digging with a dull blade forces you to apply extra pressure on your tool handle and makes gardening unnecessarily difficult. The blades on most digging tools come with a 45-degree bevel. You can maintain that angle—and the tool's efficiency—by holding the tool securely in a vise and sharpening it with a coarse 10-inch file. When sharpening a shovel or hoe, remember not to miss the corners.

Get a Good Grip

Brand-new tools come with a nice shiny coat of varnish covering the wooden handle. As the seasons pass you'll notice the varnish wearing thin in places. When this happens, take some sand-paper and remove all the varnish that's left along the entire length of the handle. With a rag, rub in boiled linseed oil for a nice smooth finish that will protect the wood.

Kink-Free Hose Care

Your garden hose will give you years of good service if you give it some care:

- Take the time to put away the hose properly after every use and you'll extend its lifespan. The best way to store it is off the ground, wound on a hose reel or hanger. Don't hang the hose over a nail or shelf bracket; this can cause a permanent kink.
- Keep the hose out of the sun when you're not using it. Too much sun exposure can crack and harden rubber hoses and damage those made from nylon and vinyl.

- Don't leave the water on in a garden hose that has a nozzle with a shutoff valve. The water pressure that builds up inside the hose can eventually weaken the walls, leading to leaks.
- At the end of the season, drain the hose and hang it inside in a dry spot.

Everything in Its Place

Your garden tools deserve a storage area all their own — to keep them out of the sun, rain, and snow and where they'll be easy for you to find. There are a couple ways to organize your tools:

- Install a large pegboard and hooks in your basement or even inside a work closet. Hang all the tools on it in a way that makes them easy to reach. Label each hook with a number and mark the handle of each tool with the corresponding number. If you don't have formal labels, masking tape works well. Now, each time you take all your tools down from the board, you will be able to match the numbers and put them away quickly.
- A variation on the pegboard approach uses a black marker instead of labels. Arrange your tools in a convenient layout on the peg board. With a black marker, trace the outline of each tool. At a glance, you'll be able to spot what tool goes where.

GRIDDLES, ELECTRIC

Safety Notes

Probe Carefully

Follow these commonsense rules for safe and effective use of your electric griddle:

- Attach the probe control to the electric griddle before plugging the cord into the wall outlet. To disconnect, turn the control to "off" before removing the plug from the wall.

- Do not wash the griddle's heat control or probe. Simply wipe them with a damp cloth or sponge, then dry thoroughly.
- Before cleaning your electric griddle, always turn the heat control to "off" and unplug the cord from the wall outlet. Allow the griddle to cool before detaching the heat control.
- If your griddle has legs, use them.
- Use handles, hot pads, and common sense. A hot griddle can give you a nasty burn if you're not careful.

Getting the Most from Your Product

Preheat, Except . . .

For most cooking, it's best to preheat an electric griddle for about 10 minutes—except when you're cooking food with a high fat content, such as sausage or bacon.

Thick and Thin

When cooking foods of various sizes and thicknesses on your electric griddle, start by cooking the bigger, thicker pieces first. Then add the smaller, thinner ones so they all finish at the same time.

Meat on the Griddle

If you follow these procedures for cooking meat on your electric griddle, you will end up with tastier food and less of a mess to clean up after dinner:

- To minimize smoke and grease, trim meat before you cook it.
- If you use salt, you should salt your meat *after* you cook it. Putting salted meat on the griddle will produce drier food because the salt will draw out the meat's juices during cooking.
- Use tongs rather than a fork to turn the meat. Piercing it with a fork lets the juices run out.

Keep It Warm

If your electric griddle doesn't have a warming well, you can still use the unit to keep food warm. Simply put the food on the griddle and cover it with an inverted bowl. Just be sure that no plastic parts, such as handles, touch the griddle. Two hours is the maximum time you can safely warm food this way—less for eggs (20 minutes) and casseroles (45 minutes).

Extend Your Griddle's Life

You can extend the life of your griddle by following these basic care and usage tips:

- Use medium to low heat for best cooking results. Extremely high temperatures can shorten the life of nonstick surfaces and cause discoloration. Always preheat the griddle on "medium" before switching to high heat, if you must use it.
- Although you can use metal utensils safely on the griddle if you're careful, it's best to use nylon, plastic, wooden, or rubber utensils to avoid scratching the surface.
- If your griddle has a warming tray or grease cup, do not place it on top of the griddle.

Cleaning and Maintenance

Battling Discoloration

Built-up grease and food residue often cause nonstick surfaces to change color. Although this shouldn't alter the griddle's performance, you may want to use one of the following along with a plastic scrubbing pad (never steel wool) to keep your griddle squeaky clean:

- Powdered mild abrasive
- Liquid mild abrasive
- Coffeepot destainer

After such a tough cleaning, you'll have to reseason the nonstick surface. Heat the griddle to medium, and using a folded paper towel or soft cloth, spread a teaspoon of vegetable oil on the surface. If food still has a tendency to stick, season the griddle again.

Also remember never to plunge a hot griddle into cold water. This could permanently damage the finish.

H

Heaters, Electric

Home Computers

Humidifiers

HEATERS, ELECTRIC

Safety Notes

Commonsense Safety

- Always use the handles to move the heater, and do not let the heater touch your bare skin—you could get a serious burn.
- Do not leave a heater that's turned on in a room with a child or an invalid.
- Turn the heater off before unplugging it, and always unplug the heater when you're not using it.
- Don't use the heater in a wet or moist environment or where it could fall into water, and don't use it outdoors.
- Never run a heater cord under carpeting; fire could result.
- Be careful where you place the heater. It's important to keep the air intake areas free of obstruction. Don't put the heater on pillows, beds, or other soft surfaces, and keep it out of enclosed areas such as closets, cabinets, and under chairs. Be sure to position it well away from curtains and other loose material.
- Never use the heater where flammable liquids are used or stored.
- Most manufacturers recommend that you not use the heater with an extension cord.
- Don't use the heater if the base has been removed.
- Never insert any foreign objects into the ventilation or exhaust openings.

Getting the Most from Your Product

Turn Down the Heat

Central heating is fine, but you don't always need it. Often your portable space heater can provide the heat you need at a lower cost. Think of using the space heater rather than the central system in the late autumn and early spring, when there's a chill in the air but it's not quite cool enough to justify turning on the big system. Just take your heater with you if you move to another room and stay comfortable for less money.

You can save money even in the middle of the winter by keeping the thermostat down and using your heater for spot warmth. If you have a quartz heater, you can spot heat even when several people are in a room. If one person likes or needs extra warmth, the quartz heater's infrared heating, which focuses more narrowly than other heaters, can keep just that individual at a toasty level, while a moderate thermostat setting suffices for the rest of the family.

Don't Make Your Heater Work Overtime

If you place your heater near a window or exterior door, you'll force it to work hard, but you won't feel the heat. That's because heat seeps out through windows and doors when the temperature inside is warmer than it is outside, so keep your heater away from these drafty openings.

The furniture, carpeting, and other objects in a well-furnished room retain heat and radiate some of it into the air, thus helping your heater warm the room. But when you operate your heater in a sparsely furnished room, it's going to work overtime, and again, you won't feel the heat. To get the most from your heater, keep it out of bare rooms.

Keep Your Heater on a Separate Circuit

Heaters draw quite a bit of current, so if you use another electrical appliance—or even a multibulb lamp—on the same circuit, you can create an overload, resulting in a blown fuse or a tripped circuit breaker. A heater should run on its own circuit. As a further precaution, occasionally check the outlet and the appliance's cord and plug for heat buildup. Shut the heater off if any of these become hot. In addition, because some heat will build up in the cord, keep it uncoiled and free of any covering, including a rug.

Cleaning and Maintenance

Keep Heating Elements Aligned

Sometimes, the heating elements in a space heater get bent. Should the element make contact with the reflector, you could get a shock from touching the appliance. Periodically check the heating elements for this condition. If you spot one leaning toward the reflector, turn off the unit and unplug it. Once the heater has completely cooled, bend a paper clip to make a hook at the end and use it to gradually move the element away from the reflector.

Don't Use Water

When it comes time to clean your heater, simply dust it with a lint-free damp cloth. If you think it needs a more powerful touch, add a bit of mild detergent to the cloth. Never dip the heater into or spray it with water or other liquid.

HOME COMPUTERS

Getting the Most from Your Product

Save Your Eyes—Buy a Monitor

Many people use their television sets as monitors for their home computers. That's fine for playing games or doing simple tasks such as keeping a recipe file. But if you or any other member of your family intends to do word processing or other work that requires looking at the screen for long periods of time, you should purchase a monitor. Monitors provide higher resolution than do television sets, so viewing a monitor over long stretches of time is easier on the eyes.

While color monitors offer a prettier picture, unless you can spend top dollar to buy the best, the usually cheaper monochrome monitors give you better resolution and are less likely to strain your eyes. Monochrome monitors usually offer characters in either white, green, or amber. European businesses have adopted amber as their standard, because many people feel it's easiest on the eyes.

Don't Buy More Printer Than You Need

There are several kinds of printers on the market. Don't be talked into buying one with capabilities that you don't need.

Dot matrix printers produce letters that look as if a computer printed them. You can see the dots that make up the letters and they appear to be not quite fully formed. In addition, some dot matrix printers are thermal printers that can print only on specially treated paper. Nonetheless, a dot matrix printer is more than adequate for most home uses. It is quick and boasts a lower price tag than other kinds of printers. If you tend to print out many drafts, a dot matrix printer will save you time, too.

Letter-quality printers produce print that resembles typewriter lettering, suitable for business letters. Your children may also need one of these for term papers if their teachers will not accept dot matrix printouts. Some electronic typewriters can also be hooked up to your computer and used as printers, though they are quite slow.

For most home applications, *laser printers* are probably unnecessarily sophisticated—and priced too high (currently, the cheapest price is $1,500), although prices are coming down. Unless you need to put out professional-quality newsletters, you'd do best to pass on this type of printer. If you do have one, be sure you use it far from any heat sources because laser printers get very hot. These printers, in particular, also need lots of breathing room, so place them at least eight inches from the wall.

Cleaning, Maintenance, and Storage

"Bust" the Dust

Whatever kind of printer you buy, it's a good idea to purchase a dust cover for it. Keep the printer covered when not in use and occasionally place the suction pipe of your vacuum cleaner near it's paper opening to remove the tiny paper particles that are shed during the printing process.

Stop the Surge

Use a surge protector to keep irregularities in your electric current from destroying your computer. Don't rely on a surge protector to protect your computer against lightning strikes. When a thunderstorm threatens, turn off and unplug your computer and printer. You can buy this device in any computer store. Just be aware that not all surge protectors are equal. Consult your dealer to make sure you have the best product for your particular computer.

On Again, Off Again

It's better to leave your computer on all day than to turn it on and off half a dozen times a day. But don't leave it on for days at a time without use because you could "burn in" the image on the screen. If you find that you often leave your computer to go do something else, and forget to go back and turn it off, consider purchasing a "screen saver." This is software that will automatically turn off only your screen, not the computer itself, whenever you have not used the keyboard for more than a few minutes.

If you're going to be away for more than a few days, unplug everything—computer, printer, monitor—to protect against power surges.

Be Careful When You Clean the Screen

When cleaning the monitor screen, be sure to use a static-free product made especially for this purpose. Household glass cleaners can damage the screen. The plastic monitor casing can also be cleaned with the same product, or simply wiped with a slightly damp cloth. Never use or place liquids on or near your computer. One accidental spill could do a great deal of damage.

Disk Dos and Don'ts

• Always make a backup of your data.

- Keep your diskettes in their sleeves when not in use to keep dust off them. This goes for the hard cartridge disks, too!
- Handle floppy diskettes with great care. Folding, bending, or writing on their paper covers with a ballpoint pen or pencil could make the data they hold permanently inaccessible. Write on the diskette with a felt-tip pen. Never touch the actual diskette surface. Also, remember that heat and direct sunlight damage diskettes.
- Never use paper clips or rubber bands to bundle disks—they can damage the disks.
- Never place disks on any part of the computer or monitor because exposure to any electrical charge can alter data on your disk. Keep disks away from the telephone for the same reason. When the phone rings it sets up an electrical charge that can alter data on your disk.

Eliminate Static Electricity

If the humidity is low in your home, beware of creating static electricity when you touch your computer. One spark could wipe out a good deal of precious data. Ground yourself by touching something metallic to discharge any static buildup before you touch the computer. There are also antistatic mats available to place under the desk. Keep a static-free cover on the computer when you're not using it. Dust and vacuum often in the area near the computer, and don't smoke in its vicinity.

Keep Disk Drives Clean

If your disk drive doors will close without a disk in place, they should be kept closed when the computer is not in use to help keep dust out. Buy a disk drive cleaning diskette. They work much the same way cleaning cassettes work in cassette tape players. Consult your dealer about what brand is best for your needs and how often you should use a cleaning diskette.

Don't Do It Yourself

There are plenty of books and magazine articles that tell you how to make minor and not-so-minor repairs to your computer, keyboard, monitor, modem, and printer. But as long as your hardware is still under warranty, it's best to avoid any do-it-yourself repairs because those repairs will probably void your warranty. This means that if you botch up the repair job, you're going to have to pay to have it fixed—and that could be a very costly mistake. Read your warranty carefully before you even consider making any repairs on your own.

HUMIDIFIERS

Safety Notes

Pull the Plug

The humidistat, the control in the humidifier that automatically starts the fan when the humidity reaches a certain level, is triggered by moisture in the air. If you're cleaning the appliance and it's been left on or is accidentally turned on, the humidistat may start the fan and you could be injured. Or, you could touch the oscillator and burn yourself. Any time you need to reach into the humidifier, whether to change the water or clean it, unplug the appliance first.

Getting the Most from Your Product

Place It Right

If you can, place your humidifier in the middle of a room, next to a staircase, or adjacent to a return register (if you have forced-air heating). Keep it away from outside walls and the thermostat that controls your heating system. Emissions from the humidifier could trick the thermostat, causing your heating system to kick on unnecessarily.

Don't Set It and Forget It

Several factors determine the best control setting on your humidifier. They include whether someone is bathing or cooking, how cold it is, and, of course, the level of humidity at which you feel comfortable. But the permeability of your house—how easily outside air can get in—is also a factor. If you move to another house or apartment, experiment with new settings on your humidifier. If you move into a house that lacks some kind of vapor barrier (for example, a plastic film in the walls), using a humidifier may damage your insulation. (Builders started putting in these moisture barriers about 1950.) Vinyl wall coverings and certain kinds of paint act as vapor barriers. Your hardware dealer should be able to recommend one that will seal in the moisture.

Setting the Humidistat Control

You might want to experiment with various control settings on your humidifier to find the humidity level most comfortable for you and your family. If you are humidifying a large area, however—a living room, which leads into a dining room and adjoins a stairway, for example—or anywhere where there is significant air circulation, start by running the machine at its highest setting. There's a good chance that you'll leave it there.

Not Too Hot, Not Too Cold

Does the temperature of the water you put in your humidifier matter? Yes. Use tap water that's approximately room temperature (in the low 70s, Fahrenheit). Colder water can interfere with the humidifier's ability to create the right amount of mist; hotter water can damage the machine.

Keep It Running

When you move or when you purchase a new humidifier, the appliance may have to run continuously—for as long as several days—to bring the humidity to the level you desire. That's because it takes a while for objects such as furniture and carpets to absorb moisture from the air. As long as they continue to absorb that moisture, the humidifier will have to keep adding water to the air.

Too Much of a Good Thing

Dry air can permanently damage your furniture, but too much humidity is also harmful. Your humidifier can create condensation that can ruin the wood in your windowsills and window frames, damage your walls, and even interfere with the operation of some kinds of household electronic equipment. How do you know when the air is becoming too moist? You'll see it—as condensation on your windows. Take this as a sign that you need to lower the setting on your humidifier or even turn it off for a while. Static electricity, on the other hand, is a sure sign of air that is too dry—and a signal to you to turn the humidifier back on.

Keep the Mist Away

Although you use a humidifier to increase the humidity in your home, the mist it produces could cause problems. Should the mist spray directly on walls, drapes, or furniture, it could cause damage. To avoid inadvertently damaging these items, position the humidifier so that its mist does not fall directly on them.

Try an Ultrasonic Model

If you know that someone in your family is especially sensitive to airborne molds, buy an ultrasonic humidifier, which emits fewer of these objectionable organisms into the air than regular humidifiers do. As a bonus, these appliances are also quieter than the ones that use a fan to disburse the moist air. There is one drawback: Minerals from hard water may settle as a white powder residue on nearby surfaces. Some models, however, now come with a mechanism that softens the water while it is in the humidifier, thus eliminating the problem.

Place Ultrasonic Units Carefully

If you have an ultrasonic humidifier, keep it away from consumer electronic items such as stereo equipment, computers, and televisions, since white dust particles that often form near this type of humidifier may be harmful to such equipment. You can vacuum these particles or wipe them away with a damp cloth.

Troubleshooting Chart

Problem	Cause	Solution
Machine gives off mist continuously, no matter what the setting.	Doors in room are constantly opened and closed, causing the temperature to fluctuate, forcing the humidifier to constantly readjust.	Keep doors closed as much as possible.
Humidifier is making squeaking sounds.	The waterwheel is touching the plastic wear pads.	Apply a bit of petroleum jelly to the wear pads.
Fan is blowing but little or no mist is coming out.	Not enough water in the reservoir.	Fill reservoir.
	Water in the reservoir is too cold.	Refill with room-temperature water or wait for water to warm up.
	Reservoir was cleaned with detergent.	Empty and rinse reservoir and refill with clean tap water.
	Humidifier is not level.	Put humidifier on a flat surface.
	Mineral deposits have accumulated in the unit.	Clean the humidifier.
	Humidity level control is set too low.	Reset humidity control to a higher level.
Unpleasant odor emanates from humidifier.	Water has been sitting in tank for too long.	Empty and refill tank with clean tap water.

(continued)

*Troubleshooting Chart—*Continued

Problem	*Cause*	*Solution*
Unpleasant odor emanates from humidifier.	Humidifier was cleaned with detergent.	Empty and rinse with clean tap water before refilling.

Cleaning, Maintenance, and Storage

Hard Water Can Give You a Hard Time

The hardness of your water is almost as crucial to the functioning of your humidifier as it is to the operation of your washing machine and dishwasher. Mineral deposits left by hard water can gum up the humidifier's working parts. If you discover such deposits when cleaning the machine, wash them off with a one-to-one solution of water and white vinegar. If you live in an area with hard water, be especially vigilant about pouring out all water before storing your humidifier. Otherwise, the water will dry and leave behind a residue of minerals that could impair the operation of your humidifier. If you don't know how hard your water is, you can call your local water company and get an analysis from them, but before you do that, here are a few tipoffs. If your water supply comes from a deep well, you have hard water. Another way of telling is to use some soap to work up a lather. If it takes a lot of effort to get the lather up but it rinses off easily, you have hard water.

Clean It Weekly

Manufacturers recommend that you clean your humidifier about once a month. But consider this: Bacteria and mold grow in the water inside your unit. People who are allergic to molds may react to the presence of these organisms in the air between monthly cleanings, and an excessive amount of bacteria in your household air isn't healthy for any member of your family. Why not play it safe and empty and clean your humidifier every week during the season? (Definitely pour out the water if you're going away for more than a few days.) Disinfect the cabinet with a diluted bleach solution (add one tablespoon to a pint of water) after you've cleaned it. Of course, follow the manufacturer's instructions about cleaning certain delicate parts, such as the filter. If the air coming from the humidifier has a musty smell, you might consider putting a smidgen of bleach in the water being vaporized.

Don't Forget the Nebulizer

Ultrasonic humidifiers have a component called a nebulizer that helps to generate a mist. Mineral deposits on this component render it less effective, so clean it every week—more often if your water is very hard. Clean it with the brush the manufacturer supplied (or a soft nylon toothbrush) and white vinegar, then rinse off with water.

Put It in Dry Storage

When you put your humidifier away for the summer, it's essential to rid it of all moisture. Otherwise, bacteria will flourish in your unit and you may be in for big trouble when you run it again next winter. The preventive measure here is an easy one: Don't cover the water storage compartment. Doing so causes moisture to linger. With the cover off, moisture evaporates within hours.

I

Ice Chests

Ice-Cream Makers

Irons

ICE CHESTS

Getting the Most from Your Product

Pack It Right

To get the most from your ice chest, you should know how to pack it correctly. Place items on the bottom of the ice chest and cover them with a few inches of ice. Ideally, the pieces of ice should be about the size of your fist. If you begin with bigger pieces, break them down to size *before* placing them in the cooler, since breaking them inside could damage the liner. If you use dry ice, wrap it in burlap or newsprint to shield it from your food and the interior of the chest.

Cool It First

An ice chest will keep food chilled for 48 to 64 hours with dry ice and 24 to 36 hours with regular ice. But don't put room-temperature foods in a room-temperature ice chest, load it with ice, and expect your food to last this long. Whenever possible, make sure your food is chilled before it gets put into the ice chest. And pre-cool the ice chest, too. This will make the most of the food storage period, and may prolong it a bit.

Wrap It Tight

Have you ever arrived at your favorite picnic site only to discover soggy sandwiches? It's easy to think you've got things all wrapped up when in fact there's a small gap in your package that's letting moisture in. To avoid this problem, place particularly vulnerable items on the shelf, if your ice chest has one. To ensure the tightest wrap, twist-tie those plastic bags or close them with rubber bands, and wrap extra bags around them.

Ice by the Quart

Tired of half-melted ice sloshing around in the bottom of your ice chest? Freeze water in resealed cardboard milk cartons in your freezer and use them as your main cooling source. You'll probably have to supplement these with ice cubes, but they will cut down on the amount of water that's left behind.

Cleaning, Maintenance, and Storage

The Baking Soda Treatment

For general cleaning, use a solution of water and baking soda on and in your ice chest. To remove lingering food odors, simply soak a cloth in vanilla extract and wipe around the inside of the chest. To further guard against offensive odors, uncap the drain plug when you're not using the chest and store the unit in a well-ventilated location.

ICE-CREAM MAKERS

Safety Notes

Before You Start

You really don't have to be aware of too many safeguards when making ice cream; even a child can do it with adult supervision. But keep the following in mind:

- Be careful not to touch any of the electric ice-cream maker's moving parts when it is in operation. In addition, keep hands—and utensils—away from the mixing blade. If you must use a spatula, turn the machine off.
- Handle the frozen chilling bucket only when your hands are dry.
- Don't heat the chilling bucket; it could rupture and injure you.

Getting the Most from Your Product

Some Like It Firm

Everyone has his or her own view as to what consistency ice cream should be. For firmer ice cream than your recipe and ice-cream maker might offer you, chill the ingredients after you mix them but before you pour them into the appliance. For a dessert that's even firmer, freeze the fresh ice cream in an airtight container before serving.

De-Stick the Scoop

It may have been funny the first time you tried to dish out ice cream and it stuck to the scoop, but by the time you scooped the third or fourth serving, you probably weren't laughing. To avoid this problem in the future, just dip the scoop in cold water between servings.

Get out of a Jam

If the ice jams while you're hand-cranking ice cream it needn't cause a major problem—as long as you don't try to force it. Just move the crank backward about a half turn. For electric models, turn off the ice-cream maker, unplug the unit, and turn the ice-cream can a few times.

Crush That Ice

Crushed ice works best in ice cream makers. And the easiest way to crush it—unless you have an ice crusher—is to put it in a bag and hit it with a mallet or hammer. For smooth ice cream texture, reduce the ice to a fine consistency.

Too Soft or Too Hard?

If your efforts seem to be producing more mush than ice cream, add more ice and salt. If your ice cream hardens before it should, you're probably using too much salt or ice that's too coarse. When things are going just right, the ice cream should resemble the consistency of mashed potatoes.

It's OK to Be Heavy

If you're new to the pleasures of homemade ice cream, you may wonder if you've done something wrong when you find you've produced such a heavy confection. Don't worry—your fresh ice cream should weigh about twice as much as most store-bought varieties because it isn't pumped up with air. And when you freeze it, don't be surprised if it freezes considerably harder than most commercial types.

Don't Add Alcohol

Half the fun of making ice cream involves inventing new varieties. Just about anything can go into this treat to enhance its flavor and texture. Everything except alcohol, that is. Refrain from adding alcohol to the ice cream mixture because it lowers the freezing point—and may leave you cranking the maker half the night with little to show for your efforts.

Cleaning, Maintenance, and Storage

Clear the Drain Hole Regularly

To successfully make ice cream, the salted water needs to flow freely out of the bucket. Should the drain hole in the bucket clog up, the water could back up into the ice cream, destroying your dessert. Check the can's drainage opening regularly to be sure that the water can flow freely.

Fight Rust

Ice-cream makers are not hard to clean—soap and hot water are all you need to do the job. But take care to dry off metal ice cream cans with a towel. If you let the water evaporate naturally, rust could form on the can. Salted water, too, can be corrosive, so be sure to get all of it out of the bucket after each use.

IRONS

Be Careful

Many appliance manufacturers warn that you should use the appliance "only for its intended use." This is imperative with irons. Using an iron improperly can easily damage it—not to mention seriously burning the person involved. Because it is such a familiar object, you may be more likely to ignore the safety precautions. Even if you've used your iron hundreds of times before, scan the list below to make sure you've developed good safety habits.

- Never immerse the iron in water or other liquid.
- Always turn the iron to "off" before plugging and unplugging it. And don't yank the cord from its outlet—always grasp the plug to disconnect it.
- Before filling and emptying the iron of water, disconnect it from the electrical outlet. Keep it unplugged when you're not using it.
- Allow the iron to cool completely before storing it.
- Be careful when turning the iron upside down. The reservoir may have a negligible amount of water in it, but just enough to cause a burn.

Getting the Most from Your Product

Plan Ahead

A little planning can save you a lot of time when you iron. If you plan to iron several items made of different fabrics, begin with the synthetics, which require low heat, and work your way up to high heat for the wools, cottons, and linens. (For garments made of more than one kind of fabric, pick the lowest heat setting appropriate for any of the fabrics.) Remember, the iron takes longer to cool down than it does to heat up.

Smooth Out the Wrinkles

Steam-ironing a large item, such as a sheet, can be an onerous, time-consuming task. To make this job easier, try removing such items from the dryer while they're still damp. You can reduce wrinkling of clothes by hanging them up after they come out of the washer or dryer. Leaving them in a pile in the laundry basket while waiting to be ironed will only make the job more difficult. Another wrinkle-fighting method is to sprinkle water on the item you're ironing, or give the item a quick sprinkle, then roll it up in a plastic bag and let it sit in the refrigerator for a few hours (to prevent mold) while the dampness permeates the fabric. And if there are still a few wrinkles—or if you have a garment with only a few wrinkles to begin with and don't want to bother with ironing—hang it over the shower curtain railing, run some hot water into the tub or shower pan, and let the steam do the work.

Reflect the Heat

To quicken the steam-ironing process, put some aluminum foil between your ironing board cover and the padding on the board. The foil reflects the iron's heat, increasing the efficiency of your iron.

Season the Soleplate

Even if you live in an area with hard water and intend to use distilled water in your iron regularly, use tap water the first few times you iron to season the soleplate. Thereafter, season occasionally by heating tap water in the tank as you would for ironing, then flush out the water. Once in a while it's a good idea to switch from distilled water to tap water because the minerals in tap water create more steam. For best results, do not use water passed through a water softener because the minerals in this water can damage your iron. And to avoid buildup of mineral deposits, always empty your iron after each use.

Inside Out Saves Your Fabric

Rayons, silks, double-knits, and certain other garments could come out with an unwanted shine after you iron them. To avoid this, put the clothing on your ironing board inside out and iron it on its inner side. If you use starch, you can prevent starch buildup on your clothes and ironing board by spraying the starch on the wrong side of the fabric and ironing as usual.

The best way to unwrinkle garments when ironing is not to press down on them with the iron and force them to straighten out, but rather to press lightly with long, gliding strokes.

A Makeshift Ironing Board

If you're traveling or if you have only one item to press and don't want to lug out the ironing board just for that, you can make do with very little effort. Fold a thick bath towel in half and slide it inside an old pillowcase. You've just made yourself an ironing board.

Irons to Go

A travel iron is a wonderful convenience on a long trip. But there are *two* adapters to be used with foreign power supplies. Your local appliance dealer or hardware store should be able to supply both:

- A converter to switch between 110 volts and 220 volts.
- Adapters so your plug can fit in any one of four kinds of sockets: flat parallel blades, round pins, flat angled blades, and three-pronged rectangular blades.

Troubleshooting Chart

Problem	Cause	Solution
Iron does not get hot.	Iron is not plugged in securely.	Check connection to wall outlet. If secure, plug in a lamp or radio to make sure the outlet is working.

Troubleshooting Chart—Continued

Problem	Cause	Solution
	Temperature selector is not set.	Set temperature selector.
Iron leaks or spits water.	Iron is not preheated.	Let iron preheat for at least 2 minutes before using.
	Selected temperature is not hot enough (when steam ironing).	Turn the temperature up if fabric can take it, and wait 2 minutes for iron to heat.
	Steam/Dry button is not in "dry" position.	Make sure iron is set correctly for dry ironing.
Iron does not steam correctly.	Steam/Dry button is not in the "steam" position; temperature selected is not in the steam zone.	Make sure iron is set correctly for steam ironing.
	Not enough water in the iron.	Fill water tank.
	Steam vents are blocked.	Push steam button up and down a few times, or use the "blast" or "burst" of steam feature a few times.

Cleaning, Maintenance, and Storage

Keep the Soleplate Clean

To prevent pitting on your iron's soleplate, store the appliance in an upright position so that moisture can evaporate after you finish ironing. Should the soleplate become marred through pitting or scratches, you can smooth it out with fine waterproof sandpaper or buff it with polishing compound (if the plate is metal); both may be obtained at the hardware store. An alternative remedy is to iron a piece of wax paper to coat the surface of the soleplate.

For starch buildup on the soleplate, make a baking soda and water paste and apply it with a damp cloth or sponge to wipe away the residue.

Vinegar Kills Clogs

You can clog the innards of your iron simply through normal use (although using hard water or water softened with a water softener could hasten the process). If washing out the iron with tap water doesn't do a good enough job, try using white vinegar instead and let the iron steam for a few minutes. Afterward, rinse it out thoroughly with tap water and wipe off the soleplate. Unclog steam vents, the steam valve opening, and the spray nozzle by *gently* poking them with a needle, pipe cleaner, or straightened paper clip—always with the iron turned off and unplugged.

Empty the Water Tank

To make sure you get all the moisture out of the tank, empty the iron while it is still hot. This ensures that the last remaining droplets will evaporate from the heat of the iron rather than being retained in the tank. Do this after each use.

J

Juicers and Juice
Extractors

JUICERS AND JUICE EXTRACTORS

Safety Notes

Beware the Sharp Edges

Does your juicer have a stainless steel strainer? If it does, take extra care when handling it, because the edges are very sharp. The strainer is one of the only parts that can be washed in the dishwasher. By taking advantage of this convenience, you can minimize your contact with the sharp edges.

Getting the Most from Your Product

Firm Is Better

When selecting fruits and vegetables to juice, always choose produce that is firm. Stay away from fruits and vegetables that are overly ripe—they may seem to be more juicy, but they will not juice readily.

Save the Pulp

Your juicer strains out much of the pulp in the process of separating the pits from the liquid. If you prefer lots of pulp in your juice—for its taste, texture, and vitamin and mineral content—don't automatically throw out what the appliance separates from the juice. Use a fork to sift through the residue and get rid of the pits. Then put the pulp back in the juice.

The Perfect OJ

There's a technique to everything, even to getting the best orange juice out of a juicer. For the "perfect" glass of orange juice:

1. Allow the fruit to warm to room temperature before you juice it.
2. Put the oranges on the counter and gently roll them around for a few seconds with the palm of your hand. This loosens the fibers and gives you more juice.
3. While holding the half-orange down against the reamer, move the fruit from side to side to extract the most juice the fruit can offer.

Prepare Fibrous Vegetables Before Juicing

If you plan on using your juice extractor to juice leafy vegetables, such as parsley or spinach, or stalk vegetables, such as rhubarb or celery, you must prepare the vegetables first so their fiber doesn't clog the machine. Roll leafy vegetables into little balls before feeding them into the juice extractor. Cut stalk vegetables into 2-inch cubes.

Don't Force It

Don't use force when feeding fruits and vegetables onto the grating disc of your juice extractor. Gentle pressure is enough. If you force material onto the disc you risk straining the motor.

Cleaning, Maintenance, and Storage

Clean Your Juice Extractor Often

Be sure to clean all parts of your appliance frequently, particularly if you juice a lot of fibrous vegetables. A buildup of pulp in the basket can cause the motor to vibrate. Wash the basket in mild soapy water, using a brush to loosen the pulp. To remove mineral stains, soak the parts in a solution of cold water and a mild detergent, then scrub the stains with a brush.

Use a Toothbrush

Your extractor probably came with a brush for cleaning the unit. It's a small tool, easy to misplace. If yours does disappear, don't bother to send for a new one. A toothbrush will work as well.

What Your Product Won't Do

Extractors Aren't for Citrus Juice

Extractors are great for making smoothies—blends of fruits like bananas, apples, and strawberries—and can give you a tall, cool glass of juice pressed from vegetables like carrots, but they're not made for making juice from citrus fruits. To make orange juice in one of these units, you must peel and pit the fruit first. Even then, the final product may be too foamy for your taste, and it may have a bitter edge, because some of the smaller pits and part of the rind may get crushed into the juice. Only a citrus juicer, which is made expressly for the task of extracting the juice from oranges, grapefruits, and the like, is good for making citrus fruit juices.

L

Lawn Mowers

Lawn Sprinklers

Lawn Trimmers

LAWN MOWERS

Safety Notes

Safe Mowing Rules

Some common sense can keep your family free from mishaps with the lawn mower:

- Enforce the lawn mowing dress code: long pants, shoes (no open sandals or bare feet), and safety glasses or goggles (even over regular glasses).
- Clear the area before mowing. Any sticks, stones, nails, and bits of debris can become dangerous projectiles when hurled by the mower blades.
- Mow grass only when it's dry and only during daylight hours.
- Keep children and pets indoors until the mowing is done.
- Should you hit a solid object or have to stop the machine and examine it for any reason, turn off the motor and disconnect the spark plug wire.
- Avoid mowing steep slopes where your footing is precarious (why not plant groundcover so you don't have to mow?). On an incline, mow across with a walk-behind mower and up and down with a riding mower.

Use an Electric Mower Safely

- Use only grounded extension cords and avoid any that are worn or damaged. Inspect the cords throughout the season.
- Never use an electric mower when the grass is wet or it's raining.
- Watch out for the cord! One way to avoid inadvertently mowing over the cord is to begin cutting the grass close to the power outlet. As you move away to mow the rest of the lawn it is easier to keep the cord behind you.
- Never leave the mower running and unattended, even for a second.
- Always make sure the mower is unplugged before doing any repairs.

Gas Mower Safety

- Fill the mower with fuel outdoors and never smoke around the gas container or the mower.
- Don't fill the tank more than three-quarters full. Wipe up spills as soon as they happen.
- If you must add more gas in the middle of the job, let the engine cool for 10 minutes. It's extremely dangerous to add gasoline to a hot machine and to open the gas cap while the machine is still hot or running.
- On models you must pull to start, avoid cuts, bruises, and sprains by gripping the rope firmly, but never wrapping it around your fingers or arm.

Make Sure It's a Safe Ride

Follow these tips for rider mower safety:

- Ride solo. A lawn mower is not safe for passengers.
- Keep your feet up and on the machine at all times and let the blade come to a complete stop before getting off the mower.
- Avoid mowing when the lawn slopes 10 degrees or more. Switch off the blade when traveling uphill at this angle. Don't drive the mower on a slope of more than 15 degrees (a rise of 2½ feet every 10 feet).

When to Cut the Engine

There are several situations that call for turning off the lawn mower's engine. They include:

- When you push the mower off the lawn to cross a driveway or sidewalk.
- When you know you hit something you shouldn't have or if you hear any unusual sounds from the motor.
- Any time you take your hands off the mower to do a task, even if it's just clearing the grass bag.

Give Your Mower a Cool-Down

Keep in mind that the engine and the engine's housing get very hot by the time you've finished the lawn. Before you put away the mower, let it sit in a shady spot until the engine housing is cool to the touch. If you're like most people, you probably have flammable material in the garage or storage shed—a spare gas can, old newspapers, and the like. Putting the mower away while it's still hot could cause spontaneous combustion.

Getting the Most from Your Product

Watch That Incline

Traction—*your* traction, not the lawn mower's—is the key to mowing a lawn that isn't level. Get out your baseball, golf, or other hard shoes that protect your feet and provide extra traction to keep you from slipping.

High Grass Needs a Second Pass

Use two passes to take care of tall grass with a reel mower. To get the best cut, keep the rear roller bar up on the first mowing. For the second mowing, lower the cutting bar to clip grass at the desired height.

Gas and Grass Don't Mix

It's amazing how often people who will work in the hot sun for hours to keep their lawn looking good will then turn around and do something that can easily kill patches of grass. *Don't service your mower on the grass.* All it takes is a little spilled gasoline and oil to wipe out a healthy patch of grass.

Starting and Restarting

You'll put less wear and tear on the engine if you always start the mower on a solid surface like your driveway (first make sure there are no stones or sticks underneath). If you do start on the lawn, do it over grass you've already cut. When starting up again after taking a break, set the speed control stick to "idle" or "slow."

Troubleshooting Chart

Problem	Cause	Solution
Mower is making unfamiliar sound.	Objects may be stuck in mechanism.	Turn off motor immediately. Disconnect spark plug, turn mower on its side to check for foreign objects. (Keep oil fill hole higher than crankcase to prevent oil leak.) Clear any obstruction and clean blades thoroughly before mowing again.
Can't open crankcase.	Crankcase plug is stuck.	Place the shaft of a screwdriver between the two protrusions on top of the plug and apply pressure.
Mower is cutting unevenly.	Tires are unevenly inflated.	Check tires, add air if needed.
Engine won't start (gas-powered model).	Gas level too low.	Fill the tank.
	Engine is flooded.	Wait a few minutes, then try to start again.
	Faulty spark plug.	Place connecting wire ¼ inch from spark plug. If there's no spark when you turn over the engine, replace spark plug.
	Poor ventilation.	Check the tiny vent hole in the top of gas tank. Clear out with a straight pin.

(continued)

Troubleshooting Chart—Continued

Problem	Cause	Solution
Engine won't start (gas-powered model).	Clogged fuel line.	Clear the line by increasing the flow of gas to the engine. Turn the needle valve clockwise with a screwdriver until the extra gas clears the blockage.

Cleaning, Maintenance, and Storage

The Ideal Cleaning Tool

You probably already own the most useful tool for cleaning your mower—a screwdriver. Wrap a piece of cloth around the blade of the screwdriver, secure the cloth with a rubber band, and you can safely probe for and remove grass and dirt from the machine. To clean away stubborn grime from the engine and metal or foam air filters, use a rag dipped in kerosene.

Feeding a Twin-Cycle Engine

Twin-cycle engines are sensitive to the ratio of gasoline to oil that you feed them and won't run efficiently if the ratio isn't right. Smoke pouring out of the engine is a warning that it's time to readjust. A gasoline-to-oil ratio of 16 to 1 is a good starting point. Be sure to blend the mixture *before* you fill the tank. If the engine still smokes, gradually increase the proportion of gasoline until the machine runs smoothly without those great clouds of smoke.

Use the Right Drive Belt

Replacing the drive belt in the motor with anything but a belt made specifically for your lawn mower is asking for trouble. No matter what anyone tells you, a generic replacement can strain and damage the motor.

Keep the Engine Oiled

Don't forget to periodically oil the engine and other parts that need lubrication. A couple of drops of light machine oil after every 35 hours of use—and before you put the lawn mower away for the winter—should keep all parts running smoothly.

The Cutting Edge

Sharpen your mower's blades at least twice a season for best mowing results. Dull blades make your mower's engine work harder and tear at the grass rather than cut it evenly. The goal is not only to have sharp blades, but to maintain the cutting angle the blades had when the mower was brand new.

When working with the blades, always wear thick gloves. Unscrew the blade bolts to remove the blades. Fit them securely in a vise grip, with the sharp edge up. Work a medium-rough flat file (or electric drill sharpening attachment) in one direction, moving from the inside bottom of the blade to its outside edge.

When you've finished sharpening the blades, you will need to make sure that you didn't unbalance them in the process. To do this, place a screwdriver through the blade's center hole and let it swing freely, pivoting on the screwdriver. If one side of the blade is heavier, file a little metal off that side (but not from the cutting edge) until the blade balances. Once the blades balance, reinstall them on the mower, making sure the lift (the bend or twist on the back edge of the blade) points upward.

The "Reel" Test for Sharpness

Reel mowers cut with a series of blades that are attached to a roller bar. The circular motion of the reel cuts the grass and, on some mowers, moves with the action of the wheels. Because the blade mechanism is so intricate, you'll have to take the mower to a professional to be sharpened. But you can periodically check the blades for sharpness with a simple newspaper test. Take a single sheet of newspaper and run one edge along each blade—carefully, of course! As long as the blades slice the paper easily, they're still sharp; if there's any resistance or ragged ripping of the paper, it's time to get the blades sharpened.

Inspect Reel Blades Regularly

Every month or so, you should check your reel mower's blades for nicks and rough spots. At the same time you should inspect for uneven areas. To see if a blade is straight, hold a straight-edge next to it. If there's any unevenness in the blade, lightly tap it out with a hammer. Try not to hit the cutting edge directly, since that will dull the blade.

Keep the Battery Charged

If your mower has an electric starter, you need to recharge the battery regularly. Once a month is a good recharging schedule for wet and dry batteries. Test the battery's strength with a voltmeter before recharging. Check the instructions on the charger to see how long you should charge your particular battery. When you remove the charger clips, be sure the charger is unplugged first.

To make sure you don't forget this important task, make it a habit on the first of every month.

Watch Out for the Sand Trap

If the soil in your yard is sandy, be especially diligent about examining the cutting blades of your lawn mower for wear. The flying grit from this kind of soil is rough on blades and can dull them quickly.

End-of-Season Care

Before putting away your mower for the winter, turn it on its side so you can remove any clumps of dried grass with a putty knife. Tape closed the air intake and exhaust openings to keep water from penetrating the mower's innards, then wash away any caked-on dirt with your garden hose.

Because gasoline evaporates, storing a lawn mower for the winter without first draining the fuel could clog sensitive parts with a sticky residue. Siphon off fuel still in the tank and empty the fuel line and carburetor by running the motor until it conks out.

Spring Maintenance Checklist

When the world turns green again, here are three important tasks you should perform before starting your mower:

1. Clean and replace the air filter and any damaged gaskets.
2. Refill the gas tank with *fresh* gasoline only.
3. Change the oil and make sure it is at the proper level.

LAWN SPRINKLERS

Getting the Most from Your Product

When Is It Time to Water?

Your eyes can be your guide for when the lawn needs a drink. Watch for these signs: the lawn takes on a bluish tinge, the grass wilts in the heat of the day, or you can see your footprints in the lawn.

The best time to run the sprinkler is in the morning—anywhere from sunrise until high noon. Evening sprinkling, contrary to an old garden tale, will not harm the grass or cause disease. The only time of day to avoid would be the hot stretch of afternoon sun.

Determine Your Lawn's Moisture Needs

How can you tell when your lawn has had enough water? Both soil and grass type determine moisture needs. Soil with a high clay content needs ½ to ¾ inch of water about twice a week, slightly more in very hot weather. Soil with a high sand content requires that much every other day. A nice loamy soil with good humus content does fine with 1 inch a week. Bermuda grass, Centipede, and St. Augustine are drought-tolerant grasses and can go longer without water. Bluegrass and ryegrass are *not* drought tolerant and need close attention. Fine and tall fescues are moderately drought tolerant.

To see how much water your sprinkler delivers, buy an inexpensive rain gauge from the hardware store. Place it within sprinkler range and check it every half hour until you see how long it takes to deliver the amount of water your lawn needs. Now you'll know how long to let the sprinkler run to give your lawn the amount it needs, and not a drop more or less.

Turn It Off and On

No matter what kind of lawn grass or sprinkler you have, there's a wrong way and a right way to water. The wrong way is to turn on the sprinkler and let it run and run until the water puddles on the lawn or starts to trickle down the sidewalk and into the street. The right way is to turn on the sprinkler for 15 minutes or so, then turn it off to give the soil a chance to soak up the moisture before running the water again.

Use the Right Sprinkler for the Job

Not all sprinklers are created equal. Some are better suited for certain jobs than others:

Fixed sprinklers work best on small to medium areas of the yard, especially corners or other inconvenient spaces. They're especially good on newly seeded sections of lawn.

Impulse sprinklers spray water over a circular area and can be adjusted to water only a semicircular or fan-shaped area. These are good to set inside a wide flower bed.

Revolving sprinklers can be adjusted to deliver low sprays of water, useful in areas of the yard where there are low-hanging tree branches.

Soaker hoses are great for rows of vegetables or narrow flower borders.

Try a Little Tenderness

Your sprinkler will stay in top operating shape longer if you treat it gently when you're moving it from place to place. Carry it when you want to change location. Dragging it along the ground by the hose risks clogging the holes with soil, grass, and grit.

Cleaning, Maintenance, and Storage

Clog-Free Watering

If you live in an area where there is a high mineral or silt content in the water, the best way to prevent clogs in sprinkler holes is to install a filter washer (some models already come with these handy devices). Remove and clean the filter washer every other week. Even in places where the water is relatively mineral-free, a filter washer isn't a bad idea. For a mere 50 cents or so you can keep clogs from ever happening.

The Clogged Nozzle Cure

When there's something blocking the flow of water through the sprinkler holes, help is as handy as the nearest straight pin or paper clip. With a steady hand and a good eye, you can quickly probe the holes to remove the blockage. Never use anything larger than a paper clip, like fork tines or metal poultry pins, since these can damage the holes.

Keep the Arm in Shape

On sprinklers with deflector arms, a once-a-month application of a waterproof lubricant will keep the moving parts in working order.

Off-Season Care and Storage

When it comes time to retire the sprinkler for the season, spend a few minutes making sure it's as dry as possible. Drain the sprinkler to get out as much water as you can, then let it sit out in the sun for the afternoon to dry up any remaining moisture. A hook is a handy place to hang the sprinkler and keep it out from underfoot.

LAWN TRIMMERS

Safety Notes

Smart Safety Sense

Lawn trimmers can make short work of many lawn chores. To make sure all your work is done safely, review the following guidelines, which apply to both gas and electric-powered models:

- No matter how much they want to help, don't let children, even preteenagers, use the lawn trimmer. Manufacturers even suggest that young children should not be allowed in the yard when the trimmer is running.
- The temperature may be in the 90s, but dress to protect your body and not to beat the heat. Always wear shoes and avoid open sandals. Trade the shorts for long pants to protect yourself from flying debris. *Always* wear safety goggles. Ear protectors can safeguard your hearing from the high decibel level of a trimmer.
- Before you begin trimming, search the area for sticks, stones, wire, and any other objects that could become dangerous missiles when hurled by the trimmer.
- Check for holes, hidden tree stumps, or any other hazards that could catch you unaware.
- Warn neighbors and anyone in your yard to stay away from the area until you're done. To be safe, keep pets and young children indoors while you're trimming.
- Because reduced visibility increases the risk of accidents, avoid using a trimmer after dark. If you must, operate it only where there is plenty of bright light.
- Never use a trimmer to cut wet grass and weeds.
- A safety harness gives you an extra measure of security and comfort, especially when you're using the trimmer for long stretches of time. A padded strap gives the most comfortable fit.

Use Electric Trimmers Safely

• Always pay attention to keep the cord out of the way of the trimming wire or blades.
• Use an extension cord with No. 12 or No. 14 gauge wire. Smaller wire (No. 16 or 18) can lead to electrical shock or fire in the unit.

Gas Trimmer Safety

• It's obvious but bears repeating: *never* smoke near the gas-powered trimmer or the gasoline container.
• Add gas to the trimmer only when it's outdoors and when the machine is cool. (If you must add gas after the trimmer has been running, let it cool down for at least 10 minutes before refilling.) Move away from the spot where you've filled the trimmer before you start the engine.
• Never store the trimmer with gasoline inside and always let it cool before you put it away.
• Save yourself from a nasty sprain or cut by starting the engine correctly. Grip the rope firmly *without* wrapping it around your fingers or arm.
• Should you hit a solid object or have to stop the machine and examine it for any reason, turn off the motor and disconnect the spark plug wire.

Cleaning, Maintenance, and Storage

Clear Away Garden Grime

Gas-powered trimmers need to have their air filters checked and cleaned after roughly every 25 hours of use. If you skip this important chore, the motor can overheat, causing damage and cutting short the life of your trimmer. To clean, remove the filter and wash it in a sudsy bucket of warm water and dish detergent. Squeeze the filter dry, then lubricate with a few drops of SAE 30-weight engine oil. Squeeze the filter to distribute the oil evenly.

On electric trimmers, particularly those where the motor is on the cutting end, keep the motor vents clean. After every use, scrape away grass clippings and other yard debris. An old toothbrush and a narrow piece of wood like a paint stirrer are handy tools for this cleanup chore.

On gas trimmers you can wash the cover and metal elements with warm water and dish detergent. However, you should *never* use water to clean an electric trimmer; water that leaks into the motor can cause a short circuit.

Take a minute to wipe the line spool and plastic spool housing with a rag before you put away the trimmer. Keeping these parts clean and in good working order ensures snag-free trimming.

Follow Good Maintenance Habits

Get into the habit of following these maintenance tips for trouble-free use of your trimmer:

- Before every use, check the power cord on an electric trimmer for signs of fraying.
- On a blade-type trimmer, inspect the blade for signs of cracked teeth or weak welds (on blades with brazed carbide tips). If there's any doubt about the condition of the blade, replace it with a new one for a safer and smoother cut.
- When you're replacing the cutting line, use only flexible nylon cord. Rope, wire, or cable pose serious hazards. Also, make sure your replacement is the correct size line or spool for your model. If not, you're likely to have a problem with a jammed spindle or a line that won't unwind.

Keep It out of Reach

When you're not using the trimmer, keep it in a dry place, out of reach of even the most resourceful child. Aside from the safety factor, keeping the trimmer out from underfoot means it's less likely to be stepped on. The plastic parts on many models break easily.

Off-Season Storage

Your gas-fueled trimmer will last longer if you retire it for the season free of fuel and oil. Once you've run the engine so that all the gas has dried, remove the spark plug and lubricate the cylinder with a small amount of 2-cycle engine oil. Pull the rope starter several times, then reinstall the spark plug. Use the dust cover and store the trimmer out of reach of children.

M

Mattresses

MATTRESSES

Getting the Most from Your Product

Ignore the Handles

Some mattresses come equipped with handles built into the sides, presumably for easy lifting. Don't use them. Not only is this an awkward way of gripping a mattress when lifting it, it also may stretch the mattress cover and shift the materials inside.

Cleaning and Maintenance

One Good Turn Keeps Your Mattress Firm

Turn a mattress about once every six to eight weeks to keep it smooth and firm. But in the first few months, do it every two weeks.

You don't have to be a Houdini to turn a mattress without injuring your back. All it takes is two people and the right method. Each person stands at a corner diagonally across from the other. Slide the mattress around on the box spring so that it ends up lying horizontally across the bed, overhanging both sides and the end by more than a foot. (If the mattress doesn't slide easily, slip some plastic trash bags between it and the box spring.) From the end of the bed, lift the mattress up on its edge and guide it so it softly flops down in the direction of the headboard. Standing at the same corners where you began, slide the mattress around in the same direction you used at the beginning of the process. Voila! One mattress turned over and reversed end to end.

Vacuum Up the Dust

It's a good idea to vacuum your mattress whenever you turn it. This picks up dust and other debris, and gives you a chance to check the mattress cover for any rips or tears. Any such tears should be repaired right away to avoid further damage.

Blot Out Stains

If you spill a liquid that soaks through to the mattress, there is a way to remove the stain. Carefully blot (do *not* rub) the spot with a damp towel until the stain begins to disappear. To draw up as much of the liquid as possible from the mattress, press firmly on the spot with a dry towel, leaving it there for an hour or so if the spot is very wet. Then let the mattress remain uncovered until the area is completely dry, to discourage mildew growth.

O

Ovens, Microwave

Ovens and Ranges,
Electric and
Convection

Ovens and Ranges,
Gas

OVENS, MICROWAVE

Safety Notes

Microwaves and Pacemakers

According to the Food and Drug Administration, the microwaves emitted by your oven should not pose a health threat to anyone who has a pacemaker. But pacemakers vary in their design, and it's possible that a person with a pacemaker could feel some brief discomfort caused by the microwaves. So, if anyone in your household has a pacemaker, ask your doctor what, if any, special precautions you or they should take when using the microwave oven.

Use Potholders

One of the often-touted features of microwave cooking is that the container in which you heat food does not get hot, even though the food does. Sometimes, however, a dish will become hot when the heated food transfers some of its energy to the dish. So it's always wise to use potholders when handling dishes from your microwave.

In Case of Fire

Foods that don't cause problems in a conventional oven can be problematic in a microwave. Some, such as a potato you over-cook or forget to pierce before baking, can even start fires. Should a fire start in your microwave oven, don't open the door. Instead, turn off the current and disconnect the appliance. Once the fire is out, let the oven cool, then clean out the inside of the oven with a mild, nonabrasive soap.

Microwave Safely

- Don't use the microwave oven for melting paraffin or drying clothes, newspapers, flowers, or other similar items not intended for use with this appliance.

- A few products—such as sealed glass jars, frozen beverages in narrow-necked bottles, and whole eggs in shells—can explode when heated in a microwave oven; do not put these in the microwave.
- Some foods, such as potatoes, whole squash, whole tomatoes, and sausage also can explode when cooked in a microwave oven. To prevent bursting of the skin or membrane, simply pierce in several places to allow steam to escape.
- Pop popcorn only in microwave-approved poppers or packages designed specifically for microwaves.
- Don't use your microwave oven for deep-fat frying. The temperature of the fat cannot be controlled and can cause serious burns.
- Always vent plastic wrap when covering a dish. To do this, turn back a small corner to allow steam to escape. This also prevents the plastic wrap from splitting during microwaving. When uncovering the dish, be sure to remove the plastic wrap away from your face to avoid steam burns.
- Don't use aluminum foil in the microwave oven. However, you can use small pieces of foil to cover areas that may burn, such as turkey wings and drumsticks. Simply secure the foil with toothpicks and add or remove the foil when appropriate during the cooking time. Don't let the foil touch the walls of the microwave oven or sparks may occur and may damage your microwave.
- Operating the microwave when it is empty is potentially dangerous and also can damage the oven. If you are experimenting, place a container of water in the oven.
- Make sure that nothing blocks the openings of the oven.
- If you plan to move your microwave oven, make sure the place you've chosen for it is at least three inches away from the edge of a countertop to avoid accidental tipping.
- Don't store flammable materials in or near the oven, and never try to heat them in the oven.

Don't Expose Yourself

If you follow these guidelines, you shouldn't worry about exposure to excessive amounts of microwave energy:

- Don't try to operate the microwave oven with the door open.

- Be sure to keep the microwave's sealing surfaces clear of residue.
- Don't use the oven if it's damaged, especially if the door is bent or if safety locks don't allow the door to close properly.

Getting the Most from Your Product

Your Microwave Needs Air

There's no flame, and the microwave oven doesn't get hot to the touch. Looking in the window can give you the impression that nothing is happening inside. Nevertheless, your microwave does need adequate ventilation to keep its magnetron tube at low temperature and to avoid harmful condensation in the cooking chamber. Therefore, make sure all vents are clear of obstructions and allow at least four to eight inches of "breathing room" between the wall and back of your unit.

Cook in Sequence

The most convenient way to cook a meal is to cook everything together. But doing that in a microwave can be difficult because of the varying densities and cooking times of the food. For an acceptable compromise, try microwaving the foods needing the longest cooking times first, such as a casserole. Often such foods require "standing time" to complete the cooking. Then you can take care of the quick-cooking foods like vegetables.

Make Quick, Nutritious Meals

The microwave oven is unbeatable when it comes to preparing good foods in a fraction of the time conventional methods take, and with fewer vitamins and minerals being cooked away. Microwaves do a great job on high-moisture foods like fish, poultry, vegetables, and fruits, as well as casseroles, sauces, and soups. Foods stay flavorful without added fats.

Prepare Two or Three Dishes at a Time

If your microwave oven comes with a middle rack, you can use it to prepare different kinds of food at the same time. Because the base of the oven's interior is subjected to stronger heating radiation than the shelf, put large quantities of food and those that require the most heat, such as casseroles, on the oven floor. Reserve the shelf for smaller quantities, or food that you only need to warm, such as pastry. While you may have to open the oven door to pull out the items on the shelf before the food on the oven floor is done, you will save time and energy in the long run.

Rule-of-Thumb Cooking Times

Unless you're cooking dishes that take 15 minutes or less to cook individually, cooking two or three dishes simultaneously in a microwave oven with a rack saves time — but how much time? Experiment with combinations of foods to see how cooking times differ. Also, be sure to use a container that's the right size. Microwaving in a dish that is too large for the amount of food will increase cooking time. Use these rule-of-thumb times as a guideline:

- If at least one dish needs to cook for 15 to 35 minutes, add the cooking times of all the dishes and subtract 5 minutes from that total to get the combined cooking time.
- If at least one dish needs to cook for more than 35 minutes, the combined cooking time will be simply that of the dish with the longest time. In other words, when you cook a roast that ordinarily takes 40 minutes, rice (11 minutes), and a frozen green vegetable (10 minutes), you will need to cook the foods together for 40 minutes.

Freeze Foods in Shallow Containers

Microwave ovens are supposed to excel at defrosting frozen foods, but sometimes there's a catch. For example, if when defrosting a deep-dish casserole you pause during the defrosting cycle to break up the frozen chunks, the outer part of the food may start cooking before the middle is even unfrozen. To ensure even defrosting, freeze foods — especially casseroles and stews — in shallow containers.

Cold Dishes Slow Down Heating Time

Heating food in a cold dish can affect cooking time. Foods that go straight from the refrigerator to the microwave take longer to heat than foods that are at room temperature. The cold dish absorbs the food's heat, making the oven work a little longer to heat the food to its final temperature. Simply allow extra cooking time when cooking in a cold dish.

Check the Wattage

Microwave ovens differ in more than just size and price. Some also produce less power than others. For certain foods— particularly cakes and other sweet confections—cooking times will be longer in ovens with less power. Most recipes assume an oven rated at 600 to 700 watts. To check your microwave wattage, look for the model and serial numbers and wattage located on the back or behind the door.

Cooking times can be as much as 20 to 30 percent slower if your appliance's output falls in the 400- to 500-watt range. Unfortunately, there's no accurate way to adjust the cooking time. And because cooking times will vary for each dish, always check the food to see if it's done before you remove it from the oven.

Cooking Evenly

The size of the container in which you microwave food makes a big difference in how evenly it cooks. When heating anything that requires more than a small dish, stir often. Otherwise, you may end up with the outer edges overdone and the middle undercooked. (Contrary to what some people think, microwaves don't cook "from the inside out." The actual cooking energy reaches only two inches into the food from its surface; heat penetrates farther into the food through conduction.) The shape of the dish also determines how evenly food cooks. Round shapes are best for even cooking.

The Cookware Test

Use this simple test to see if a container is appropriate for use in your microwave oven. Put the dish in the oven next to a glass of water. Now run your microwave oven for about a minute. If you end up with hot water but a cool dish, the container passed the test and you can cook with it. If both water and dish are warm, the dish won't be suitable for use in the microwave oven.

Which Frozen Dinners Can You Cook?

Increasingly, frozen dinners are being sold in containers designed for use in a microwave oven. But can you cook food that comes in a metal tray? The answer is "no," because you should never use metal in a microwave oven; the rays actually bounce off metal, damaging the microwave. However, you can defrost a frozen dinner (don't use the microwave to do it!) until it's warm enough to transfer to a dish that's microwave safe.

Take an Accurate Temperature

Use these methods to make sure your oven's temperature probe accurately measures the doneness of food:

- For liquids, put a spatula or wooden spoon across the center of the bowl and rest the probe on it, allowing the probe tip to dunk into the middle of the liquid.
- Place the probe tip into the center of a casserole dish before you begin to heat it. Remember to carefully reinsert the probe after stirring the food.
- Find the thickest part of a roast and pierce the center of it with the probe tip, taking care not to let the tip touch bone or fat.

Keep Cooking Records

Why not set up a formal recordkeeping system for your microwave cookery? Keeping track of how you prepared each dish should help you produce more consistent results. Include recipe information and cooking time as well as notes on what type and size of container you used. Leave room for general comments and refer to your notes as you would refer to a recipe book.

A New Twist

Most manufacturer's manuals warn you to remove metallic twist-ties from bags before putting them in the microwave oven, yet very few suggest a substitute for this little convenience. Here's a safe and simple substitute: a rubber band.

Troubleshooting Chart

Problem	Cause	Solution
Oven does not turn on.	Fuse is blown or circuit is tripped.	Check fuses and circuit breakers.
	Door is not closed properly.	Check door.
	Controls are not set properly.	Check timer, "start" button, and other controls.
Moisture collects on the oven's interior.	Food is giving off moisture.	This is normal.

Cleaning, Maintenance, and Storage

Wipe Up Each Day

Clean the microwave with a damp cloth each time you use it. For stubborn food stains or particles, use a plastic scrub pad and a nonabrasive cleaner. Don't use cleaning pads or steel wool, and don't be tempted to use a knife or sharp object to scrape. You could easily damage the oven.

Steam Clean Your Oven

Cleanup is easier when you soften food splatters on your microwave's interior walls before wiping them off. To do this, boil a cup of water in the unit, and when you see some vapor inside, turn off the oven and let the condensation work on the food scraps for a few minutes. Then open the door and wipe them away.

Borderline Cleaning

Food that spills on the edge where the oven door seals may prevent the door from closing completely. The resulting gap may not look like much to you, but it may be enough to slow cooking times or even cause the oven to shut off. So carefully sponge off these spots with the same mild, nonabrasive soap you use on the rest of the oven.

Don't Confuse Your Oven

If foods take longer to cook than the time suggested by your recipes, you could be running into the problem of "microwave confusion." This condition is caused by food particles left on the walls of your microwave oven from previous dishes. The oven's microwave energy cooks everything inside; it can't distinguish between the food you put in to heat and the scraps you forgot to wipe up. A buildup of food on the oven's walls means somewhat less energy available for cooking tonight's dinner. The solution, of course, is to clean up food particles after each use.

The Aromatic Oven

Leftover food particles not only confuse the microwave oven, but also can make it smell bad. Heating food scraps over and over will leave your appliance with a less-than-desirable odor. After cleaning the oven, give it a fresh scent by combining ½ cup of lemon juice and one cup of water in a bowl and boiling it for a few minutes in the microwave. Let the mixture stand for another 5 minutes before opening the door.

Bring Your Microwave to Room Temperature

You could damage your microwave oven by operating it when it's colder than the surrounding air temperature. This could happen if you temporarily store it in the basement and then use it as soon as you bring it upstairs to the kitchen. Or it could occur if you turn on a new oven as soon as you bring it home or too soon after it's delivered in the winter. At any of these times, give the appliance plenty of time to warm to room temperature before cooking with it.

What Your Product Won't Do

It's Not Good for Multiple Drinks

Even though microwave ovens boast faster cooking times for most foods, sometimes it's more efficient to use a conventional oven or stovetop. As you gain experience with microwave cooking, make a chart with cutoff points showing where it's sensible to switch to gas or electric cooking. For instance, when you make one cup of tea, the microwave is your best choice. If, however, you want more than one cup, you should switch to the stovetop, because the time it takes to boil the water increases with each additional cup.

Not Better the Second Time Around

Using recycled paper products may be environmentally sound, but it could be dangerous in your microwave oven. Avoid using plates and bowls made of recycled paper; they contain tiny metal fragments that might set the paper aflame during the cooking process. The package should tell you whether the paper products contain recycled material, but if you have any doubts, don't take the chance.

Plastics Aren't Always Safe

Plastic containers are suitable for certain microwave applications—for example, boiling water—but not for others. They particularly don't work well for cooking food with a high fat or sugar content for long periods of time. These foods can heat quickly, possibly causing the plastic to melt. Use glass or other microwave-safe cookware instead.

OVENS AND RANGES, ELECTRIC AND CONVECTION

Safety Notes

Range Safety

Although there are marked differences between gas ranges and electric ones, many of the safety precautions are similar. Refer to the "Safety Notes" for gas ovens and ranges later in this book, as a supplement to the information below:

- Electric heating elements get hot even before they start to turn color. Until you get used to cooking with electric ranges, exercise extra caution with the burners' coils.
- Use pots that are large enough to cover the surface elements. If you use a pot that is smaller than the heating element, you run the risk of exposing yourself or your clothing to the hot burner.
- Don't immerse the removable heating elements in water or other liquid.
- If you're using a high setting on the range, keep an eye on what you're cooking. Food that boils over may ignite.
- Use drip pans, if they come with the range. Cooking without them may damage wiring or other internal components. Don't line the drip pans with aluminum foil, or you could give yourself a shock or cause a fire.
- Never use the oven to heat a room.
- Teach your children to respect the oven. Don't leave them alone in the kitchen with a hot oven.
- Do not store flammable items in or near your oven.
- Use dry chemical or foam-type fire extinguishers on grease fires, not water.
- Use *dry* pot holders to protect yourself when handling pans going into and out of the oven.
- Be careful when you open the door to your convection oven. Hot steam is likely to come out, and carelessness can result in burns.

- Make sure that the vents of your convection oven are free of obstructions.
- If you have a self-cleaning oven, do not use commercial oven cleaners, and do not touch the oven or range top when the cleaning cycle is in progress.
- Keep all knobs in the "off" position when the oven and range are not in use.

Repair Cooktop Breaks

A broken glass-ceramic cooking surface is dangerous as well as inefficient, because any liquid—whether it's a spill or a cleaning solution—can get inside and cause electric shock. Inspect the cooktop periodically for any cracks or breaks. If you notice damage, promptly call a repair person.

Safety above the Range

What do you keep in the cabinet above your range? While the temperature is not likely to create problems for most household goods stored in this space, it may heat up enough to do unpleasant and dangerous things to volatile liquids and aerosol sprays. Take an inventory of what you have in that cabinet and find another place for these substances or others about which you have any doubts. While you're at it, remove any items that may interest children; you don't want to tempt the little ones to climb all over the range.

Hands Off the Cooktop

To avoid a dangerous encounter with a solid-element cooktop that's hot to the touch, wait until you have a potful of food ready and in place before you turn on the burner. The design of these elements causes them to conduct more heat along the cooktop than do coils. If there's no pot on the range to absorb the heat, much of it transfers to the cooktop.

Getting the Most from Your Product

Tips for the New Electric Range User

Most of the tips for using gas ovens and ranges apply as well to electric ones. However, if you've used a gas range in the past and are now changing to electric cooking, bear in mind these essential *differences* between electric ovens and ranges and those fueled by gas:

• Effective electric cooking on the range top usually involves starting with a high temperature and finishing with one that is somewhat lower.

• Electric heating elements, unlike gas burners, continue cooking even after you've turned them off, because the elements cool slowly. That means you'll have to remember to remove the pot from the stove when you're finished cooking.

• The bottom of the pan must be flat to maintain even contact with the heating element. That old warped pan you used with your gas stove will not work well on your electric range. Trivets and the like are also out, because they can leak condensation onto the heating element, causing corrosion.

• Pots and pans should not overlap the trim ring of the heating element by more than an inch and should not rest on the cooktop, the area surrounding the burner.

How Many Volts?

While most appliances need 120 volts to operate, your electric range probably requires more. The standard wiring supplies your range with either 208 or 240 volts. Because it reduces building costs and saves energy, your outlet may have been wired to supply 208 volts. (Use a volt meter to check this out, or consult an electrician if you're not sure which you have.) Either 208 or 240 volts is sufficient, but if you receive only 208 volts from the line, give special attention to:

Preheating. Extra preheating time is required at this voltage.

Baking time. If your oven seems to bake more slowly, it may be because you have a 208-volt line. For some foods, this could mean a 25 percent increase in baking time.

Broiling time. The lower voltage could cause a slowdown

here. But you can deal with it by moving the rack closer to the heat source.

Cooking on the heating elements. When you use the top of the range, figure that foods will take a bit longer to cook.

No matter how your house is wired, a brownout will probably affect your electric cooking in the same way. So if the power company cuts your voltage—possibly during a summer heat wave—be ready to slightly alter cooking times.

Use the Correct Heat Setting

Need a guide to heat settings for the top burners on your electric range? As in all cooking, you will discover what the best settings are for you and your equipment by trial and error. But if you're new to electric range cooking, the following guidelines should help, although you'll still have to make adjustments for your particular range. Starting from the lowest setting on your dial, the settings are: Warm, Low (25 percent), Medium (50 percent), Medium High (75 percent), and High.

Warm. Use this setting for keeping heated foods at a ready-to-serve temperature and for cooking cereal and steaming rice.

Low. This is the basic cooking temperature after you begin with a brief period on "high."

Medium. Use "medium" to brown, saute, and simmer food.

Medium High. Pan broil and fry at this setting; also use it to bring pasta and similar foods to a rolling boil.

High. Reserve the hottest setting for getting most dishes started and for boiling water.

Save Energy and Money

Want to save money on electricity? Here are a few ways to do it:

- When you make tea or coffee, measure out the amount of water you need, cup by cup, rather than simply filling the pot. This draws less current and gets your beverage on the table much faster.
- Turn off the heat a few minutes before the cooking is finished, since the element holds the heat for some time before it cools.
- Never place a small pan on a large burner. The exposed area of the heating element wastes energy.

Solid Elements Save Energy

If the burners on your range top are solid heating elements rather than the more familiar coils, be aware that solid elements take longer to heat up; but they hold that heat longer than coils. Therefore, you save even more energy by turning them off sooner than you would coil elements. You can also save energy and money by starting with lower heat settings than you would on a range with coil elements.

Solid Elements Need Flat Pans

While all electric ranges work more efficiently with flat-bottomed cookware, appliances with solid heating elements are even more sensitive to this need than those with coils; so you should test any pot in question. To test if a pan is truly flat, boil an inch of water in it. If the bubbles aren't uniformly distributed across the bottom, the pan is unsuitable for use over a solid heating element.

Kebab Tips

If you have a grilling facility built into your electric cooktop, you may already have purchased a kebab accessory. Here are some tips for using it:

- Try piercing foods with a toothpick before you skewer them — it often makes inserting the skewer much easier.
- Kebabs can dry out if cooked for too long, so use the highest setting for the shortest cooking time.
- For best results, cut meat into 1-inch cubes before cooking.
- If you like your meat well done, space the pieces farther apart on the skewer.

Ventilate for Fresh Air . . . and More

If your cooktop has a ventilation system, you can use it for more than just getting rid of range top smoke and odors. Cool your baked items and hot utensils with it. Put the food or utensils on the grill with the fan turned on, but don't block off the entire vent. You also can use the fan when cutting up foods with strong odors, such as onions, near the range.

Eliminate Smoky Grilling

If smoke gets in your eyes while using the grill component despite diligent ventilating, you may be undercutting the ventilator's effectiveness. Do you have cross-ventilation in your kitchen? Are the windows open? The breeze from open windows could be pulling the smoke into the room with just enough force to overwhelm the ventilator's efforts. Try closing the windows. If that doesn't work, you might consider installing a fan.

Converting Recipes for Your Convection Oven

When you cook food in a convection oven, you can still use standard recipes, but you'll have to adapt them for different timing. After about 75 percent of the cooking time has elapsed, check to see if the food is done. If it isn't, keep close tabs on it until it is. Test the food by sight or with a utensil; don't rely on time and temperature alone.

Try these two rule-of-thumb guides for conversions. They will vary a little, depending on different foods and the quirks of your particular unit:

• For roasting, reduce the cooking time by about one-third.
• For baking, cut the oven temperature by 75°F, but not lower than 300°F.

Dark Pans Work Best for Convection Cooking

Dull or dark pans work best for baking in the convection oven because they absorb heat more quickly, whereas shiny ones reflect heat. Using the darker pans will speed baking time and brown crusts more readily.

To ensure sufficient air circulation, always maintain at least ½ inch of space between your baking pan and the walls of the oven, so be careful to choose your pan sizes accordingly. If you're using more than one pan, make sure they do not touch one another. As an added measure, stagger the pans—one behind the other—for the greatest air circulation.

When to Choose Convection

If you have both a microwave and a convection oven, how do you know which oven to use for which food? For heating leftovers and TV dinners, the microwave is superior. If browning the food is not crucial, the microwave could also be your first choice with many fresh foods. But for roasts, baking, and slow cooking, use the convection oven.

When preparing fresh foods such as baked potatoes, choose your appliance according to the quantity you will be cooking. For example, a microwave oven will make fast work of a single potato. But once you increase the quantity to two or more, the cooking time also increases, making the convection oven the more convenient appliance.

No Need to Preheat

As a general rule, preheating your convection oven is not recommended unless you want to bake foods that rise or broil foods that need browning. Even casseroles can be cooked in a cold oven; just check them 5 or 10 minutes before they would be done if baked in a conventional oven.

From a Frozen Start

You can cook a frozen roast in your convection oven without first defrosting it, but the cooking time will be a bit longer than if you'd let it thaw. If you do pop the roast in the oven right from the freezer, add an extra 15 to 20 minutes of cooking time for each pound. You need a bit less time per pound for small roasts (less than 5 pounds) and more for the bigger ones. This works only with meat; frozen poultry requires defrosting first.

Can You Trust the Thermostat?

There's an easy way to see if your convection oven's thermostat is providing reliable information and cooking control. Buy some cake mix and bake a cake exactly as the recipe on the box specifies. If the cake is soggy and underdone or dry and over-done, the thermostat must be adjusted.

Avoid Two-Toned Baked Goods

Cakes and cookies that unintentionally come out with dark bottoms and pale tops are disappointing. You can avoid the dissatisfaction by keeping these questions in mind before you bake:

- Are you using the right size pan? Using one that's either too large or too small could result in unevenly baked goods.
- Did you preheat the oven? It's especially important with most baked items that the oven be hot when you put them in.
- Are you putting too many pans on a rack? Or, have you placed several pans directly over each other on the racks, thus creating uneven air circulation?
- Is the rack you're using too close to the bottom of the oven? If you think about it, it's easy to see why this would darken the bottom of your baked goods.
- Is the oven door closing completely? Or, on the other hand, have you been opening it just a bit too often? Heat that escapes can cause uneven baking.

When to Use Radiant Bake

If you have both radiant (conventional) and convection heating in your oven, use the mode most appropriate for what you're cooking. Generally, cook items in the following list using radiant bake, and everything else with convection heat. You can cook tender cuts of meat with radiant bake, but they cook faster with convection heat. For best results, use radiant bake for:

- Less tender cuts of meat.
- Any meat you cook in a cooking bag.
- Meat prepared in a Dutch oven.
- Meat prepared in a covered roasting pan.

Troubleshooting Chart

Problem	*Cause*	*Solution*
Nothing on the range works.	Fuse is blown or circuit breaker tripped.	Check fuses and circuit breakers.
	Cord is not properly connected to the wall outlet.	Check plug connection.
Oven does not heat.	Some models have separate controls for turning on the oven and setting the temperature.	Make sure controls have been set properly.
	Time controls are not set properly.	Check timer.
Self-cleaning process does not go on.	Controls or timer are not set properly.	Check controls, timer, and current time of day on the clock.
	Door is not locked.	Lock door.
Oven did not clean well.	There were unusual spills in the oven.	Clean excessive spills before turning on the self-cleaning process.
	Oven needs a longer cleaning time.	Clean again; next time set the clock for a longer cleaning time.
Oven door cannot be unlocked after self-cleaning (if oven has a lock light, it should be on).	Oven needs to cool to a safe temperature.	Let oven cool (45 minutes to 1 hour); make sure knob is still in the "clean" position.
Some smoke emanates from the oven and/or a small flame can be seen through the oven window during self-cleaning.	Oven is heavily soiled.	This is normal.

(continued)

Troubleshooting Chart—Continued

Problem	Cause	Solution
Convection oven does not work at all.	Fuse may be blown or circuit tripped.	Check fuses and circuit breakers.
Cooking results in convection oven are poor.	Pans are positioned badly.	Stagger pans.
Convection oven is baking unevenly.	Oven isn't properly installed; oven rack is uneven; pans aren't staggered correctly.	Call dealer or service company; check rack with a level; stagger pans and don't let them touch the oven walls.

Cleaning and Maintenance

Cleaning the Reflector Pans

The reflector pans, which act as drip protectors, can be made of one of several types of materials, each of which requires different cleaning methods.

Wash *porcelain* with soap and water in the sink or use your dishwasher. Porcelain will also stand up to your oven's self-cleaning process; just turn the pans upside down and put them on one of the racks. For troublesome stains, try soaking them in a mixture of ½ cup ammonia to 1 gallon of warm water.

Wash *chrome* in your sink as you would any other chrome utensil—with hot water and a plastic scrubbing pad. Don't run them through the dishwasher or put them in the oven during the self-cleaning cycle. You can, however, use an oven cleaner on the chrome to get out tough stains.

You can put *aluminum* in the dishwasher, but it may spot. If you'd rather wash the pans by hand, use hot water and a plastic scrubbing pad.

For *stainless steel* trim rings, scrub stubborn stains with a nonabrasive cleaner, otherwise just use hot water and a mild detergent.

Solid Elements Are Easy to Clean

Unlike coils, solid heating elements do not need reflector pans to catch spills. Cleaning involves just wiping up the burners with a damp cloth. However, wait until the element is cool enough to clean safely but still warm enough to wipe the spill before it hardens. Drying the element is even easier: Just turn it on at its "medium" setting for a minute or two.

A New Use for Aluminum Foil Pie Plates

You can save yourself much cleaning time by placing foil pie plates under the burners. The tins will collect anything that boils over, and it's a lot easier to take them out and clean them off (or replace them) than it is to soak and scrub the surface under the burner.

The Lowdown on Self-Cleaning

When using your self-cleaning oven, a little smoke, a small momentary flame, and a slight odor are not signs of trouble. Some ash deposits and/or film left behind after the cleaning process is finished are also normal. Simply wipe them away with a damp sponge. However, if these deposits are dark or you consistently get a lot of them, try running the oven on self-clean more frequently and for a longer period of time. Never use a commercial oven cleaner, which can damage the oven's surface.

Save on Self-Cleaning

You can save money and also time on self-cleaning if you start the self-cleaner just after you bake or broil. The oven won't take as long to reach the necessary temperature, which means less time and less energy.

A Solution for Sticky Racks

Do you leave the oven racks in when you use the self-cleaning cycle? If so, you may notice that they become harder to slide in and out afterward. To lubricate them, spread a light coating of vegetable oil on the bottom of the rack edges and on the oven rack supports after the self-cleaning operation has run its course and the appliance has cooled.

Lemons Clean the Oven Window

A greasy window may resist your oven's continuous or self-cleaning action. To cut through the grease, coat the inside of the window with lemon oil. After an hour, remove the oil with a stainless steel pad and wipe thoroughly with a dry cloth.

If you don't have a self-cleaning oven, use a commercial glass cleaner or soapy water. Be careful not to allow liquid to run down into the door's air vents.

Grill Cleaning Made Easy

Range top grills do not require an excessive amount of cleaning. In fact, giving your indoor grill the cleaning workout you give your outdoor charcoal grill could be damaging. Instead, just clean the grill each time you use it. You can put it in the dishwasher or clean it with a plastic scrubber. For the occasional stubborn stain, soak it in ammonia and water.

It's Soap for the Griddle

Messy as this cooking surface gets, you can usually clean it easily with soap and hot water—but wait for the griddle to cool to approximately room temperature before immersing it. For tough spots, use a plastic scrubber and a nonabrasive cleanser.

Cleaning a Glass-Ceramic Cooktop

If you own one of the newer electric ranges with cartridge cooktops, you may have parts made of a combination of glass and ceramic. This substance is sensitive to dirt, so keep it as clean as possible. Before using the cooktop, wipe any dirt from its surface and be sure the bottoms of your pots and pans are clean.

A mild dishwashing liquid should suffice for daily cleaning, but a burned-on spill requires special handling. Mix water and baking soda (or any common, nonabrasive household cleanser) to form a paste. Apply it to the spot and then lift it off with either a paper towel or a nonabrasive scrubber made of plastic or nylon. If the stain won't come off easily, leave the paste on (covered by a moist paper towel) for about 45 minutes. And if that fails, scrape off the stain with a single-edge razor blade, being careful not to scratch the surface.

OVENS AND RANGES, GAS

Safety Notes

Stove Safety

You obviously would not touch a hot pot or put your hand near an open flame on your gas range. But when you're in a rush to prepare a meal, it's sometimes easy to overlook the less obvious safety precautions, such as:

- Keep loose clothing away from the burners. Be especially careful if you're wearing a bathrobe or housecoat with big, droopy sleeves.
- Take items out of cabinets above the range *before* you start to cook. If you need to get something from up above once you've started cooking, turn down the burners and reach over cautiously. If you have children in the house, make sure that there is nothing of interest to them in those cabinets.
- Keep dry, thick pot holders near the stove. That dish towel you grab without thinking could be much too thin to protect your hand from a hot handle.
- Turn pot handles toward the side or back of the range when you're cooking so you or your children cannot accidentally knock over a pot with scalding contents.
- Allow a pan of hot grease to cool—preferably on a back burner—before storing or disposing of it.
- Add or remove food from your oven by pulling out the rack rather than reaching in for the food.
- Take the broiler pan out of the oven as soon as the food is done, eliminating the possibility that the leftover grease will ignite.

- Keep the broiler grid (on which the food rests when it broils) clear, not covered with aluminum foil. Although it may look like a shortcut to cleaning up, covering the grid defeats the purpose of the grid/drip pan combination and keeps grease close to the flame (it also produces fried rather than broiled food). For the same reason, avoid disposable broiler pans.
- Prevent grease from accumulating on the ventilating hood or filter. Many restaurant grease fires get started because this apparatus is not kept clean, and your home is subject to the same danger.
- Light a burner only with a pot in place above it. The pot then becomes a shield between you and the flame if it should flare up when you light it.
- Keep the flame under the pot. Your food may cook a little faster with the fire licking up the sides of the pot, but everything near the burner will be at risk—including you.

Use Pot Holders with Care

Pot holders are often taken for granted, but if they're not used safely they can cause problems in the kitchen. The first precaution is obvious: Keep pot holders away from an open flame. The other: Don't use a damp or wet pot holder. It can be extremely dangerous. If the pot holder is soaking wet, using it to touch a hot utensil can send up enough steam to scald you. Even if there's only a spot of water on the pot holder, the moisture reduces the insulating qualities of the fabric.

Chill before Baking Automatically

Timers that allow you to bake automatically—sometimes hours after you put the food in the oven—are a handy feature. It's a good idea, however, to forgo this luxury when baking with eggs, milk, pork, fish, or any other foods that spoil easily, especially if they are likely to be sitting in the oven for some time before the baking process begins. If such foods are chilled well before being put in the oven, you'll have a little more leeway.

Dealing with Grease Fires

Kitchen grease fires are scary. Most of the restaurant fires you read about originate with burning grease. If it happens in your kitchen, do you know what to do? If the fire flares up in the oven or broiler, turn off the oven and keep the door shut. The fire should burn itself out. If it happens on the range top, throw baking soda on the flames or use a fire extinguisher designed for the kitchen. Another possibility is to first throw a pan on top of the blaze to contain it, then put it out. It's a good idea to keep such a pan handy—hang it on a hook where you can reach it quickly.

Getting the Most from Your Product

Use the Right Size Flame

Vary the size of the cooking flame on your gas range according to the material of the pots and pans you are using. Keep the flame low to medium when using cookware that transfers heat slowly, such as those made of cast iron, enamel, glass, glass/ceramic, and stainless steel, and cookware with nonstick surfaces.

Cover It If You Can

There are several good reasons to cook on your gas range with a covered pot or pan whenever possible:

- Temperatures stay at a more even level in a covered pot.
- A covered pan retains steam, making for more efficient cooking and a more comfortable kitchen.
- Odors remain in the pot instead of permeating your house.
- You need less water when you cover the pan, decreasing the amount of vitamins cooked out of the food.

A Test for Flat-Bottomed Pots

On a gas as well as an electric cooktop, pots with flat bottoms give the best results. But how can you tell if the pot's bottom is truly flat? An easy way is to place a ruler's straightedge against the bottom. Now rotate the ruler, and you will spot any unevenness in the surface very quickly.

Rolling vs. Gentle Boiling

Does your food cook faster at a rolling, dramatic boil, than if it's barely boiling? No! It doesn't cook any faster. You can't get water any hotter than 212°F. So unless you're cooking spaghetti, which calls for vigorous boiling, save on gas by using only as much energy as you need.

Keep Air Vents Clear

If you plan to install kitchen carpeting, keep in mind that you can easily block your gas oven's air vents. Before your carpet is installed, inspect the stove's location to make sure the surface is hard and flat.

Fry Dry

When frying food, take note of a simple precaution that will help prevent a mess in the kitchen. Water gets in the way of effective frying. Its presence on frying foods can cause fat to bubble up during cooking and possibly spill over the side of the pan. So if you defrost food that you're going to fry or if you wash off fresh food before placing it in the frying pan, be sure it's dry before you start to cook.

Make a Foil Drip Catcher

Many people like to put aluminum foil on the bottom of their ovens to catch drippings and thus ease the cleaning burden. If you do this, take care not to cover the bottom entirely; you need to leave some openings clear for ventilation in a gas oven. Better yet, instead of using the foil directly on the oven bottom, place a foil-covered cookie sheet on the oven's lowest rack, directly under whatever you've got cooking. This is especially helpful if you're baking a fruit pie, where a gooey bubble-over is always a possibility.

Warm and Thaw Foods in the Oven

By all means use your gas oven to keep food warm for a while, but use this practice selectively. For example, rare and medium-rare cuts of meat can cook just enough under these circumstances to end up a shade darker than you may intend. Vegetables can dry out, so cover them tightly with aluminum foil while keeping them warm and try adding a little water to them. Generally, keep food in warm storage for no more than about an hour. If you just want to warm up a serving dish, set the oven at 170°F.

You can also use the oven to thaw frozen foods. Set the oven at 155°F and thaw frozen food for about one-fourth the time you would at room temperature.

Use the Right Size Pot or Pan

One of the keys to cooking efficiently with a minimum of splatter is to use a pot or pan size appropriate to your cooking task. Roasting, for example, requires a shallow pan not much bigger than the size of the roast. But when baking other foods that will have a lot of liquid, use pans with deep sides to prevent spills as you remove the food from the oven. On top of the range, choose cookware that will be nearly filled by the quantity of food you wish to prepare—but always allow enough extra space for any food you will add while cooking and for a certain amount of bubbling up.

Place Pans for Even Cooking

When you have more than one dish in the oven, there's a trick to baking efficiently: Place the pans to maximize heat circulation between them. This means keeping the pans near the middle of the racks, arranging them so that none is directly above or below another.

Cooking in a Power Failure

You can still cook on your gas range when the electricity goes out, by carefully lighting the burners with a match. It is *not* safe, however, to light the oven. If the power were to come back on while you were trying to light the oven with a match, the automatic ignition would kick in, possibly giving you a serious burn.

A Hot Tip for Broiling

Do you or does someone else in your house like your meat dark on the outside but blood-red inside? There's a trick to pulling this off every time without fail: keep your oven door open just a bit when you're broiling and you want a really rare steak.

Troubleshooting Chart

Problem	Cause	Solution
Nothing on the range works.	Fuse is blown or circuit breaker tripped.	Check fuses and circuit breakers.
	Cord is not properly connected to outlet.	Check plug connection.
Burners won't light or flames are yellow.	Burner ports are clogged.	Clean ports with toothpicks and soapy water.
Flame is uneven.	Burner ports are clogged.	Clean ports with toothpicks and soapy water.
Oven burner doesn't light.	Controls aren't set properly.	Make sure controls are set properly.
	Time controls aren't set properly.	Check timer.
Control knobs won't turn.	Knobs aren't being pushed in as they are being turned.	Push in knob as you turn it.
Burner makes a popping noise when it is on.	Burner is wet from washing or spills.	Let burner dry before using it.
Self-cleaning process does not go on.	Controls or timer are not set properly.	Check controls, timer, and current time of day on the clock.

Troubleshooting Chart—Continued

Problem	Cause	Solution
	Door is not locked.	Lock door.
Oven didn't clean well.	There were unusual spills in the oven.	Clean excessive spills before turning on the self-cleaning process.
	Oven needs a longer cleaning cycle.	Clean again or set clock for a longer cleaning cycle next time.
Oven door can't be unlocked after self-cleaning (if oven has a lock light, it should be on).	Oven needs to cool to a safe temperature.	Let oven cool (45 minutes to 1 hour) and make sure control knob is still in "clean" position.
Moisture condenses on oven window.	This is normal when you cook foods that have a high moisture.	Leave oven door open just a crack for a few minutes at beginning of baking period or when preheating.

Cleaning and Maintenance

Keep the Ports Clean

A good gas flame should be blue. This comes from the right mixture of air and gas. If the flame is yellow or makes a noise, or if soot covers the bottoms of your pots, you're not getting the correct air/gas mixture. Yellow flames are cooler than blue ones, which means that it will take more time and more gas for foods to cook.

One reason for yellow flames is that food may have spilled over at one time and is now clogging the ports. Another possibility is that the burner air shutters aren't adjusted properly, giving you the wrong proportion of air to gas. You can clean the burners by lifting them out and using toothpicks and soapy water to clear the ports. Dry the burners before putting them back on the range. Then give them a try. If the flames are still yellow, call a repairperson to adjust the air shutters.

Clean the Drip Trays

If your older model gas range has drip trays under the burner, slide them out periodically and wash them. Not only does this keep the appliance clean, but it also eliminates a prime food source for cockroaches.

Get Out the Worst

Not all spills are equal in their ability to damage the finish on your stove. Most of the worst offenders have a high acid content. They include foods such as citrus juice, marinades, sour milk, tomato sauce, and vinegar. Getting to these spills quickly with a dry cloth will prevent problems later. When the stove has cooled, wash the spot with soap and water.

Clean the Burner Grates Two by Two

It's easy to put off the unpleasant task of cleaning burner grates and drip pans until burned-in grease makes this a job to dread. On the other hand, if you do it often, it makes the task as easy as doing the dishes. Instead of washing all four burner grates at once, make the job easier by doing only two at a time. Wash the grates and drip pans with your dishes; with frequent cleaning you won't need heroic measures to free them of grease.

Bake Burners Dry

If you put washed burners back in service while they are still wet, you could get an uneven flame. Water in the burners might also prevent them from lighting automatically. To dry them easily, replace the burners and then set your oven to 170°F and "bake" the burners dry—about half an hour should do it.

Use a Fan for Less Grease

You can avoid a lot of dirty work by using a range hood with a fan filter mechanism when you cook greasy foods. Over the course of a year, this system will cut down substantially on the amount of cleaning you have to do. When the hood filter eventually gets greased up, you can just clean it in the dishwasher.

(Not Always) Continuous Cleaning

Most of the time, your gas oven's continuous cleaning mechanism will get the job done. But it's often less effective on sugar and starches than on other spills and splatters. For these spills, use a nylon brush to remove as much of it as you can. Loosen the rest by spraying on one of the common household cleansers, such as Fantastik. After about 15 minutes, you should be able to brush off most of the residue with a wet brush or nylon scrubbing pad. Use a damp sponge to finish it off. Don't use commercial oven cleaning products. If they become trapped in the porcelain enamel surface, the cleaners can give off harmful fumes.

Beware of Commercial Oven Cleaners

Did you ever carefully read the label on a commercial oven cleaner? You might think that a person should wear a space suit for safety when using one of these preparations. But an older oven or one that does not have a continuous cleaning surface can still be cleaned without resorting to these commercial cleaners. First, stop food buildup on the spot by pouring salt on spilled food as soon as you see it—but wait to wipe it off until the oven has cooled. For general cleaning, dampen a rag or sponge, apply baking soda, and scrub. For heavier duty cleaning, wipe inside the oven with ammonia, close the door for three hours, and then scour away what's left.

Stagger the Oven Racks

Do you dread cleaning the oven racks? If you don't have a self-cleaning oven, use this tip to cut your scrubbing time in half: Clean the two racks simultaneously. Stagger one on top of the other so you can scrub them both at the same time.

Smoke Signals

You may hear a crackling sound while your gas oven is self-cleaning. That's a natural sound from metal expanding and contracting as it's heated and cooled. But if your oven also begins to emit a large quantity of smoke during this process, you have a problem.

The smoke is caused by a buildup of dirt in the oven—just too much for the self-cleaning procedure to dispatch without complaint. You probably don't need to call the fire department—you don't have a fire—but you do have some extra cleaning to do. Turn off the oven, open the windows, and wait at least 45 minutes before you open the oven. (Of course, if the smoke hasn't abated after this time, you might want to consider calling in the fire department.) Wipe away the offending soil once the oven is cool and restart the cleaning cycle. In the future, clean the oven more often.

What *Not* to Clean

The prohibition against cleaning the gasket that helps create a firm seal between your oven and its door is worth heeding. You could easily damage the gasket should you subject it to normal cleaning. If it becomes discolored, live with it. If the dirt becomes too much to tolerate, moisten a sponge and gently dab at it.

P

Power Tools

Pressure Cookers

POWER TOOLS

Safety Notes

Know the Basics

When it comes to power tools, safety is of paramount importance. The possibility of serious injury is far greater when using power tools than when using any other home product. Here are some safety basics:

- Familiarize yourself with the tool you're using. Know what it can and can't do.
- Check your shop's outlets for correct polarity and grounding continuity. (You can buy a tester to do this at an electric supply shop for about $5, or you can have an electrician do it.) If any problems are discovered, have an electrician correct the wiring. For greatest safety, install ground-fault circuit interrupters (GFCIs) on all circuits in your shop.
- Always use a properly-grounded three-pronged plug with tools that require them. Don't use grounding adapters.
- Keep your work area clean. If anything sharp or slippery falls on the floor, stop work and remove it immediately.
- While you work, make your shop off-limits to everyone, especially children. If you have children, child-proof your work area: Install a master switch well out of a child's reach and remove starter keys when not using them.
- Use tools only for the purpose for which they were intended.
- Wear safety glasses or whatever other protective facial covering is appropriate for the tool you're working with.
- Always disconnect tools when you're not using them or when servicing or changing attachments on them.
- Avoid wearing loose clothing and jewelry while working in the shop, and keep long hair tied up and covered.
- Hold your work with a clamp or vise whenever possible.
- Lay out your work area so you won't have to reach over power tools for anything. Take extra steps rather than reach too far and possibly lose your balance.

- Clean and sharpen tools regularly and repair (or replace) damaged tools promptly.
- If you saw or drill into a wall, keep your hands away from the tool's metal parts, because you might hit a live electric wire.
- Keep any flammable or explosive substances out of your shop while you use power tools.

Paint Removal Safety

Using a paint removal attachment on your electric drill could pose a health hazard if you're working in an old house where lead-based paints may have been used (60 percent of homes built before 1940 contain lead paint). It's safest to leave lead-based paints *undisturbed;* either paint over them, or build another piece or component to cover the lead-painted part. If you *must* disturb woodwork painted with lead-based paint:

- Wear a filtered respirator
- Tape plastic drop cloths to isolate the work area from the rest of the house
- Keep everyone away from the work area, especially children
- Don't smoke during or after working in the area
- Wear long-sleeve shirts, long pants, gloves, and a hat; discard these clothes after you've finished working with the lead-painted woodwork
- Use a dustpan and broom to collect all paint chips and dirt; discard the dustpan and broom when finished
- The safest approach is to pry out the lead-painted woodwork and discard it totally; then make new woodwork to replace it
- Check with your local municipality to determine where you should take the paint chips, dirt, dustpan, broom, and woodwork for safe disposal

Getting the Most from Your Product

Control Your Drilling

The trick to drilling accurately is to maintain as much control as possible over the tool. To do this:

1. Punch a slight indentation in whatever you're going to drill to get started.
2. Holding the drill firmly, apply a moderate amount of pressure on a straight line.
3. If it stalls, stop the drill and check the problem rather than try to unstall it by pulling and letting go of the trigger in quick succession. Breaking clear through the piece you're drilling can stall the machine. To reduce the odds of this happening, ease up as you get close to breaking through.
4. Continue to run the motor while extracting the bit from a hole to reduce the risk of jamming.
5. Except when working with cast iron and brass, always drill metal with a lubricated bit—even bacon fat will do.

Use Both Hands

Large, professional electric drills have handles for both hands to give the user greater control and steadiness. Smaller drills can be used with just one hand on the handle, but to make the drill steadier and keep it from slipping, grasp the body of the drill with your other hand. This also lets you know when the motor is becoming hot from overworking. If the body is getting hot, turn off the drill and wait for it to cool down. If you find that your drill continues to overheat, it's probably because the material you're drilling is too hard for that particular drill. Either use a speed reducer or use a larger drill.

Keep Saw Blades Sharp

Sharpened blades are essential to success when using a power saw. A dull blade can cause motor overload and slow your work. Don't get caught without a usable tool when you send a blade out for sharpening—stock a few spares. Keep in mind that the price of sharpening is not that much less than the cost of a new blade.

Make the Most of Your Circular Saw

To make good, clean cuts with your circular saw:

- Start with a sharp blade.
- Be sure you've set the correct depth of cut with the adjusting knob. Don't expose too much blade depth beyond what you need for your cut.
- Always give yourself a cutting reference by marking the piece you're working on with a pencil.
- Remember to move the saw smoothly, applying minimal pressure. Don't force the saw, or it may bind and overheat.
- Always cut wood with the "good" side facing down to minimize splintering.

Know Your Circular Blades

In general, circular saw blades with few, coarse teeth cut quickly and roughly, resulting in a piece that needs quite a bit of finishing work. On the other hand, saw blades with many fine teeth cut more slowly and leave a finer finish, resulting in less finishing work.

Start Slowly with Your Table Saw

A table saw combines the cutting capabilities of crosscutting, ripping, beveling, and cutting compound angles. Beyond these four basic cuts, the table saw offers the ability to cut mortises, dadoes, and many other more artistic efforts. But if you're not a real pro, start slowly. Because table saw blades cut from behind and beneath the piece you're working on, there's a lot more opportunity for mistakes than with other power cutting tools. So, start your work slowly. Spend a few extra minutes setting up. Mark your work piece with pencil to help you correctly adjust the saw. Then try your cutting on a piece of scrap wood before you go to the real thing.

Cut Right with a Sabre Saw

To make controlled, accurate cuts with an electric sabre saw:

- Clamp down the material you are going to cut.
- Hold the saw with both hands.
- Start the motor so that the blade is in motion before it begins the cut.
- Rest the saw on its base and use its guide to keep the blade on the cutting line.
- Turn off the saw before you remove it from the material being cut. Otherwise, it may jab the surface and break the blade as it comes out of the cut.

Planing Basics

A planer can save you time and enhance your ability to turn out quality work. If you're just beginning to use this tool, follow these basics for best results:

- The way you work with a piece of wood depends in large measure on the nature and condition of the board. For best results, test plane a scrap of the kind of board you're using, especially if you're working with this type of wood for the first time or with wood that is difficult to work with.
- If you're dealing with warped stock, flatten one edge of it on a jointer before starting to plane.
- Face the flattest side of the board down and cut with the grain if you can. If you can't plane with the grain and you're beginning to chip out pieces, use a lighter cut.
- When planing a long board, make sure you support it enough at either end to keep it level during the entire operation. If you do enough of this type of work, buy an adjustable-height table to provide that support.
- Start planing a bent board with the end that curves up.

Sander Savvy

Sanders take a lot of drudgery out of woodworking and speed up the time required to finish projects. To get the most from them:

- Begin with a rough grade of sandpaper, moving to finer grades as you take off more material. Synthetic abrasives will give you the most for your money when you're doing power sanding.

- Check to be sure your sandpaper is firmly attached to its pad.
- Don't let the sander touch the wood you're working with when turning the tool on or off.
- Use the sander only when it's reached full speed.
- Use a light touch, moving the sander constantly.

Helpful Hints for Hole Saws

- Firmly secure the piece that you are working on, because the turning saw can make it spin out of your control.
- Begin your cut with the saw at a 90-degree angle to the piece and supply steady pressure as you work the saw through.
- Keep your piece free of chips by working the saw in and out.
- Except with cast iron, use a cutting oil.

Cleaning, Maintenance, and Storage

Motors Must Stay Cool

The life span of any motor is severely diminished by excessive heat, so it is absolutely essential that the air vents in the housing of your power tools not be obstructed. Cooling air must be allowed to circulate freely through the housing to keep the motor running at its peak. It's easy for vents to become clogged with sawdust and dirt. Check them regularly and keep them cleaned out, either by using a clean, dry paintbrush, small stick, or cotton swab.

Replace Circular Saw Brushes

Several times during the year, remove and inspect the circular saw's motor brushes. Replace any worn brushes as soon as possible to maintain full cutting power.

Keep Blades Clean

Your saw blades will work more efficiently if you keep them clean and free of deposits from sawn wood. Don't try to remove deposits by scraping the blades. Instead, simply soak the entire blade in warm water and mild detergent. Wipe it with a cloth while it is submerged, then thoroughly dry it before storing it or using it. If there are stubborn deposits, apply a commercial pitch remover with an old toothbrush.

Before you store a blade, be sure it is completely dry. Coat it with a very light film of paste wax, rubbed to a polish.

Store Them High and Dry

Store your power tools where you can find them, but out of reach from curious children. A good place for power tools is a locked cabinet. (Be sure to keep the key to the cabinet out of reach, as well.) And be sure your storage area is dry. The amount of moisture in your basement or garage may cause metal to rust. You can keep rust from forming by coating metal surfaces with a light film of oil, wax, or petroleum jelly. Be sure to apply these protectants only after the metal has been cleaned.

Hook Your Blades

You can store circular saw blades easily by hanging them on hooks spaced far enough apart so the blades won't touch each other. If you don't have the cabinet space to do this, use long hooks that can hold several blades, with heavy cardboard or other soft material used for spacers between the blades.

Hang band saw blades in a single loop. If you don't have room for this, you can fold the blade so it forms three loops and tie the loops together with soft covered wire or cord. Then hang it up on covered hooks or pegs.

PRESSURE COOKERS

Safety and Maintenance Musts

Use your pressure cooker carefully. Improperly used, it can cause scalding and severe burns. The following tips can help you reduce your risk of injury.

- Do not fill the pressure cooker more than two-thirds full. If you're cooking rice or dried vegetables that expand, do not fill the cooker more than half full.
- Do not cook applesauce, cranberries, hot cereals, pasta, pearl barley, rhubarb, split peas, or other foods that tend to foam and froth while cooking; they may block the vent pipe.
- Check the vent pipe to make sure it's open every time you use the pressure cooker by holding the cover up to a light. You should be able to look through the vent pipe if it's open. Clean it with a pipe cleaner if it's blocked.
- Always check to make sure that the cover is closed securely.
- Never open the pressure cooker until you're sure that the pressure has been reduced, the air vent/cover has dropped, and the pressure regulator has been removed. No steam should escape when the regulator is tilted, and the cover should come off easily. If this is not the case, cool the cooker before trying again. Never force the cover off the pressure cooker pot—and always remove the pressure regulator before opening.
- If your model has a pressure dial gauge, do not turn it or remove it until the pressure is completely reduced.
- Replace the overpressure plug at least every two years. It should be replaced each time you put in a new sealing ring or when it becomes hard or deformed.
- Never use the pressure cooker for pressure frying with oil. Even pouring oil into an overheated cooker is dangerous—the oil could flare up and cause serious burns.
- Periodically tighten the screws of the cooker body and handles.

- Protect the rim of the pressure cooker from nicks and dents that may allow steam to escape.
- Never pour cold water into a dry, overheated pressure cooker.
- Always have some water or other liquid in the bottom of the pressure cooker.
- Never use the cooker cover for keeping foods warm in the pot after you've finished cooking. Use a saucepan cover or a piece of aluminum foil instead.
- Since high heat can damage the sealing ring in the top of your pressure cooker, take care not to place the pot's cover on top of the stove.
- Even if the air vent and pressure regulator indicate that it's safe to remove the cover, stop immediately if the cover does not come off easily. Let the pot stand until it's cool enough to comfortably remove the top.

Before Canning

Each time you start to can, you must check the pressure dial gauge:

- Make sure the pointer moves forward and backward freely and steadily when you build the pressure up and then let it down; do this check before you start canning in earnest.
- Check that the pointer returns to zero when the pressure is down.
- As a final check, take note of the prescribed cooking times and your actual cooking times. If the recipe time matches your real time, your pressure gauge—most likely—is still in good condition.

Getting the Most from Your Product

Cool It Fast

Some recipes call for quick cooling. You can accomplish this by running cool tap water over the top of your pressure cooker. But you must be very careful not to let water flow into the automatic air vent. As an alternative, you can cool the pot by placing it in a pan of cool water, which is the less risky method. Remember, quick-cool only when it's called for; never quick-cool when canning.

Sterilize with Your Pressure Cooker

Has it occurred to you that you can use the high heat and pressure provided by your pressure cooker to sterilize? Place the objects you wish to sterilize in a closed glass jar and heat for 15 to 25 minutes in a few inches of water.

High-Altitude Cooking

Standard recipe times for your pressure cooker will hold true up to about 2,000 feet above sea level. Thereafter, for every additional 1,000 feet, increase cooking times by 5 percent.

Adapt Recipes and Save Time

You can adapt recipes for use with your pressure cooker by following this general guideline: Cooking times are generally about one-third the time needed with conventional methods. Keep in mind that you also need less liquid, since very little evaporates with pressure cooking.

Can Do

If you have a combination pressure cooker/canner, you can enjoy the fruits of your garden or your favorite store's in-season produce, meat, and fish at any time. For best results, look for:

- Firm and fully ripe fruits and tomatoes
- Fresh poultry (cook until virtually all the pink color near the bone is gone before canning)
- Fresh fish, thoroughly cleaned and gutted
- Lean meat, free of gristle and large bones (precook until light brown)
- Young vegetables—even immature—unbruised and tender (can them as soon as possible after picking)

Expert Advice

Did you know that the United States Department of Agriculture county agent or Extension home economist can come to your assistance if you run into pressure cooking problems? You can consult these professionals for information and advice about pressure cooking; and if your cooker has a pressure gauge, you can bring it in and they will check to make sure it's working properly. Look in the phone book under United States or state government listings for the office nearest you.

Troubleshooting Chart

Problem	Cause	Solution
Moisture under the pressure regulator when cooking.	Temperature of pressure regulator is lower than the rest of the pressure cooker; vent pipe is loose.	A small amount of condensation at start of cooking is normal. If you notice moisture throughout the cooking process, tighten vent pipe with an adjustable wrench.
Leakage between cover and body.	Sealing ring has shrunk from prolonged use.	Replace sealing ring and overpressure plug.
Excess leakage around air vent/cover lock during cooking.	Cover lock is not properly engaged.	A small amount of leakage at start of cooking is normal. Check alignment of cover handles; periodically clean air vent/cover lock in warm, soapy water.
Continuing leakage around overpressure plug during cooking.	Overpressure plug is dirty or needs to be replaced.	Clean or replace overpressure plug.
Overpressure plug forced out of its cover opening while cooking or canning.		Do not use the pressure cooker again until serviced by a professional.

Cleaning, Maintenance, and Storage

Remove Dark Stains

Minerals in foods and cooking water may stain the inside of the pot. Although this will not affect your cooking, you may wish to remove the discoloration for aesthetic reasons. Mix 1 tablespoon cream of tartar with 1 quart of water and add enough of the solution to cover the stains (be careful not to fill the pot more than 60 percent full). Cover the pot and heat until the regulator begins to sway. At that point, turn off the heat and let the pot stand for about 2½ hours before opening. Cleaning with steel wool also will remove the stains.

Boil Away Stuck-On Food

If you come up against stuck-on food scraps that elbow grease won't rub off, fill the pot with enough water to cover the scraps. Pour in ¼ cup of vinegar and bring the uncovered pot to a boil. Turn off the heat and drop in a teaspoon of baking soda. By the time the mixture cools, you should be able to wash off that food with ease.

Avoid Unpleasant Odors

Storing the pressure cooker with the lid tightly in place will probably create an unpleasant smell in the pot. Avoid this by turning the cover over and placing it loosely over the pot.

Wash the Cover

Because you're cooking with steam, your pressure cooker cover needs only a simple rinse and wipe inside and out to stay clean *except* when you've cooked meat. Always wash the cover thoroughly in hot, soapy water after cooking meat. Once in a while, you may have to do a more thorough cleaning. Disassemble the air vent/cover lock and wash the sealing ring in hot, sudsy water. Dry and replace carefully.

R

Razors, Electric

Refrigerators

Roofing and Siding

Rotary Tillers

RAZORS, ELECTRIC

Safety Notes

Safe Shaving

Follow these safety precautions when using an electric razor:

- Avoid using a razor with a broken comb (the cutter housing), which could cut you.
- When using the razor, plug the cord into the razor first, then insert the other end into the outlet. Always unplug the razor before cleaning it.
- Do not use your razor in the same area where someone is using an aerosol spray or administering oxygen.

Getting the Most from Your Product

Troubleshooting Chart

Problem	Cause	Solution
Motor won't run.	No voltage to receptacle; fuse has blown or circuit breaker tripped.	Check receptacle with a lamp; replace fuse or reset circuit breaker.
	Defective cord.	Check for breaks or tears; replace if necessary.
	Battery is dead (on cordless models).	Recharge or replace battery.
Not cutting well.	Cutters damaged or dull.	Replace cutters and shaver head.

Cleaning, Maintenance, and Storage

Razor Maintenance

• Clean the razor head with the brush provided after every shave. This gets out whiskers and any preshave powder.
• Always keep the protective plastic cap on the head when you are not shaving.
• Every month, detach the head and cutters and rinse them under hot water. After reassembling the shaver, put two drops of light machine oil on the head while the shaver is running.
• Keep hard objects, which can damage your razor, away from the heads.
• As with other electrical appliances you use in the bathroom, keep your electric razor well away from water.
• Trimmer teeth should be lubricated twice a year with a drop of light machine oil.

Don't Drop It

All it takes is a slight flaw in the screen or blade of an electric razor to cause it to nick. If you should drop your razor, inspect it for tiny breaks or dents in the screen. If you find any, replace the screen.

REFRIGERATORS

Getting the Most from Your Product

Keep It Level

Your refrigerator must be level in order for the doors to close tightly. If your floor is uneven and you can't seem to get your refrigerator quite level using the leveling screws, try folding a piece of cardboard under the side that needs balancing. To see if the unit is standing correctly, open the door at about a 45-

degree angle. When you let it go, it should gradually shut by itself. If it doesn't, adjust the tilt until it does.

A Warm Room Is Best

Try not to let the temperature in the room where you have your refrigerator drop more than a degree or two below 60°F. Anything colder could cause the unit to shut down for long periods, making it all but impossible to maintain the necessary low temperature in the freezing compartment.

Take the Cooling Test

How do you know if your refrigerator is working properly? For an easy way to test its cooling action, leave a glass of water in the refrigerator compartment for 24 hours. At that point, the temperature of the water should register between 35° and 40°F, or just slightly higher if it's a hot day, if the food compartment is full, or if you've been opening and closing the door a lot.

You can also follow a similar procedure for your freezer compartment, except you should use a plastic container of cooking oil instead of a glass of water. After one day, measure the oil's temperature. If your freezer is working properly, it should register between 0° and 8°F.

An Open and Shut Case

These suggestions can help you minimize the opening and closing of your refrigerator door and keep your appliance working effectively:

- Think through an entire meal before beginning to prepare it and remove all the necessary ingredients from the refrigerator at once. This will not only keep the refrigerator closed as much as possible, but also will make your cooking easier by having all the ingredients ready.
- Store quantities of the same or similar items together in the refrigerator. A sensible layout will help you locate the right food faster.
- Place food that's been in the refrigerator longest near the front

instead of buried in the back where you can't see it; this will encourage you to use it before it turns bad.

Use It Wisely

Try these simple steps to keep your refrigerator running at peak efficiency and save energy, too:

- Cool hot foods completely before storing in the refrigerator.
- Don't stock the refrigerator too full and don't put items in that really do not need refrigeration.
- Don't stare into a wide-open refrigerator while you think about what you need. Make your decision before you open the door.

When the Power Goes Out . . .

Assuming the refrigerator door remains closed, your food will keep for 24 to 36 hours after the power goes out. If you use dry ice, you can extend the period for another few hours. But remember to cover your hands before handling dry ice and to keep layers of cardboard or newspaper between the dry ice and the food to prevent freezer burn.

If, after a power outage, you have any doubts about the freshness of any of your food—especially uncooked meat, fish, or poultry—throw it out immediately.

Humidity Control

If your refrigerator has a control that allows you to regulate the humidity in your produce storage compartments, use these guidelines to make sure it is set properly:

- Set it on high for all leafy vegetables.
- Set it on low for anything with a skin, such as pears, apples, tomatoes, or green peppers.

Refrigerator Compartment Storage

Follow these guidelines for storing food in the refrigerator compartment:

Food	Storage Time
Cheese (hard)	4 weeks
Cheese (soft)	4–7 days
Eggs	2 weeks
Fish (fresh)	1–2 days
Fish (cooked)	3–4 days
Fruits and vegetables	3–4 days
Leftovers	3–4 days
Meat (fresh)	4–5 days
Meat (chopped)	1–2 days
Milk and cream	3–7 days
Poultry	2 days

Fresh in One Step

Want a one-step method for keeping vegetables fresh and crisp in your refrigerator? Put a moist towel over them. And to keep your lettuce extra crisp, lay the leaves flat on a length of paper towel and roll it up. You'll never have to worry about soggy salads again.

Proper Packing for Freezing

When packing food for the freezer, choose materials that keep external moisture, odors, and air out. Polyethylene plastic containers made for this purpose, freezer paper, and aluminum and plastic wraps (nonpermeable) are fine for this task. Materials to avoid include waxed paper and wax-coated freezer wrap, bread wrappers, and nonpolyethylene plastic wraps and containers.

To store food in the refrigerator or freezer, wrap it in material that is about 30 percent larger than the diameter of the food, using the butcher's wrap method. Simply place the food in the center of the wrapping material. Bring the long ends of the wrapping over the food and fold together about one inch of the edges. Fold over again two or more times until the wrapping fits flat and tight against the food. Press the wrapping to squeeze out the air. Crease the ends and fold them over the package toward each other. Secure the ends to the package with freezer tape.

Get the Air Out

When sealing food in bags, be sure to press out the air and twist-close the top of the bag. Getting the air out of the bag is especially important when storing poultry since it is very perishable. One good way to accomplish this is to fill a large pot with water and put the bag under water with just the opening sticking up above the surface. Press the bag against the food to remove air bubbles. Then remove the bag and twist-close the end.

When Can You Refreeze?

Refreezing foods that have thawed—even partially—results in lowered quality of taste and texture. And if the food has reached room temperature, it could spoil. However, there are times when you would like to put food back in the freezer. According to the U.S. Department of Agriculture, you can do this safely only if the food is still cold (below 40° F) and still contains ice crystals.

How Much Can Your Freezer Digest?

There's a limit to how much food you can expect your freezer compartment to freeze at one time without overtaxing your unit. Most refrigerator/freezer combinations can freeze approximately two to three pounds per cubic feet of freezer space. Don't force your freezer to handle more, or all the food may freeze too slowly and may spoil as a result.

Freezing Food Efficiently

If you want your freezer to work at maximum efficiency, fill it to capacity, but not beyond. The frozen food helps maintain an even temperature in the box, even when you open the door.

Most freezer compartments maintain a uniform temperature throughout the compartment, except the shelves on the door. Because of the higher temperatures at this spot, avoid keeping anything there for too long.

Old Ice—Not So Nice

No, it's not your imagination. Ice left in the freezer compartment too long will shrink from the movement of cold air over its surface. This most likely happens in a frost-free model, since it isn't defrosted manually, forcing the owner to make new ice.

Cubes are also more likely to stick together with age and to acquire odors from surrounding foods. To prevent this, change the ice regularly—at least once a week.

Troubleshooting Chart

Problem	Cause	Solution
Water is leaking from refrigerator onto floor.	Drain pan is cracked.	Replace drain pan.
	Drain hose is cracked.	Replace drain hose (unscrew condenser coils first).
	Drain holes at bottom of freezer or refrigerator section are clogged.	Clear drain holes with piece of wire, flush with baking soda and water solution.
Refrigerator drawers don't slide smoothly.	Side channels of drawers need lubrication.	Lubricate with petroleum jelly.
Refrigerator door sags.	Hinge screws need adjusting.	Use screwdriver to loosen hinge screws at top of door. Realign door and tighten screws.

*Troubleshooting Chart—*Continued

Problem	Cause	Solution
Too much condensation forms on outside of refrigerator.	It may be too hot or humid for unit to work without forming condensation; interior temperature is too cold, causing unit to overwork.	Make sure freezer is set above 0°F.
	Door gasket is worn.	Replace door gasket.
	Doors opened too much.	Reduce time doors are opened.
Refrigerator runs but does not cool.	Temperature control is set too low.	Set temperature control to next-highest (warmer) level.
	Defective door gasket.	Replace gasket.

Cleaning, Maintenance, and Storage

Cleaning Tips

- Use mild soap and warm water to clean your refrigerator. For extra freshness, add a teaspoon of baking soda for each quart of water.
- To keep the vegetable bins from sticking, lightly spray vegetable oil on them.
- Clean the door gaskets about every six months.
- Use a brush and vacuum cleaner to clean away dust on the condenser coils in the back and at the bottom behind the front grill. Since they're partially hidden, it's easy to forget about both sets of coils, but dusty coils will lower the efficiency of your unit. If you have a pet, you may need to clean the coils more frequently, since your animal's hair could add to the dust buildup.
- To clean under the refrigerator easily, tie an old cloth to the end of a yardstick with rubber bands. Then just slide the stick under the unit and wipe around.

For That Showroom Finish . . .

Commercial car rubbing compounds will do an excellent job of restoring the finish on your refrigerator. Use undiluted hydrogen peroxide to get stains off glass components and a paste of baking soda and water to deal with stains on your unit's interior walls.

Don't Buy Fixed Shelves

Thinking of buying a new refrigerator? Many newer models come with fixed shelves that can't be removed. This makes them harder to clean. Unless such a unit has a wealth of other features and a marvelous price to recommend it, look for models with removable shelves.

Get Rid of Sticky Ice

If you have minerals in your water, you may find your ice cubes sticking to the tray. If you have that problem and notice a filmy residue in the tray, wipe away the film with a cloth dampened with vinegar (be sure to wash out the tray afterward). You may have to do this each time you clean the refrigerator to keep the trays reasonably clear of film.

Prevent Odors

You can prevent odors from transferring from one food to another inside the refrigerator by keeping food covered and leaving an open box of baking soda in the refrigerator compartment. Put plastic wrap over the lids of storage bowls, use paper towels in the meat compartment to absorb juices (discard the towels regularly), and add some lemon juice to your cleaning solution.

When to Defrost

For owners of manual-defrost refrigerators, this is a chore that's easy to put off. If you defrost regularly, haven't been opening the door too much, and it's not summer, a delay in defrosting won't hurt. But if you notice that the frost has grown to a ¼-inch thickness, don't delay any longer or you risk damaging your freezer permanently.

Defective Lights Cause Trouble

Something as simple as a light bulb that won't go off when the door shuts could warm the interior of your refrigerator. You obviously can't be inside the unit to see if the light stays on when you close the door, but you can test to see if this is the case. Open the door and press the button that turns the light on and off automatically. If it doesn't turn the light off, the switch is defective and a new one should be installed.

When Should You Turn It Off?

Should you leave the refrigerator on while you're on vacation? If you have a frost-free model, you may wish to let it run. If you do not own a frost-free model, or you will be away longer than a month, put the unit in warm storage. Use up all the food and discard or give away what's left. Clean the interior, turn all controls to "off," *and leave the doors open*, which will help keep the unit smelling fresh and clean.

What Your Product Won't Do

It Can't Be Outside

It might seem like a good idea to use your old refrigerator on your porch or patio for the summer. Unfortunately, even in the summer, it's likely to be too cool in the evening and way too hot in the daytime for your unit to work properly. It's better to keep your unit just inside the door to the porch or patio.

ROOFING AND SIDING

Up on the Roof

In order to inspect or repair a roof you must, of course, get up on it. To do so safely, choose a day that is not windy or rainy and be sure that the ladder you climb has it's "feet" pushed into the dirt so it doesn't slide around. If it is resting on a hard surface, be sure the feet are covered with rubber. The safest angle for a ladder is when the feet are ¼ the height of the ladder away from the house. A 16-foot ladder, for example, should be angled with the feet 4 feet away from the house.

Once you're up on the roof, make sure you stay there by tying one end of a sturdy line around your waist and the other end around the chimney or an immovable object on the other side of the house. Wear shoes with soft, rubber soles to assure a firm footing and always walk with a stoop—never walk fully erect on a sloping roof.

Getting the Most from Your Product

Don't Be Hasty to Reroof

Age is no indicator of how well your roof will stand up. For every 10-year-old roof that is leaking, there are dozens of 25-year-old roofs that are still in fine shape. If your roof isn't leaking and still looks good (no cracks, splits, or curled shingles), don't rush to have it redone just because someone told you that a roof has a specific lifespan.

You Need a Pitch for Shingles

To use wood shingles on a roof, its pitch must be at least 3 inches in 12. To use asphalt shingles, the roof's pitch must be at least 4 inches in 12. For flatter roofs, tar and gravel is best.

Extend the Life of Your Roof

If you have an asphalt-shingle or asphalt-roll roof, water falling off the roof can curl back under the roofing at the eaves instead of falling straight to the ground. Once you start to get water under your roofing, leaks are not far behind. To prevent this, your roof should have drip edges—L-shaped aluminum strips that are nailed along the edges of the eaves and rakes. They're not needed with wood and other stiff roofing materials because these materials overhang the roof edges farther than asphalt roofing does. If drip edges weren't installed with your roof, you can easily add them.

Use Guards to Stop Snow

If your roof has a steep slope, you may find that piles of snow catapult off the roof after a heavy accumulation. To stop the snow from crashing down, you should install several rows of snow guards well up from the eaves, spaced about 1 foot apart in rows 2 feet apart.

White May Not Be Bright

If you live in a warm climate, you may be tempted to replace your roof shingles with white or very light-colored asphalt shingles because they reflect the sun's rays and keep the house cooler in hot weather. While a white roof will, indeed, keep the house cooler, you may want to reconsider if your house is surrounded by overhanging trees. In a very short time, the light-colored roof will become so dirty and discolored that it will ruin the appearance of the house.

Cleaning, Maintenance, and Storage

Hose Down Siding

You can keep your siding clean by hosing it down at high pressure at least once a year. This will flush away any corrosive materials on the surface.

Keep Mildew at Bay

Remove mildew from siding by scrubbing with a mixture of equal parts ammonia and water. Household bleach also works well, and can be sprayed onto the siding with a chemical sprayer. One word of caution: it could bleach your paint and harm foundation plantings.

De-Moss the Roof

To get moss off a wood shingle roof, scrape and brush it off. Let the shingle dry out, then saturate it with a wood preservative. To keep the moss from returning, you will need to reapply preservative about every five years.

Cover Up Paint

If you spill paint on asphalt roof shingles, you're out of luck. Even when the spill is fresh, you can't get the paint off. The best you can do is hide the spill by brushing on asphalt roofing cement (for dark gray or black roofs) or a matching-color aluminum roof coating (for other colored roofs).

Flatten Raised Shingles

Raised asphalt shingles can be made to lie flat again. Wait until a warm, sunny day, when the shingles will be pliable, then apply asphalt roofing cement under the raised edge and stick them down. Any loose nails can be tapped back into place, with the nailheads covered with the roofing cement.

Plug Asphalt Shingle Holes

Small holes in asphalt shingles can be made watertight by lifting the shingle tabs and applying asphalt roofing cement under the holes. For larger holes, slip a sheet of aluminum flashing or piece of asphalt shingle under the damaged shingle. Make sure it's long enough to extend well up under the shingles in the course directly above the damaged one. Tap it into place.

Replace Those Damaged Shingles

Damaged roof shingles are an invitation to leaks. Make it a habit to periodically inspect your roof. If the shingles are too far gone to be repaired, they must be replaced. If there are only a few, you can do it yourself, but if the damage is widespread, you probably need a new roof. Here's how to replace damaged shingles:

Asbestos: Slide a hacksaw blade up under the damaged shingle and cut off the nails holding it in place. Pull out the shingle and replace it. Drill a hole through the joint between the overlying shingles and drive a galvanized roofing nail flush with the face of the new shingle. Tap a piece of aluminum flashing up under the joint, over the nail.

Asphalt: Cut out the damaged part, then cut a new shingle to the correct width and long enough to extend up under the shingles in the course directly above the damaged one. Hold it in place with roofing cement applied under the bottom edge.

Slate: Leave slate replacement and repair to a professional roofer.

Wood: Slide a hacksaw blade up under the damaged shingle and cut off the nails holding it in place. Pull out the shingle and replace it. You may have to cut notches in the top edge of the new shingle to get it to fit around the nails holding the shingle in the course above. Tap the new shingle into place, then fasten it to the roof by smearing roofing cement under the bottom edge.

Pull Out Aluminum Siding Dents

While aluminum siding requires no maintenance other than an occasional hosing down, it does have a tendency to scratch and dent. You can touch up scratches with aluminum siding paint. To remove dents, drill a small hole in the dent and insert a self-tapping screw. Pull on the screw with pliers until the dented metal is level with the rest of the siding. Carefully remove the screw and fill the hole with a metal filler. Sand it smooth, then prime and paint.

Weather Your Leftover Vinyl Siding

Because vinyl siding will fade over time, it's a good idea to expose several pieces of leftover siding to the elements. That way, if you need to replace a section, you will have a good color match.

Cleaning Gutters and Downspouts

Every spring and fall you must clean debris that may have accumulated in the gutters and downspouts over the previous six months; otherwise, water will not flow freely. To minimize this task, you can install a plastic or metal screen at the point where the gutter and the downspout meet. Then, all you have to do is clean the screen.

In addition, you should also repair any faulty connections you come across. To check for leaks, pour water into your gutters and ask someone to watch for leaks and other problems from below. Pay particular attention to the point where the water enters the downspout.

If the downspout is stopped up, unblock it by inserting a plumber's snake through the gutter outlet. If you spot a leak, clean the surrounding area with a wire brush and a rag and seal the leak with asphalt roofing cement.

For holes larger than ¼ inch, however, begin the sealing process with a thin layer of cement. On top of that place a canvas patch measuring a bit larger than the spot you're mending. Press it down and cover it with a heavier coat of cement.

This is also the time to tighten any loose gutter hangers. If you have the type with straps, use galvanized nails or screws to tighten the hangers and replace any defective straps. If you have the hangers with sleeves and spikes, tighten with an aluminum or galvanized spike. You may have to adjust the slope of the gutter if water does not drain from it completely.

ROTARY TILLERS

Tilling with Care

Here are some safety rules that can make using your tiller a productive, not hazardous experience:

- Before you till, walk through the area to remove any rocks, bottles, bones, sticks, or bits of wire. Any of these objects kicked out by the tiller's tines could turn into a dangerous projectile.
- Dress for the job. Wear shoes and long pants to protect your lower body and goggles to guard your eyes.
- Always stay alert and be prepared for surprises. Hard-packed soil, buried rocks, large roots, or other debris—or unexpectedly rough terrain—can cause the rotary tiller to jump upward or forward unexpectedly. If you're working less-than-ideal soil, stay behind and to one side of the tiller, guiding it with one hand. Make several passes at a slow speed, going a little deeper each time.
- If the tiller does lurch out of control like a bucking bronco, don't try to tame it. Instead, hang on and gently guide the handle to counter the erratic movement until the unit returns to normal operation.
- The safest way to use a rear-tine tiller (meaning the best way to stay in control) is in a low gear at a slow speed. With a front-tine tiller, push down on the handlebars to keep weight on the tines.
- Remove or disengage the tines when using the tiller as a snow plow.
- Start the engine only in neutral.
- Steer clear of places where underground electric cables, phone lines, pipes, or hoses are likely to be found.
- Avoid tilling up or down a steep hill. A gradual slope poses less of a danger; just be sure you have good footing.
- Stay clear of fences or the sides of buildings. If you come too

close and the tines touch, that could send the tiller out of control.
- Watch out for the muffler! It gets *hot* and can burn your skin or possibly start a fire if it touches something combustible. Even after you've turned off the tiller, the muffler is still dangerous since it stays hot for a while. Keep young children away.

Getting the Most from Your Product

The Right Tiller for the Right Job

Front-tine tillers are best suited to working the soil in established garden beds where the soil is soft and free of large rocks and other debris. Hard-packed, rocky, or weed-choked soil can send these tillers leaping out of control. Rear-tine tillers are heavier and tend to behave better when faced with hard, rock-strewn conditions or soil that hasn't been tilled before.

Beware of Bone-Dry or Soggy Soil

To get the best use from your tiller you have to be able to judge when the soil's in the right condition to work. That means when it's not too wet and not too dry. A tiller that plows through soggy soil creates clods; when the sun dries these clods they become rock-hard lumps that are nearly impossible to get rid of. If you try to till bone-dry soil, the tiller won't be able to do much more than scratch at the top few inches.

Dry, hard, and compacted soil can be readied for tilling by soaking it with water for two to three hours about three or four days before you want to till. To test when the soil has the right moisture content (the same test to use on rain- or snow-soaked soil), take a handful and form it into a ball. Poke at the ball with one finger; if it crumbles apart easily, start up the tiller. If the ball dents rather then breaks apart, let the soil dry a little longer before tilling.

Avoid Weedy Entanglements

If you've ever plunged into a weedy patch full speed ahead with your tiller, you've probably regretted it. A rotary tiller and tall weeds are a poor match. The weeds can become so tangled around the tines that you must stop and spend time cutting them away. There's an easy way to avoid this sort of entanglement. Two to three days before tilling, cut the tall weeds with a lawn mower or scythe. Then, when you till, you'll have smooth going.

Tilling-In Soil Builders

One of the handiest things the tiller can do for the garden is to turn under mulch, compost, leaves, peat moss, and other soil-enriching materials. The easiest way to do this is one thin layer at a time. If you spread too thick a layer on the soil, the tiller will push it into a pile or move it around—everything but churn it in the soil where you want it.

Cleaning, Maintenance, and Storage

Tending the Tines

- Unless damp soil is clinging to and building up on the tines, there's no need to clean them after every use.
- When a tiller is working its way through tall or thick masses of plants, stems and other pieces can become wrapped around the tines. To clear them, first disengage the tines and turn off the engine. Next, disconnect the spark plug wire. Only then is it safe to wrestle with the matted tines.
- Some tillers come with self-sharpening tines, but for those that do not, you will need to provide the sharpening. Use a smooth, flat file (6- to 10-inch bastard mill file) to create a 70- to 80-degree angle on each blade (or close to the original angle). Bent or very worn blades should be replaced.

In-Season Maintenance

Your tiller works hard for you, so it deserves a regular schedule of attention to make sure all the parts are in good shape:

- To keep dirt from infiltrating the carburetor, clean the air filter often and make sure you replace it properly after each cleaning.
- The motor oil in the tiller cleans, cools, and lubricates. Fresh

oil is therefore a must for a smoothly running machine. Don't operate your tiller for more than ten hours or so without changing the oil.

• The air-intake screen and the cooling fins play an important part in keeping the engine from overheating. Clean them regularly by wiping them with a small brush.

• After each use, clean around the engine openings with a dry rag to remove traces of oil and gas.

Keep Moisture Out

Moisture can damage the tiller's engine. To seal moisture out, close both engine valves whenever you put away the tiller. To do this, simply pull slowly on the starter rope until you feel resistance.

S

Sewing Machines

Shampooer-Polishers

Silver and Silverware

Slow Cookers

Smoke Detectors

Snow Blowers

Spas and Hot Tubs

Sump Pumps

SEWING MACHINES

Safety Notes

Change Parts Safely

Always make sure the power switch on your sewing machine is turned off before you change a needle or the presser foot, or put on an attachment. That way there's no chance of accidently starting the machine if the speed controller is pressed.

Getting the Most from Your Product

Find Your Rhythm

No matter how experienced you are at sewing, always start the machine on a low speed. This keeps the fabric from "running away" from you, especially when you are using a new type of stitch. Starting slowly allows you to find the sewing rhythm that best suits you—without ruining the piece you're working on.

Pick the Best Stitch Length

A good rule of thumb is to use shorter stitches for lightweight fabrics and longer stitches for heavy fabrics. Always test the stitch length and tension on a scrap of the fabric you'll be using; if there are problems they are easy to adjust before working on the actual project.

Feeding Fabric through the Machine

You can guide most fabrics through your sewing machine by gently pushing from in front of the pressure foot. But for fabrics like nylon tricot, cire, velvet, and synthetic knits, you'll get better results by holding the piece of material in the front *and* back to apply gentle tension. For stretchy fabrics, apply firm tension in the front and the back.

Troubleshooting Chart

Problem	*Cause*	*Solution*
Machine moves around on work table when in use.	Motion is normal but can be prevented.	Glue foam rubber or felt pads to bottom of machine.
Thread winds unevenly on bobbin; one side is fuller than the other.	Bobbin thread tension is incorrect.	Adjust bobbin thread tension guide. You may have to experiment with several settings before you find one that doesn't make thread clump unevenly.

Cleaning, Maintenance, and Storage

Keep Your Machine Well Tuned

Keeping your machine oiled and the needle sharp will make sewing easier and extend the life of the machine. Oil it regularly according to the manufacturer's instructions. Use oil specifically for sewing machines. After you've added the oil, use an old rag to soak up any excess that might stain your fabric.

The Less Dust, the Better

Always treat your sewing machine as you would any precision instrument. Wipe it off with a soft cloth after each use and make sure there are no loose threads that could become tangled in the mechanism. If you keep it out on your work table, cover it when not in use or dust it frequently. Any dust or foreign matter that reaches the inside of the machine could damage it.

SHAMPOOER-POLISHERS

Safety Notes

Maintain Control

Your floor shampooer-polisher can take on a life of its own if you let it. Its momentum can make it dance out of your grasp and go off for a reckless waltz around the room. Avoid this unscheduled performance by holding the handle at an angle, not straight up.

Getting the Most from Your Product

Delay the First Shampoo

Carpeting comes with a protective coating that shampooing removes. Once you shampoo it, the carpet will get dirtier more quickly, and you will find yourself cleaning it more often. So wait until you have no choice before that first shampoo. (For more information on carpet care, see pages 54–57.)

Test Your Carpet

If you just bought a shampooer-polisher, if you want to clean a carpet that hasn't been cleaned before, or if you're trying a new shampoo formula, there are two tests you should perform on your carpet before you shampoo the entire area. First test your carpet to make sure the color won't run. Dab a little of the shampoo solution on an inconspicuous spot of carpet (under a piece of furniture that doesn't get moved.) Rub the spot with a white cloth. If the cloth doesn't pick up the color and the color of the test spot doesn't change after it's dry, you can proceed to the next step, which is to test the effect of the shampoo and the shampooer on the carpet's texture. Shampoo a small section of the carpet. Make sure your final pass with the shampooer (and with the brush you'll use after the shampoo) is in one direction. You should feel no more than a slight change in the carpet's texture.

Test Your Shampoo

All carpet shampoos are not alike. In addition to knowing the differences between brands, you should also be careful about using shampoo that may have been sitting around for years. Using the wrong shampoo on your carpet could cause more harm than good. Here are two ways to test a suspect shampoo:

- Make sure the shampoo is not too alkaline by testing it with pH test paper (available at any pet shop that sells aquariums). The shampoo should have a pH of no greater than 9.5.
- Make sure the shampoo doesn't leave residue. To test for residue, take a piece of clear glass and dip half of it into the shampoo. After the shampoo dries, sprinkle talcum powder over the entire piece of glass. Then tap the glass. If more talcum powder sticks to the shampooed section, you're likely to have a dirty carpet not long after you use this shampoo.

Clean Out-of-the-Way Places by Hand

The best way to clean out-of-the-way areas of your carpet (such as the areas under and behind radiators) is to wash them by hand. Pour the shampoo solution into a bowl or pan and use a small brush to spread the liquid. Afterward, be sure to discard the solution—it now contains lint and pouring it into your shampooer could gum up the machine.

Get Out All the Soap

How do you know if you've gotten out all the soap after shampooing your carpet? The next time you vacuum it, look for loose fibers. If you pick up a lot of them with the vacuum, it's an indication that leftover soap has been breaking down the carpet's fibers. To stop this process, rinse your carpet after you shampoo it with a solution of 1 cup white vinegar to 1 gallon warm water. Wipe it off as you go along. Refresh the solution often to avoid suds buildup.

Wait Before Polishing

If you wet-scrub your hard floors with your shampooer-polisher and then go to polish them, the machine may leak some dirty water even after you think you've discarded it. If you proceed to polish the floor, the leftover dirty water could get on the polisher's pads and brushes and ruin the wax. To ensure that all the water from the scrubbing has dried out, wait at least a day before polishing.

Close the Gap

Most shampooer-polishers have two brushes for waxing wood floors. There is a slight gap between the brushes that you must account for as you wax. Be sure to wax in a straight line, with the grain, and make sure your up and down strokes overlap. Otherwise, the gap between the brushes could leave an uneven shine.

Protect Waxed Floors from Scratches

Here are two ways to protect your waxed wood floors from scratches:

• Wax the arc of the rockers on rocking chairs.
• Put winter-weight socks on furniture legs when you must move heavy pieces.

Troubleshooting Chart

Problem	Cause	Solution
Machine won't run.	Fuse blown or circuit breaker tripped.	Replace fuse or reset circuit breaker.
	Cord is damaged.	Inspect cord, replace if necessary.
Machine lacks power when polishing.	Brushes are worn.	Replace brushes.

Cleaning, Maintenance, and Storage

Keep It Clean

Your shampooer-polisher must be kept clean. After every use, empty out any unused shampoo or wax from the tank. This will prevent clogging of the dispensing tubes. If the tubes do get clogged, empty the tank and refill it with hot water. This will loosen the buildup and it will flow out.

Check the Brushes

Several times a year, detach the brushes from your polisher and remove any dirt and debris from the shafts. When you replace the brushes, be sure they are snapped securely on their drive shafts.

Iron out Wax

You can actually iron out problems with wax buildup on your floor polisher pads. Simply pack the pads in several sheets of paper toweling and press with a warm iron; the wax will come off on the toweling.

What Your Product Won't Do

It Can't Make Up for Neglect

Shampooing will not restore a rug that's been neglected or that is well past its prime. In fact, shampooing may highlight matting and other results of years of wear.

SILVER AND SILVERWARE

Getting the Most from Your Product

Use It Often

If anything ever deserved the old adage, "It gets better with age," it's silverware. More specifically, it gets better with use: the more often you use it, the more beautiful it will look as its patina develops. So don't save your set only for special occasions. Try to use it every day and use it *all* on a regular basis. Set up a rotating system to ensure that each piece gets used often. Put knives, forks, and spoons on the bottom of the stack after you wash them, so that pieces you did not use will be on the top and ready for the next meal.

Avoid Nicks

Do not use steak knives with your finest silverware. When you hold the meat with your fork, you risk nicking the fork tines with the knife's cutting edge.

Cleaning, Maintenance, and Storage

Get Food Off Quickly

Silverware needs attending to after dinner: It will tarnish if you leave it lying around with food scraps stuck to it (especially foods rich in salt). If you can't wash the silverware right away, at least rinse it, then dry immediately. Do not soak the pieces. Extended contact with water may cause the silver to tarnish.

When cleaning your silver, do not wear rubber gloves, because rubber can leave dark marks.

Silverware in the Dishwasher?

While you can use your dishwasher to safely wash your silverware, you're better off doing the job by hand—especially if you have hard water. Use hot water and a gentle detergent, rinse with even hotter water, and dry with a soft cloth. If you want to wash your silverware in the dishwasher, follow these precautions:

• Wash sterling silver knives by hand. Running them through the dishwasher can weaken the cement that attaches the blades to the handles.
• Rinse the silverware first, and do not put it in the dishwasher with stainless steel (an electrolytic action between the two metals can cause pitting of your stainless). Be sure to keep fork tines from poking through the basket and touching anything else in the dishwasher.
• To minimize spotting, use a wetting agent. If your dishwasher doesn't have a wetting agent injector, buy the block-type wetting agent and use it as directed.
• Remove the silverware before the drying cycle starts, and dry gently with a soft cloth.

Twice-a-Year Polishing

With the proper care, you won't have to polish your silverware more than twice a year. When it does tarnish, use either a commercial silver polish or a solution of 1 tablespoon baking soda per quart of water. Boil the solution and bathe the silverware in it for a minute or two.

Use a reputable brand of polish. Although spray and dip varieties are fine for quick jobs when company is coming and you're pressed for time, they can cause excessive wear, actually removing some silver from each piece. If you can, use a paste, liquid, or soap that contains a substance to guard against tarnish (check the label). Or make your own polish by mixing a little ammonia with powdered white chalk to form a paste. Wearing plastic (*not* rubber) gloves, apply the polish with gentle, even strokes in the same direction. To reach into crevices formed by patterns, dab some polish on a cloth and use your fingernail to guide the cloth into these areas; or use a cotton swab, a sponge, or a soft toothbrush.

A Silver-Cleaning Shortcut

Jeweler's rouge, which comes in a stick that you rub on a piece of flannel, is sometimes used to clean silverware. When you use the flannel to polish your silverware, however, you do have to be careful, because the rouge can flake off and discolor just about everything within reach. You can buy jeweler's rouge at crafts stores and at jeweler's supply stores.

Keep It Airtight

Although it may be convenient, avoid storing your silverware in the kitchen, where cooking vapors can tarnish it. It's best to keep silver in airtight chests or drawers lined with antitarnish cloth. Add a piece of chalk or gum camphor, too, to absorb moisture. Felt bags also work fine for storing silver, as do plastic wrap or plastic bags, providing you carefully squeeze the air out and seal the bags with string rather than rubber bands. Your silver dealer probably carries antitarnishing strips (3M makes them), which you can place in the bag with the silverware.

SLOW COOKERS

Safety Notes

A Safe Location for Your Slow Cooker

Unattended cooking is the reason why most people buy slow cookers, but it causes them some misgivings. What if their units malfunction while they're away? While such a malfunction is not at all likely, it can happen. Prudence dictates a few simple precautions:

- Keep anything flammable away from the slow cooker. Because it uses electricity, there is always the chance of a short.
- Be certain to place the slow cooker on a solid, steady surface,

away from the edge of a counter or table, especially if you live in an area prone to even mild earthquakes (or where you can feel vibrations from traffic).

• Never leave a child alone in a room with a slow cooker that's in use.

• Use a rack or drain board under the pot to provide sufficient drainage. This will prevent liquids from a cracked or over-flowing pot from accumulating in the area at the base of the appliance where the electrical wiring is located.

Safe Extension Cord Use

Don't use an inadequate extension cord for your slow cooker. The rule of thumb is to divide the number of watts your appliance uses by 120 to arrive at the amp rating you need in an extension cord. For example, if your cooker uses 1,800 watts, you need a 15-amp extension cord.

Hot and Cold Don't Mix

You can put frozen foods in a slow cooker if your recipe calls for them—but only when you first fill the pot. Once the unit is hot, anything frozen could cause the pot to crack on contact.

Be on the Safe Side with Pork

The familiar warnings about undercooking pork apply even more strongly to slow cooking. If you have not yet become familiar with your appliance's abilities and limits, cook pork dishes at least as long as called for by your recipe. Don't worry about overcooking; a slow cooker *won't* burn your food. At worst, cooking the meat too long will make it a bit less firm than you might like.

Getting the Most from Your Product

Leave the Lid On

Many users of slow cookers often are tempted to keep lifting the lid to "see how it's doing," especially during the initial hour or two of cooking, when nothing much seems to be happening.

But lifting the cover slows down the cooking process, which works by the retention of heat and steam in the pot. The pot may need 15 minutes or so to regain the right temperature after you lift the lid. If you want reassurance, carefully touch the side of the pot after about 20 minutes into the cooking. If it's hot, the slow cooker is working.

Too Much Liquid?

Because a slow cooker cooks your meal for a long time with the cover on, liquid won't evaporate as it does with other kinds of cooking. In fact, when you adapt a recipe for use with your slow cooker, you may find that there is an excess of liquid at the end of the cooking period. If this should happen, turn the control to the "high" position, leave the lid off, and run the cooker for about 45 minutes to reduce the liquid.

Converting Recipes

You can convert most recipes designed for oven and rangetop cooking for use with your slow cooker. But bear in mind that beans should be cooked before going into your pot; rice and pasta also should be cooked before adding them to other foods in the cooker; and cream, sour cream, and milk should be added to your recipe no more than about an hour before the dish finishes cooking. Use the following cooking times flexibly—you don't have to worry about overcooking. And remember that meat and vegetables cooked together always require a minimum cooking time of 8 hours at the "low" setting:

Your Recipe	Slow Cooker Time
Under 30 min.	Low: 5 hrs. High: 1¾ hrs.
30 to 45 min.	Low: 8 hrs. High: 3½ hrs.
45 min. to 3 hrs.	Low: 12 hrs. High: 5 hrs.

Substitutions Allowed

When using your slow cooker, you may substitute any liquid for the liquid called for in a recipe. The key, however, is always to maintain the same amount of liquid.

Go Easy on Liquids

Do you often end up with too much liquid when making a roast in your slow cooker? Keep in mind that you only need to add a small amount of liquid when roasting because fat in the meat will keep it moist. However, when adding vegetables to the pot, you do need the liquid to soften and properly cook the accompanying ingredients. Just remember that adding too much liquid, or not trimming excess fat from the meat, could result in overcooked food.

Starting with a Frozen Main Dish

If you start a slow-cooker meal with frozen meat or poultry, add at least 1 cup of warm liquid to the pot. This avoids any sudden temperature changes in the meat that could result in overcooking the outside and undercooking the inside. Your recipe probably calls for adding water to frozen foods; if it doesn't, add water or a sauce. And bear in mind that you will have to increase the cooking time to allow for thawing. For most frozen meats, add 4 to 6 hours to the cooking time on the "low" setting or 2 hours on the "high" setting.

Fill at Least Halfway

Slow cookers do not generate direct heat at the bottom of the pot, as does cooking on a range, so be sure to increase the distribution of heat to the food by letting a substantial amount of food touch the sides of the pot. You will find that your unit cooks more efficiently—and finishes your dish at the time specified by your recipe—when it's at least half full.

Don't Stir

Wondering whether you should occasionally stir the food in your slow cooker? Generally, stirring is not recommended because it can extend cooking time by letting heat escape from the pot. When you cook on "high" for brief periods, however, a little stirring helps to blend flavors throughout the food. Recipes designed for slow cookers will state whether you should— or should not—stir.

Spice It Up

How you add herbs and spices to your slow cooker will make a big difference in the way your food ends up tasting. Use them whole if they are to cook all day with the food. If you're using ground herbs and spices, stir them in about a half hour before your dish is done.

Making Gravy

To make gravy or to thicken natural juices in your slow cooker, you can add flour and water to the juices left in the pot and cook for 15 minutes. However, there's a quicker and easier way: Add a package of minute tapioca to the pot when you start cooking.

Cleaning and Maintenance

Slow Cooker Care

- Always turn the control to "off" and unplug the cooker before cleaning.
- Never immerse the base of your slow cooker in water or other liquid.
- After emptying the slow cooker, fill it with hot, soapy water. Do not use abrasive cleaners to remove stuck-on food; a nylon or plastic scrubbing pad should do the trick.
- To remove stains from nonstick surfaces, use 3 tablespoons of commercially available nonstick-surface cleaner and enough hot water to cover the stain. Then just cook away the discoloration by setting your slow cooker to "high" for 2 hours.
- If you have a stoneware pot and it begins to discolor, simply

wipe the crockery with a soft cloth dampened with vegetable oil.

Almost Cleans Itself

Do stuck-on scraps of food in your slow cooker make you dread washing it? The easy way out is to pour water and dishwashing detergent into the pot and turn it on. In less than an hour, the food will wash away easily.

What Your Product Won't Do

Don't Reheat

A slow cooker is not good for reheating food. For this task, use your gas or electric range or microwave oven.

SMOKE DETECTORS

Getting the Most from Your Product

Place Them Right

Placing smoke detectors properly is crucial to their lifesaving role. Locate them where smoke from a fire is likely to pass, but not near anything that could trigger a false alarm. For example, don't put a smoke detector right outside a bathroom door. The warm air that rushes out after someone takes a hot shower will trigger the alarm. Most important, place them where your family will hear the alarms. In addition, keep these considerations in mind:

- In a multi-story house, put a smoke detector at the top of each flight of stairs, provided that no door or other barrier would prevent smoke from wafting up to this spot.

- Hallways more than 40 feet long require detectors at each end.
- Install a detector in any bedroom where the occupant closes the door at night, smokes, or uses a humidifier or portable heater.
- Install at least one smoke detector on each floor of your house.
- If you have slanting ceilings, mount the smoke detector in a spot 3 feet from the ceiling's highest point.

Test Your Detector Regularly

It's a good idea to test your smoke detector regularly—about once or twice a month. Simply press the test button on the detector. Although it may seem logical, holding a match near the detector—which many people do—is not only unnecessary, it may actually damage the device. Besides, a detector's job is to sniff out smoke, and a match doesn't produce much of it.

Cleaning and Maintenance

Keep Your Detector Detecting

Aside from testing the battery, you need only change the battery and clean the smoke detector to keep it in top working order. Change the batteries annually, and clean the detector at least as often, if not more so. Fortunately, your detector will tell you when its batteries need replacing through some kind of audible (and, on some models, visual) signal. But why wait? The batteries should last about a year, so why not mark a date on your calendar to change them, instead of taking the chance of having them run down just when an emergency occurs? When you install new batteries, also remember to vacuum the dust from the unit.

What Your Product Won't Do

Where They Don't Work

Smoke detectors are sensitive, tricky gadgets. Many things besides smoke from a fire can set them off, so it pays to place them carefully. Locations likely to make it difficult for the detector to pick up smoke, or induce it to give false alarms include:

- Places infested by insects, since the bugs can get in and start the beeper going.
- The area where a wall meets the ceiling or the apex of a peaked roof. These are known as "dead air spaces," areas where smoke generally will not reach.
- Anywhere that it's dirty and dusty. Dirt can set off the alarm, or it may obstruct smoke from activating a warning in a real fire.
- Locations too hot or cold for the smoke detector to function properly. Smoke detectors work most effectively in the general range of 40°F to 100°F.
- Near any source of heat, such as your furnace or kitchen range (keep the detectors at least 20 feet away), or where household air currents will carry that heat to the detector.
- Close to sources of high humidity. For example, keep a minimum of 10 feet between a smoke detector and a bathroom.
- Away from areas in which fans, air conditioners, or any other appliance that moves air is likely to blow smoke away from the detector, thus disabling it.

SNOW BLOWERS

Safety Notes

Safe Snow Removal

Take these precautions when you use your snow blower:

- Replace all worn or cracked parts with parts made by your snow blower's manufacturer. Generic replacement parts, especially the auger shear bolts holding the auger gear case together, can make your machine unsafe.

- Always use tire chains on your tires to avoid losing control of the blower and causing an accident.
- Always stop the engine and disconnect the spark plug cable before replacing any parts or making any repairs.
- Always wear protective clothing and heavy shoes or boots — never sneakers — when using your snow blower. It's easy to slip on ice or snow when operating your machine.
- Keep children away from the snow blower and don't ever let a child operate it alone.
- Never leave the snow blower, for no matter how short a time, without disengaging the auger and drive clutches and turning off the engine.

Getting the Most from Your Product

Raise the Blades

Always raise the augers — the blades that churn up the snow for the blower to clear — to their maximum height when using your snow blower over gravel. To do this, adjust the auger height skids upward.

Even if you take this precaution, however, you may occasionally hit a stone or other obstruction with the blades, snapping the bolts that fasten the augers to the auger shaft. That's why it's a good idea to have an extra supply of these bolts on hand. Be sure to order them directly from the manufacturer or get identical replacements from your dealer, since it's crucial that any replacement parts be matched exactly to your equipment.

Troubleshooting Chart

Problem	*Cause*	*Solution*
Snow blower vibrates excessively.	Bolts are loose.	Examine all bolts and tighten.
Unit is turned on but won't throw snow.	Discharge chute is iced up.	Check chute for ice; chip out ice.
	Oil level in auger gear case is low.	Check and fill with fresh oil.

Troubleshooting Chart—Continued

Problem	Cause	Solution
	Impeller belt is worn.	Check belt for wear and replace if necessary.
	Snow is very wet and causing machine to run sluggishly.	Run engine at a higher speed and put transmission into a lower gear.
Unit is hard to steer.	Oil level in transmission gear case is low.	Check and refill if necessary.
	Tires not properly inflated.	Check tire pressure. Inflate or deflate as needed.

Cleaning, Maintenance, and Storage

Preseason Maintenance

If you regularly perform some simple maintenance tasks, your snow blower should give you many long years of service with very few problems. On the other hand, careless maintenance and storage can cause this otherwise sturdy machine to break down when you need it most. Make sure to perform the following maintenance tasks regularly:

- Before snow season begins, check the oil level in the transmission gear case, and refill with fresh oil. At the same time, replace any leaking oil seals.
- Check and adjust the drive disc clearance, cleaning any grease or oil from the disc with solvent.
- Replace any broken or cracked parts with the same parts made by the same manufacturer only. Generic parts can cause safety problems.
- Check frequently for worn belts or chains and replace well before they wear through completely.
- After each 10 hours of use, lubricate all control linkages, bearings, and chains with lightweight motor oil.

Dry It Out

If you always put your snow blower away when it's wet, it won't take long for rust to form on vital moving parts. Perform this simple task after each use: Wipe all wet surfaces dry with a towel and lubricate as indicated in the maintenance tips above.

Drain the Gas

Before you put your snow blower away for the spring, make sure you drain all the gas from the tank. Otherwise, the fuel could clog sensitive parts of the machine with a sticky residue as it slowly evaporates. Siphon off the fuel still in the tank and empty the fuel line and carburetor by running the motor until it's out of gas.

SPAS AND HOT TUBS

Safety Notes

Tubbing It Safely

Soaking in a spa or hot tub is a soothing way to relax. But danger lurks in these heated bodies of water. Follow these precautions to keep your spa or tub experience a safe one:

- Never let the water temperature exceed 104°F. If children under the age of 5 are going to be using the spa or tub, keep the water under 98°F. Check the spa or hot tub's thermometer and confirm the water temperature subjectively by putting your hand in it before entering the water.
- Don't drink just before you get in or while you are in your spa or hot tub. Alcohol and heat can be a deadly combination.
- Until you get used to spending long periods of time in hot water, limit your stays to about 20 minutes, then gradually increase the time.

- Don't settle into your spa or hot tub directly after strenuous exercise. Allow your body to cool down first.
- Never let children use the spa or hot tub without adult supervision.

Don't Let the Heat Get You

Under certain conditions, prolonged exposure to hot water can cause hyperthermia—a type of shock that can kill you. Children are more susceptible to this reaction than adults; adults who have diabetes, high blood pressure, circulatory disorders or heart disease, and those drinking alcoholic beverages before entering the spa or hot tub or while in it are also at risk.

At the first signs of hyperthermia—profuse perspiration, drowsiness, and a flushed complexion—get out of the water and wrap yourself in a towel or blanket.

Getting the Most from Your Product

Check for Leaks

It's a good idea to check your unit periodically for leaks. Since you have to drain and refill the tub at regular intervals, use these occasions as an opportunity to observe all connections, valves, and so on for water seeping through.

If you've recently purchased a wooden hot tub, there may be some water leakage during the first few days. This will stop once the staves absorb enough water to tighten against the metal hoops on the outside of the tub.

When the Rains Come

If rain has significantly raised the water level in your spa or hot tub, drain the excess water, filter the water remaining in the tub, and check its pH level to make sure it hasn't strayed from the correct range.

You may want to buy a cover for the tub. This not only keeps out rain, leaves, and other debris, but also keeps the water from evaporating and protects children from accidentally falling into the tub.

Cleaning, Maintenance, and Storage

Hose Down the Filter Cartridge

You can usually clean your filter cartridge by spraying it with a garden hose. But if that's not enough to get it clean, do the following:

1. In one plastic pail, mix 1 cup of automatic dishwasher soap with 5 gallons of water; in a second pail, mix 3 cups of muriatic acid with 5 gallons of water. Follow all cautionary instructions on the container of muriatic acid.
2. Soak the filter in the first pail for an hour and then hose it down.
3. Now soak it in the second pail for two hours and wash it off, taking care not to splash any of the liquid containing the acid.

Use Fresh Chlorine

Unless properly stored, granulated chlorine—the most popular disinfectant—does not have a long shelf life. So don't be tempted to buy it by the case. Instead, buy one or two bottles at a time and keep them in a cool place with the bottle caps securely fastened. Avoid inhaling the fumes or touching the granules and wash your hands after using chlorine. If you go away for a week or more, put an automatic disinfectant dispenser in your spa or hot tub.

Maintain the pH

The pH balance of your water—its relative alkalinity or acidity—is crucial to the longterm functioning of your spa or hot tub's electrical components. It also plays a significant role in controlling surface scaling (mineral deposits) in your spa.

Several factors affect the pH balance. Hard water, for example, increases alkalinity, while a chlorine disinfectant will raise the acidity of the water in the tub. Your dealer has chemicals that regulate the pH of the spa water. Use those made specifically for spas rather than anything made for swimming pools.

Change the Water When You Have Suds

Soap film from your skin and bathing suit will collect in the water in your spa or hot tub after about two or three months of regular use, making it necessary to drain and refill the unit. When you change the water, always disconnect the power cord and don't plug it back in until you have refilled the tub.

Winterize Your Hot Tub

Just because you live in a northern climate, there's no reason why you can't enjoy your hot tub year-round. To winterize your tub:

• Buy or build a wooden cover and keep it on the tub when it's not in use.
• Locate your heater, pump, and filter indoors, in a shed, or in a homemade covered wooden box that's lined with insulation.
• Bury the plumbing pipes well below the frost line.
• Once winter sets in, set your tub's thermostat to 50°F and leave it there until spring. Turn it up to 104°F only when you plan to use the tub.

Polish Scratched Acrylic

If your spa shell is made of acrylic and it gets scratched, repair it with an automotive polishing compound. Finish the job with auto paste wax and a power buffer.

SUMP PUMPS

Getting the Most from Your Product

Buy a Backup

During a flood, just when you need your sump pump most, the electricity powering the pump can go out. To avoid the hassle of bailing out the water, you may want to consider installing a battery-powered backup sump pump.

This backup pump, installed either next to or above your present unit, has a control valve that automatically opens when the water level rises, permitting water from your house to flow into the main pump. When the water level recedes, the backup sump pump shuts down automatically.

Troubleshooting Chart

Problem	Cause	Solution
Pump doesn't turn on.	Pump isn't plugged in; power cord is frayed.	Check plug and cord; replace cord if necessary.
Breaker or fuse blows when pump is turned on.	Circuit is overloaded.	Use pump on another circuit.
Pump doesn't pump as quickly as it should.	Float valve is stuck.	Replace float valve.
	Caked-on grime is hampering operation.	Clean and lubricate the pump.

Cleaning and Maintenance

Watch Out for Rust

Since many parts of your sump pump operate under water, rust and corrosion—at least on the outside of the machine—may be a problem. That's why it's important to treat all bolts and screws to a liberal dousing of a penetrating oil so they can still be turned if you need to get at the motor inside.

Regular cleaning and lubrication will help fend off corrosion. No matter what you do, however, there's a good chance that rust will still get to your sump pump. Because of this, parts such as the suction head and the floats will have to be replaced fairly often.

Keep Dirt Away

While the suction heads of the sump pump are usually equipped with a filter to trap any materials floating in the water, you should keep dirt, lint, and other waste away from the sump area. Any foreign matter that gets sucked up into the unit can jam the motor.

What Your Product Won't Do

It Can't Stop Leaks

Finding water in your basement after each heavy rain is not reason enough to go out and buy a sump pump. While the pump will get rid of the water entering the basement, it won't stop the basement from leaking. So before you install a pump, patch up any holes in the basement walls and floor and coat the walls and floor with a good waterproof sealer. Then go outside and make sure that the soil around the foundation is angled *away* from the foundation and not toward it. You may have to berm soil away from the house and plant groundcover to encourage better drainage. If these steps don't eliminate the water problem, it's time for a pump.

T

TELEPHONE ANSWERING MACHINES

Getting the Most from Your Product

Recording Your Message

If recording the message on your telephone answering machine makes you nervous, write it out and rehearse it a few times before recording it. Play some soothing music in the background—both to relax you and to serve as a background for what you're going to say. (Music that's too loud, however, will sound distorted.) The actual message should be whatever you're comfortable with and one that will elicit the information you want from your callers. Make sure you ask callers to leave their names and numbers after the tone or beep. If your answering machine doesn't have a time/date stamp that tells you when the message was received, also ask your caller to mention the date and time of the call. Be sure to never let callers know that you're out of town, on vacation, and so forth. That's an open invitation for a burglary.

Cleaning and Maintenance

Keep the Tapes Clean

Treat your answering machine's tapes with as much care as those that contain your favorite music. Occasionally clean the heads on both the outgoing and incoming message recorders with a cotton-tipped swab dipped in alcohol.

Troubleshooting Chart

Problem	Cause	Solution
Machine cuts off incoming/outgoing message before allotted time is up.	Tapes are worn or heads are dirty.	Replace tapes, clean heads.

Troubleshooting Chart—Continued

Problem	Cause	Solution
Sound on outgoing message is distorted.	Background noise or music is too loud.	Re-record message with lower background noise.

TELEPHONES

Safety Notes

Water and Telephones Don't Mix

You may think of your telephone as a perfectly safe appliance, able to be used anywhere. But you could give yourself and the person you're talking with an electrical shock if the phone gets wet. Never talk on the phone while in the bathtub or while doing the dishes. And it's a good idea not to use the phone during electrical storms; lightning can travel through telephone lines.

Phone Safety for Children

Do you have small children at home? An accident, an intruder, or any other threat to their safety or to the well-being of their caretaker could require them to make a telephone call. While they may be too young to dial a phone or read a name on a programmed phone, your children know your picture when they see it. Put a small photo of yourself next to the phone, with your work number beside it. Tell your children that in an emergency they should dial the numbers for mommy or daddy. You may also want to cut out a picture of a police officer and a picture of a doctor or nurse along with their corresponding emergency numbers and add it to your illustrated phone list. Be sure your children know their complete names, home phone number (including area code) and complete address. Many emergency response efforts are slowed because the dispatcher receives incomplete information from the caller.

Getting the Most from Your Product

Pulse or Tone?

If you have a pulse phone and are wondering if it's worth the few dollars extra per month for tone service, you first must decide whether you want to take advantage of what's available only through a tone line: access to information stored in computers, as in bank-at-home services; and less expensive long-distance services. If you aren't interested in information-retrieval systems and you make very few long-distance calls, you're probably better off sticking with your pulse phone.

You May Be on a Party Line

Before you rush out to by a cordless phone, keep in mind that cordless phones in proximity have been known to interfere with each other. Try to get your dealer to guarantee your money back if you get the phone home and discover that your connection is really a party line or if you are receiving calls meant for someone else.

Save on Service Calls

When phone trouble develops, you might save yourself the price of a service call if you run this quick check first: Switch the troublesome phone with one from an extension and see if you still have the problem (if you only have one phone, borrow one from a neighbor). If the test phone works, you know the problem is with your phone. If it doesn't, the trouble is in the line and you should call the phone company.

Speaker Phones

Once you buy a speaker phone, your room's acoustics become important. Remember that hard surfaces reflect sound. To make using the speaker phone more pleasant both for you and the person you're talking with, place the phone where sound will be absorbed by carpeting, drapes, and other furnishings.

Two people talking at once never makes for a good conversation. But with a speaker phone, it can actually make conversation impossible. The circuits in your unit give priority to the sound with the higher decibel level, and may not reproduce the sound of the softer voice at all.

Static on the Line

Like any electrical appliance, telephones are susceptible to the effects of static electricity. During the winter, when drier air makes static a problem, ground yourself before touching the phone by touching a nonmetallic surface near it.

Cleaning, Maintenance, and Storage

Cleaning the Small Spots

The little holes on your telephone headset through which you hear and speak are ideally shaped to trap dirt and grime. To clean them, unscrew the caps containing the holes and wash them in warm water and a liquid dishwashing soap. Dry them thoroughly before replacing them. If you can't unscrew them, carefully poke out the dirt with a toothpick. Clean between the buttons or beneath the dial with a cotton-tipped stick.

TELEVISIONS

Safety Notes

Know When to Turn It Off

- To prevent damage during lightning storms, unplug the television from the wall. Lightning and power surges may damage the unit.
- If you are away from home for long periods of time, unplug the television from the wall. It's a good idea to disconnect it from the cable system, too, and disconnect the outside antenna.

Not a Do-It-Yourself Project

Today's televisions are complex appliances. Always call a qualified television repairman. Never attempt to repair your unit unless you have been specifically trained to do so. Attempting to do your own repairs can void any warranties you might have and can result in a television that does not function properly. And just the act of trying to take your television apart can expose you to all sorts of hazards — electrical and otherwise.

When to Call for Help

Call a qualified serviceman:

- If the electric cord is damaged
- If any type of liquid gets spilled into the internal workings of the television
- If the television has been dropped or damaged in any way
- When there is a noticeable change in the way the television operates
- If someone has pushed any kind of object through the vents at the back of the television

Placement Is Important

Never place a television near a bathtub, bathroom or kitchen sinks, laundry tubs, or a swimming pool. Always place a television on a stable surface, preferably a table made especially for the television. The vents at the back of a television are for a purpose: to keep it running well and to keep it from overheating. So, never block these vents by pushing the television against a wall or against furniture. Don't place a television over a hot-air register or too close to a radiator. And if you place a television in a built-in storage unit, make sure you provide holes for ventilation.

Respect This Electrical Appliance

Never place a television in a room so that the electric cord is positioned where people can trip over it. Also, never run the electric cord under a rug. Don't overload an outlet by plugging several appliances into it. And never push any kind of object through the vents of the television.

Cleaning and Maintenance

A Damp Cloth Will Do

Before you clean your television, unplug it first. Never use a liquid cleaner or an aerosol product to clean the television. A damp cloth will do the job just right. Be careful not to spill any kind of liquid onto the television.

THERMOMETERS

Safety Notes

Beware of Digital Probe Covers

Digital fever thermometers usually come with a supply of plastic probe covers that fit over the thermometer's tip. While you may want to use these covers when taking rectal temperatures, do not use them when taking an oral temperature, particularly that of a young child. A child can easily choke on the plastic cover if it is swallowed or inhaled.

Getting the Most from Your Product

Use Your Food Thermometer Wisely

Professional chefs never rely on touch or sight to determine the doneness of foods, such as meats, or the readiness of particular ingredients, such as boiling sugar. Instead, they rely on their food thermometers. You can benefit from your food thermometer by using it correctly:

- Never allow the thermometer's tip to touch a bone or nestle into a pocket of fat.
- Never force the probe into place.
- Always warm the thermometer in hot water before plunging it into boiling liquids or hot meats.
- Don't place the thermometer in cold food and then cook the food—you'll get an inaccurate reading. Instead, wait until you're near the end of the estimated cooking time to take the food's temperature.

Boil Your Meat Thermometer

With continual use, your meat thermometer may become less accurate. The easiest way to test for proper calibration is to put the instrument in boiling water: if it doesn't read 212°F, it's off. You can adjust the thermometer (if your model allows for this), make a mental adjustment when you read it (allowing for the number of degrees of deviation you noticed when you tested it), or buy a new one.

Make Allowances

You can't assume that every—or any—spot inside your oven will heat to the exact temperature you specify when you set the thermostat. And if you cook on both shelves, bear in mind that the level of heat on each may not be the same, and that neither may be the right temperature. To adjust your cooking to the peculiarities of your oven, test each rack in your oven. Place your oven thermometer in the center of the middle rack first (where readings are most accurate) and follow this procedure:

1. Pick a thermostat setting and warm the oven for 20 to 30 minutes.
2. Write down the temperature your thermometer records. Take additional readings every 15 minutes for 1½ hours thereafter.
3. Average those readings. If the average reading deviates by more than 15° or so from the temperature you selected on the oven's heat dial, you will have to make an allowance for that difference when you cook.

4. Repeat this for the upper and lower racks to see where the hottest and coolest spots in your oven are.

Take Your Freezer's Temperature

It's a good idea to have a thermometer in your freestanding freezer. You don't want your freezer's temperature to ever exceed 4°F because at that point, enzyme action within the frozen food will alter its flavor, color, and texture. Keep the following in mind when reading your freezer thermometer:

• The temperature will rise when a lot of unfrozen food is added to the freezer.
• You will get a warmer reading near the top of a chest freezer and a colder reading at the bottom.
• You will get a warmer reading near the door of an upright freezer and a colder reading at the back.

Cleaning, Maintenance, and Storage

Wash Fever Thermometers

A fever thermometer, whether digital or glass, should be cleaned one of two ways: wash the tip with soap and lukewarm water, or wipe the tip with a cotton ball soaked in rubbing alcohol. Don't immerse a digital thermometer in water or splash water on the readout.

Wipe Food Thermometers Clean

Food thermometers should not be immersed in water. The best way to clean them is to simply wipe them clean with a damp cloth.

Safe and Secure

Treat all glass thermometers with care. Store them in a safe place, out of the reach of children, and not anywhere where they're likely to be knocked about (such as in a kitchen drawer) or dropped (such as sitting on an open shelf).

THERMOSTATS

Getting the Most from Your Product

Check the Cover

If your furnace isn't kicking on despite a high thermostat setting, check the cover. A thermostat cover that is put on incorrectly or inadvertently struck can jam the thermostat and
prevent the furnace from turning on or off. Take the cover off
and check to see if one or more of the clips that hold it in place is
bent. If so, restore it to its original position. With the cover still
off, rotate the dial to be sure the parts move freely and turn the
furnace on and off. If they don't, you must replace the
thermostat.

Keep Static Away from Programmed Thermostats

Dry indoor air in the winter can indirectly play havoc with your
electronic thermostat. All it takes to erase the program you
laboriously entered into the instrument is for you to walk across
the rug and touch the unit. That spark of static electricity
leaping between your hand and the thermostat can wipe out the
thermostat's directions in an instant.

If this happens to you, take the thermostat off the wall and
remove at least one of its batteries. When the display on the
front of the thermostat has disappeared completely, replace the
battery, reinstall the unit on its base on the wall, and re-
program it. If this is a frequent occurrence, consider buying a
humidifier to keep the static electricity out of the air.

Keep It on the Level

If you've recently removed a mercury thermostat (to paint or
paper the wall, for example) or have removed its cover and now
find that it isn't working properly, it may not be level. Mercury
thermostats must be perfectly level in order to operate correctly. Check the thermostat with a carpenter's level. If it needs

to be realigned, carefully remove the screws from the base and readjust its position slightly until you've got it just right.

Stay Away from Hot and Cold

Few things are as useless as a thermostat placed in a spot where it can't obtain a correct temperature reading. To be sure that your thermostat can determine the actual temperature in your house, don't put it:

- in a recess in the wall, or in an interior hallway
- in a draft or dead spot, such as behind a door or in a corner
- in direct sunlight
- too close to exterior doors, large windows, glass walls, or any other cold-producing areas
- too close to televisions, radiators, heat registers, large incandescent lamps, or any other heat-generating appliances

Turn Down the Heat

Whether you must adjust the thermostat manually or you have an electronic thermostat that automatically sets back the temperature, you *will* save energy dollars by lowering the thermostat at night. For the best savings, turn the thermostat down about 7°, or no more than 10 percent of your normal daytime setting.

Cleaning and Maintenance

Treat Your Thermostat with Care

You can perform simple maintenance on your thermostat because it is easy to take apart. However, keep in mind that the thermostat is a sensitive instrument. When working on it, use a light touch and avoid bending the bimetal coil (the roll of metal that sits behind the dial) and damaging other sensitive parts. Be sure to turn off the power to the heating system at the main service panel before you get started.

Banish Dust and Dirt

Dust and dirt can reduce the sensitivity of a thermostat, causing temperature swings that leave you uncomfortable. Take the cover off your thermostat. What you're now looking at is the thermostat body. This is screwed into the base that attaches to the wall. Carefully dust inside the body with a lens brush (available at camera shops). Pay special attention to the bimetal coil—turn the dial as far as it will go in both directions to expose the surface of the coil. Next, unscrew the body from the base. (Be careful not to bend the bimetal coil.) Take a strip of white bond paper and slip it between the switch levers and the contacts. Move the levers from side to side and slide the paper to clean them. Then remount the thermostat body and attach the cover.

TOASTER OVENS

Safety Notes

A Matter of Inches

Your toaster oven gives off a tremendous amount of heat, especially near the heating elements. If you use glass casserole dishes, keep them at least an inch from the heating coils. And keep the appliance itself at least six inches from the wall or any nearby object.

Lower the Temperature

If you're using your toaster oven for broiling and you hear the grease "popping," lower the oven's temperature. While it is unlikely that a grease fire will start, it's better to be safe than sorry.

Toast and Broil Safely

Follow these safety tips when using your toaster oven:

- Do not immerse the toaster oven in water.
- Do not cover the broiler pan or crumb tray with aluminum foil—it may trap grease and cause a fire or cause the oven to overheat.
- When broiling foods with a high fat content, set the shelf in the lowest position.
- Do not try to dislodge stuck-on food when the appliance is plugged in.
- Never put anything on top of the toaster oven when it is in use.
- Do not use glass covers on pans in the toaster oven.
- Use an extension cord only if you must, and make sure it's rated for at least 15 amps.

Avoid Slow Cooking

While toaster ovens are capable of slow cooking, they are not designed for this cooking method; they are likely to keep food at temperatures low enough and long enough to foster bacteria growth. If you want to slow-cook foods, use a slow cooker, such as a Crockpot, instead.

Cool It

Wait for the toaster oven to cool before removing the oven rack, bake/broil tray, and door for cleaning; and always unplug it first.

Getting the Most from Your Product

The Fewer the Better

Which is cheaper to use: your toaster oven or your electric range? For a few servings, such as four hamburgers, the toaster oven costs less. But when you're cooking for a crowd, your range is not only more convenient but cheaper to run.

Oven Running Hot—Or Not?

Toaster ovens are not terribly exact in their thermostat readings, and extensive use and wear can throw them off even further. Test the appliance by running it on "bake" for half an hour with an oven thermometer inside. A reading that's off by more than 25°F suggests a faulty thermostat. If you observe consistent discrepancies, you can take a grease pencil and re-mark the dial to reflect the oven's true settings.

Use Aluminum Foil

Use aluminum foil for both warming and baking in your toaster oven. When keeping foods warm, cover them with foil to preserve their moisture. Use it for baking when your recipe calls for it, but be sure to tuck the foil under the baking pan so the aluminum will not accidentally touch the unit's heating elements or block the thermostat.

Look Before You Bake

When you bring home a new toaster oven, be sure to test all your pans for fit before you use them for baking. Then store these pans apart from the others so you know which ones to reach for.

Troubleshooting Chart

Problem	Cause	Solution
Toaster oven doesn't heat.	Defective outlet; fuse blown or circuit breaker tripped.	Plug a lamp into outlet to test; replace fuse or reset circuit.
Toaster control won't latch or click into place.	Toaster oven is overheated.	Shut toaster oven off and allow to cool before using.

Cleaning and Maintenance

Keep It Clean

Toaster ovens with continuous-cleaning seem to be the perfect solution for people who hate to clean. But in reality, they are not all that labor-free. No matter what the manufacturers claim, to keep a truly clean oven you must clean it yourself periodically. It's worth the extra effort to clean the inside bottom of your oven to a shine, since this part of the appliance reflects heat upward at the food. Use a nylon scouring pad (never steel wool) and mild detergent or noncaustic cleaner.

Want to make sure you remove food particles that you might miss in a quick cleanup? After the toaster oven cools, turn it sideways and shake out anything that's left inside.

TOASTERS

Safety Notes

Toaster Tips

Even if you've been using a toaster for years, read over these safeguards, especially if you have children who are learning how to use the appliance.

- Use knobs and handles; don't touch the toaster's surface, which can be very hot.
- If toast becomes lodged in the toaster, unplug the appliance, let it cool, then try to remove it with your fingers. Never try to free it with a knife or other utensil. You run the risk of electrical shock or damage to the interior of the toaster.
- Most toaster manufacturers recommend that you move the control to an "up" or "off" position before disconnecting the plug from the wall outlet.
- When cleaning the toaster, don't use any metal scouring pads;

tiny pieces of the metal may break off and cause electrical shock.
- Don't try to stuff oversized food into the toaster; it could start a fire.
- Don't immerse the toaster in water or other liquid.

Getting the Most from Your Product

Shake Out Small Pieces

If a torn piece of bread gets stuck in the toaster's mechanism, pull the plug and wait about 10 minutes to allow the toaster to cool. Then press the handle down as if you were going to make toast, turn the appliance upside down, and gently shake the bread free.

If you want to toast small pieces of bread, keep them from sticking in the toaster by running toothpicks through the tops of the bread. The toothpicks will rest across the toaster slots, keeping the bread from dropping to the bottom when you push down the handle.

Don't Toast Frozen Food

It's best not to toast food straight from the freezer because it will end up being unevenly toasted—well cooked on the outside and still cool in the middle. Instead, let the food come close to room temperature before popping it in the toaster.

Troubleshooting Chart

Problem	Cause	Solution
Toaster doesn't heat.	Defective outlet; fuse blown or circuit breaker tripped.	Plug a lamp into the outlet to test. Replace fuse or reset circuit.
Toaster smokes.	Crumbs are stuck inside toaster.	Clean out crumbs.
Toast is brown on only one side.	Defective heating element.	Have toaster repaired.

Troubleshooting Chart—Continued

Problem	*Cause*	*Solution*
Toaster handle won't stay down or gets stuck when switching settings.	Toaster is too hot.	Let toaster cool down for 10 minutes before using again.
	Pieces of toast stuck in toaster.	Clean thoroughly.

Cleaning and Maintenance

Clean Out the Crumbs

You should clean your toaster every time you use it. Unplug it, turn it over after it cools, and shake it gently. Assuming you use your toaster regularly, clean the crumb tray by brushing it out once or twice a month.

Keep It out of Water

Never put your toaster in water. When cleaning the outside, be sure to unplug the toaster first, then use a damp sponge to wipe away fingerprints and small crumbs. For a shine, use any commercial glass/metal cleaner and a soft cloth.

TOOTHBRUSHES, ELECTRIC AND DENTAL IRRIGATORS

Safety Notes

Don't Brush in the Bath

As convenient and timesaving as it might seem, don't use your electric toothbrush while bathing or showering—after all, it's an electrical appliance that could give you a nasty shock.

Don't Clean under Your Tongue

Be sure to keep the sharp flow of water from a dental irrigator away from the area under your tongue, where it could harm delicate tissues.

Getting the Most from Your Product

Some Things Never Change

Keep in mind that you must still practice certain dental hygiene techniques when using an electric toothbrush. To get the most from your toothbrush you should:

- Hold the brush at a 45-degree angle to the gum line to scrub out food that has lodged between your gums and your teeth.
- Floss as part of your dental hygiene routine—an electric toothbrush can't replace the benefits that flossing provides.

A Spare Brush Comes in Handy

Do you have a spare brush for your electric toothbrush? If you do, you could turn your electric toothbrush into a cleaning device for those hard-to-get-at places, such as around bathroom and kitchen faucets or into corners. It's also useful for cleaning the grime from jewelry.

Not Before Bedtime

When's the best time to use your dental irrigator? Since you should exercise a certain amount of caution when using this appliance, don't wait until bedtime; that's when you're likely to be bleary-eyed and not terribly alert. Try earlier in the evening or first thing in the morning instead.

An Irrigator is Not a Toothbrush

Don't maneuver your dental irrigator as if it were a toothbrush. For best results, use a smooth, continuous motion across the gum line, rather than a brushing one.

Dental Irrigator Don'ts

- Don't use salt water in your dental irrigator—sediment will accumulate in the unit and could eventually cause malfunctioning.
- Don't keep your dental irrigator near radiators or heaters— high temperatures cause the plastic parts to bend or become brittle.
- Don't use glue to secure the tubes to their fittings—runaway glue can wreak havoc inside the irrigator, and the solvents in some glues melt plastic parts.

Cleaning and Maintenance

Flush with Warm Water

If you use a mouthwash in your dental irrigator, flush out the reservoir with warm water after each use. Keep the jet tips clear by washing them occasionally in warm soapy water. You may have to clear them with a thin wire or fine-bristle brush.

Troubleshooting Chart

Problem	Cause	Solution
Electric toothbrush seems sluggish.	Gears are stripped.	First test by running the unit while pushing down on the brush. If you can hold the brush steady and the motor doesn't stall, the gears are stripped. Have toothbrush repaired. If the motor stalls, the gears are fine.
	Unit needs recharge.	Recharge toothbrush, keeping in mind that a completely charged battery will run the unit for an hour, but it takes 13 hours to recharge fully.

TRASH COMPACTORS

Safety Notes

Compactor Cautions

Follow these precautions when using your trash compactor:

- Never allow children to play with the compactor.
- Never push trash into the compactor with your hands or feet. You could encounter broken glass, cut metal, and other hazardous objects.
- Never stick your hands into the compactor for any reason when it is plugged in, even if you have turned it off.
- Be careful of glass shards when you're cleaning the

compactor—not just the interior of the cabinet but also on or in the surface of the bucket.

• If your compactor has a drawer handle, make sure the handle is in place before compacting.
• Avoid spilling liquids into the compactor.
• Do not set hot items or electrical appliances on top of the compactor, and don't use its top as a cutting board.
• Use caution when lifting the compacted trash in a bag. Don't pick up the bag by its sides, and always hold it away from you.

What Not to Compact

Even though your compactor is designed to handle just about anything you'd want to throw out, there are a few items you should never put in the trash compactor. These include:

• Aerosol cans containing hazardous or flammable materials, including hairspray. (Spray cans that contained shaving cream, cheese spread, whipped cream, and the like can be compacted.)
• Flammable items such as paint, lighter fluid, and paint thinner cans; and rags soaked in thinner, paint, or oil. (The vapors from these items could cause spontaneous combustion.)
• Toxic chemicals such as insecticides and other poisonous materials (The fumes from these products are hazardous.)
• Firearm cartridges, fireworks, and so forth.
  If you're unsure about the safety of an item, don't compact it.

Keep It Locked

At their maximum thrust, household trash compactors exert a force of about one ton. The easiest way to keep children from playing with these potentially dangerous appliances is to keep the key that operates it out of their reach. Place the key on a shelf you know they can't get at, or put a key hook in the wall high enough so that it's out of reach even if a child moves a chair or stepladder up to it.

Compact Glass Safely

To keep glass shards from dispersing in your compactor's container, always put glass containers on their sides in the middle of the compacting area and surround them with newspaper. Even better, place the glass in a milk carton or cereal box.

You can avoid being cut by glass protruding from the compactor's disposable bag by wearing a heavy-duty apron and gloves when carrying the bag and always gripping the bag by the top and not the sides.

Getting the Most from Your Product

Load It Right

Misloading the unit is the most common cause of trash compactor failure. Placing a can or bottle on the side, instead of the center, of the compacting area may cause the object to become wedged between the crushing plate and the interior wall of the unit. Should your machine stop for no discernible reason, turn it off, open it, and move everything to the center. And remember, always place bottles on their sides.

Keep It Piling Up

Your trash compactor works best when there is a lot of previously compacted trash in the unit, and then just a small amount of new garbage is added each time. Since the ram only descends about ¾ of the depth of an empty container, it works by flattening new material against already-compacted trash. So, compact trash often, but don't empty the container until it's almost filled—and don't operate the compactor with an empty container.

How Full Is Full?

While there is a physical limit to how much you can have in your trash compactor and still operate it, there's a more practical consideration: You need to be able to close the bag at the top to lift it out for disposal. Try closing the bag before adding more trash to an almost-full compactor. After a while, you'll know when there's enough just by glancing at the compacted trash level.

Prolong the Pressing

You can get the most force from your compactor—and squeeze the most trash into the least amount of space—by prolonging the compacting cycle. If your unit has a setting that allows you to maintain the ram in its down position, use it to press the trash for several hours, even overnight. If you don't have this switch, turn the key to the "stop" position when the ram has reached the bottom of its piston-like action. You can tell when it is at this point by the change in the sound coming from the machine. When you're ready to return the compactor to the beginning of its cycle, just turn the knob to "start."

Keep Your Compactor out of the Cold

The logical place for a compactor is either in your kitchen or out in the garage, depending on where you produce most of the trash you place in it. However, in colder climates, the garage presents a problem; winter's cold can hinder the operation of the unit. If you have an unheated garage, try to place the compactor just inside the house. The ideal place would be a utility room, workshop, or laundry room next to the garage.

Troubleshooting Chart

Problem	*Cause*	*Solution*
Compactor door won't close.	Trash is stuck behind container.	Unplug unit; look behind bucket and remove any trash.
Compactor doesn't operate.	Fuse blown or circuit breaker tripped.	Replace fuse or reset circuit breaker.
	Defective cord.	Check cord for breaks, replace if necessary.
	Drawer isn't firmly shut.	Check drawer.

(continued)

Troubleshooting Chart—Continued

Problem	Cause	Solution
Compactor doesn't operate.	Lock isn't in "on" position.	Turn lock to "on" position.
	"Start" button wasn't pressed.	Press "start" button.
	Motor overloaded.	Let cool for 10 minutes.

Cleaning and Maintenance

Watch Out for Glass

You can be cut by tiny glass shards when cleaning your compactor. To avoid injury, shine a flashlight in the drawer or container and in the rest of the unit's interior before you wash it out. You'll find the glass by its sparkling reflections. Use a stiff brush to sweep it out.

Fight Odors

Your trash compactor is fighting an uphill battle in disposing of most food substances without causing a stink. You can minimize the odor by wrapping food in newspaper before feeding it to the unit, or dispose of such items with your regular garbage. Dirty diapers, raw meat and fish trimmings, even grapefruit rinds, should go into the trash bag, not the compactor. A good rule of thumb: If it's soft enough to squeeze, don't put it in the compactor.

Many compactors come with deodorizers—either aerosol or solid. If your unit has a deodorizer but you're beginning to notice odors, it's time to replace the deodorizer.

V

Vacuum Cleaners

Vaporizers

Video Cassette
Recorders and Video
Cameras

VACUUM CLEANERS

Safety Notes

Use Your Vacuum Wisely

It may seem as though a vacuum is a perfectly safe appliance, and for the most part it is, but you should be aware of these safety precautions when using your machine:

- Never use the vacuum to clean up damp or wet surfaces unless it is specifically designed for this purpose.
- Never use the vacuum to clean up cigarette butts, matches, or live ashes. Sharp objects should also be avoided.
- Be careful not to run the vacuum over its electrical cord.
- Use the vacuum cleaner base only on the floor; don't place it on chairs, tables, or other furniture.
- Switch the machine off before you unplug it.
- Never vacuum in an area where people are using flammable or combustible liquids or where there are flammable fumes.
- If your machine has an automatic cord rewind feature, don't let it spring back by itself. Grasp the plug when disconnecting it from the wall outlet, then guide the cord as it rewinds into the machine.
- Don't vacuum without proper foot protection—that is, not in bare feet, sandals, or open-toe shoes.
- When you're operating the vacuum, guard against getting your hair, fingers, clothing, and so on near the suction intakes and revolving brushes.
- If you have a central cleaning system, don't put any objects into the wall inlets and always disconnect the hose cord before attaching or removing the power nozzle cord.

Getting the Most from Your Product

Scout Around First

Certain objects can damage your vacuum cleaner, so it's a good idea to survey the area you're going to vacuum before you turn on the machine. Sharp items, for example, can damage the dust bag. Fine-textured substances, such as corn starch, face powder, and plaster dust, can act as a seal on the filter, reducing the suction available for cleaning. Small, hard objects such as pebbles can cause serious damage if you vacuum them up and they strike the fan.

When Push Becomes Shove

What do you do when your vacuum cleaner gets harder to push? Check the height adjustment of your unit's nozzle for the kind of flooring you want to clean. If the setting seems right but you're still huffing and puffing, the problem could lie in an excess of suction—say, too much for a particular type of carpeting. Too much suction makes for inefficient and difficult cleaning, because the unit is cutting down on the amount of air (and dirt) the machine can suck in. To correct it, simply adjust the suction regulator, which is usually found on the power nozzle, to reduce the suction.

Cleaning a Lightweight Area Rug

If your upright vacuum cleaner tries to eat up your area rugs while you're cleaning them, try this: Push down on the handle just before you reach the end of the rug; this should lift the business end of the cleaner off the floor enough to weaken its pull on the rug. Move the vacuum off the rug, turn it around, and get the area near the edge of the rug that you skipped; place your foot on the rug's edge and lower the nozzle to the rug's surface, moving the appliance forward over the skipped area.

Don't Keep It Running

Some vacuum cleaners—primarily uprights—work through the action of rotating brushes that sweep dirt and dust into a suction hole so the machine can pick it up. Leaving such a unit in one spot can mar carpeting or bare floors because the brushes continue to rub one spot. Turn off your vacuum if you must stop for a moment.

Replace Bags Before They're Full

Common sense dictates that it's time to replace disposable filter bags when they're full. But here, common sense is wrong. With little empty space left in the bag to help create suction, your vacuum is already beginning to gasp as it strains to do its job. You're getting lowered efficiency and putting considerable wear and tear on the cleaner's parts. To get the most from your vacuum, replace the bags when they're about 75 percent full.

Central Cleaning Systems

The newest innovation in vacuums is the central cleaning system. If you have one, keep in mind the following tips:

- Don't use the flexible hose if you can see the colored inner skin through the outer skin; that means the hose is damaged.
- Don't use the system if the filter is not in place.
- Empty the dust receptacle at least twice a year.
- Clean the filter at least twice a year, more if you've been picking up a lot of fine dust.
- If the cleaner picks up a large obstruction, it may trip the thermal protector and shut the whole system off. Stop cleaning and disconnect the hose if this happens. Wait at least 15 minutes for the system to cool before turning it on again.

Uprights vs. Canisters

Upright vacuum cleaners work best only on carpeting, while canisters work best on bare floors. If you have carpeting *and* bare floors in your home, buy an upright for the carpets, then save yourself money and purchase an electric broom, rather than a more expensive canister, to clean the wood floors.

Get the Most from Your Cordless

If you want to get the best performance from your cordless vacuum:

- Clean out the dirt collection chamber after *each* use. This collection area is small and fills up fast.

• Discharge and recharge the batteries every few months. To completely discharge the batteries, simply leave the vacuum cleaner on until it runs out of juice.

Vacuum Efficiently

To get the most from your vacuum cleaner:

• Empty an upright's dust bag when it's about 75 percent full. After this point, suction diminishes. The same applies to a disposable bag.
• Adjust the cleaner head to the height that produces the most suction when vacuuming level or multilevel pile or textured loop carpets. For cut- and loop-pile varieties, adjust the cleaner head upward for maximum agitation of the pile.
• Work your way slowly across carpeting with short strokes, allowing your machine to pull in dirt from deep in the pile.
• Vacuum each area several times—make about seven passes to be sure—and in every direction. Finish by guiding the unit across the carpet *with* rather than *against* the grain of the pile.
• Vacuum twice a week. If that's not possible, do so at least weekly.

Troubleshooting Chart

Problem	*Cause*	*Solution*
Vacuum won't run.	Plug isn't firmly connected to outlet.	Check plug.
	Fuse blown or circuit breaker tripped.	Check fuses and circuits.
Vacuum doesn't pick up well.	Belt is worn or broken.	Replace belt.
	Brushes are worn.	Replace brushes.
	Dust bag is full.	Empty bag; replace if disposable.

(continued)

Troubleshooting Chart—Continued

Problem	Cause	Solution
Vacuum doesn't pick up well.	Hose is clogged.	Clear hose outside the house by attaching it to exhaust port and blowing out obstruction. If this fails, slide a broom handle through hose.
	Nozzle adjusted incorrectly.	Adjust for correct carpet height.
	Filter clogged or dirty.	Clean; replace if damaged.

Cleaning and Maintenance

Keep the Filter Clean

Canister vacuums have a foam or felt dust filter that sits on top of the fan housing. Remove the filter and wash it in warm soapy water every few months, or more often if you've been vacuuming a lot of dust. Be sure to allow the filter to dry completely before reattaching it.

Test the Brushes

To test the rotating brushes in your upright vacuum or canister power attachment, unplug the machine, then hold a card across the brush opening. Now turn the shaft to which the brushes are connected. If the bristles don't scrape against the card, you need to replace them.

Check the Hose

It's a good idea to check the vacuum's hose from time to time, keeping an eye out for small rips or breaks. You can cover small holes with vinyl tape, but if they grow larger, you will notice a definite loss of suction. In that case, it's best to replace the hose.

Replace a Worn-Out Belt

The belt in an upright vacuum or in the power attachment of canister models is the vital link between the motor and the shaft, which turns the agitator that sweeps dirt into the cleaner. A damaged belt undercuts the effectiveness of your vacuum and puts unnecessary stress on the motor. To locate the belt on an upright vacuum or power attachment, turn the unit over and unscrew or unclip the plate that covers the agitator. The belt is worn out and needs to be replaced if:

- It's stretched—this should be obvious at a glance.
- It's cut—a torn belt can't provide the precise level of tension needed to efficiently transmit energy from the motor to the shaft.

To replace the belt, detach it from the pulley and lift out the agitator. Remove the old belt on the agitator, replace it with a new one, and snap the agitator back into place. Then place the other end of the belt over the pulley on the vacuum. Replace the bottom plate.

VAPORIZERS

Getting the Most from Your Product

Pointing the Nozzle

To use your vaporizer most effectively, point the nozzle toward the center of the room, not directly at the occupant. In addition, take care to keep the mist from flowing directly at sensitive electronic equipment, such as computers, which don't respond well to moisture.

Why You Should Avoid Low Water Levels

As long as there's water in the tank, your unit will produce vapor. But the unit's sensitive parts are more likely to corrode if you run it when the water level in the tank is low. That's because at a low water level, the minerals in the water become more concentrated. To prevent this, simply refresh the water supply in the vaporizer frequently.

Lowering the Steam Output

If you feel the room getting clammy, you need to reduce the vaporizer's output. Unfortunately, many models do not have controls that permit you to do this, or humidistats that allow you to set the machine for a specific level of humidity. But there is one thing you can do. If you have been adding salt to the water to foster electrical conductivity, cut down on the salt and pour tap or distilled water into the unit. This will cut down on the conductivity—and the steam.

Cleaning, Maintenance, and Storage

Cleaning Up Mineral Deposits

Your vaporizer generates heat in its internal parts, so wait until it has had sufficient time to cool before cleaning or storing it. Let it cool for at least fifteen minutes before you handle it.

The very thing that makes this appliance work creates quite a cleaning problem. Unlike most appliances, it thrives on—and needs—minerals in the water it processes. In fact, softened or distilled water undermines the unit's effectiveness. The minerals in hard water allow it to conduct electricity, permitting a pair of electrodes immersed in the water to generate steam. Some manufacturers even tell you to add substances such as salt or baking soda to the water to increase conductivity.

But those minerals do leave a harmful residue, and if they build up too much, they can corrode the electrodes. Prevent this by cleaning your unit often. If you use your vaporizer sporadically, once a month should be enough. But if you use it more often, clean it once a week. In either case, it's best to use a toothbrush or other very small brush dipped in a mixture of vinegar and water to wipe away deposits. You can also soak the components overnight in this solution if stains prove stubborn.

VIDEO CASSETTE RECORDERS AND VIDEO CAMERAS

Safety Notes

Keep It Dry

Never use your VCR—or your video camera—very near a water source, such as a swimming pool. Not only will the machine be permanently damaged by water, but the resulting electrical shock could be fatal. If any of your video equipment is ever exposed to moisture, such as rain or even extremely high humidity, unplug it immediately and have it inspected by a service technician before using it again.

Cleaning Precautions

Always unplug your VCR before cleaning it, and never use any cleaning fluids that could drip into the unit's vents and cause electrical shock. Exposure to large amounts of grease and dust could also cause internal damage.

Keep the Kids Away

The VCR may seem like a wonderful and mysterious plaything to young children who want to stick their fingers or other objects inside. Contact with some inner parts can result in serious electrical shocks, and objects dropped inside can break the machine or cause a fire. So keep your video equipment out of reach of curious kids.

Getting the Most from Your Product

A Timely Tip

Do you like to tape late-night programs for viewing at more reasonable hours? If so, don't take the television listings in your newspaper or *TV Guide* too literally. The program may start later than the schedule says it should, for reasons as varied as public television fund-raising drives, football games, or a presidential press conference. To make sure that you tape the entire program you want, set your VCR to record for at least 15 minutes longer than the program is scheduled to run.

Those Old Home Movies

Do you have old 8-millimeter color movies of the kids (or ones your parents took of you when you were a child)? Get them out of storage before they fall to pieces. Not only are they physically fragile, but the color is also probably already fading. If you had figured on simply using a video camera to copy them from the screen while showing them with your old projector, don't waste your time. It's virtually impossible to make the transfer that way without distorting the image. You're much better off using one of the many professional services that can do the job right. Look for them under "Video" in the yellow pages.

You can convert color slides to videotape with the help of one additional piece of equipment. Buy a tele-cine adaptor at an electronics store. They're not hard to use and they cost less than $50.

Erasure Insurance

To prevent taping over a video recording you want to keep, punch out the tab on the plastic video case after you've made the recording. Removing this lock-out tab prevents a VCR from recording on the tape; it can only play it back. And, should you ever change your mind and want to use the tape again, you can simply place a piece of adhesive tape across the gap where the tab was, enabling your machine to record on it again.

Do Tapes Live Forever?

Your video cassette tapes should last at least as long as you do and, if stored under the ideal conditions, even your children should be able to enjoy them throughout their lifetimes. According to the Electronic Industries Association, tapes won't start shedding oxides (the coating on which the magnetic signals are recorded) on your VCR heads until they have been played about 200 times. And you're not likely to watch *anything* that many times, even the kids' first steps. However, you could easily record that many times on a tape. So if you use one tape just for recording, either keep track of how many times you use it and throw it out when it nears the 200 mark, or figure out some reasonable replacement schedule based on how often you tape.

Don't Record Sun Spots

Don't point your video camera at the sun. Like your eyes, the camera could sustain permanent damage from "looking" directly at such a bright light for more than a very brief time. With prolonged exposure, the sun could burn a permanent spot on the camera's pick-up tube, and that spot will be transferred to every tape you make thereafter.

A Battery Saver

The electronic viewfinder on your video camera is a great feature that allows you to display what you're recording as you're recording it. But it also saps battery power. If you are taping with the camera on a tripod, you don't really need to use the viewfinder after the initial setup, so disconnect it and save your batteries.

Consider a Tripod

Many people think that tripods are only for professionals. But these handy accessories are even more useful to amateurs now that video cameras have become light enough to hold by hand. A tripod comes in handy when your arm starts to grow tired, plus it's the only way you'll get to be part of the film along with everyone else.

If the 5 or 10 pounds the tripod weighs puts you off, consider buying a monopod with only one leg. You still have to be there to steady the camera, but this gadget weighs less than a pound and collapses like an umbrella to fit in a small bag.

Lights, Camera, Action

Video lights are great for supplementing indoor light during taping. They work indirectly by bouncing their rays off the ceiling. If the ceiling or the upper part of the walls where you're taping is painted any color but white, you may be disappointed in the results. If the light first hits a color and then reflects onto your subject, the light will pick up some of that color and it will show up in your tape.

Editing from a Master Tape

With your video camera you can turn out tapes that are much more professional than you ever thought possible (assuming you have a VCR). The secret is in the editing. Follow these steps to assemble a smooth, edited version of the hodgepodge of images you've collected with your camera:

1. Begin with high-quality raw material by using only the best recording tape for shooting. In addition, make sure to run it at the fastest speed setting on your video camera.
2. View the results and set up a "story board" for your editing. To do this, keep track of which segments you want to use, the order in which you will use them, and where they are on your original (master) tape.
3. Play the original tape on the video camera, since playing it on any VCR might introduce slight distortions that you would not want to end up in your edited version.
4. Connect the video camera to the VCR using both audio and video cables, rather than one cable transmitting a signal containing both the audio and the video. This is the highest quality transfer you can make.
5. For clean edits, put the VCR on pause at the end of each transferred segment and quickly locate the next section you

will use on the master tape. Start to play it and release the pause button on the VCR as soon as you come to the spot in the master segment where the edited version should begin.

The Possibilities Are Endless

Now that you have a VCR and have rented movies and perhaps recorded television programs, you might want to look into the endless number of nonfiction tapes available for sale or rent. Most people don't realize that informative and how-to tapes now deal with many subjects besides home exercise. Virtually any subject you can find in books is also covered on videocassettes that can be rented or bought, including: duck hunting, home repairs, child-proofing a house, looking for a job, choosing wines, making homemade pasta, and learning to use a computer. If you've been renting from a small neighborhood store, check the stock of some of the bigger stores in town, and buy a copy of one of the video magazines that runs ads for specific tapes and for catalogues that list thousands of available cassettes for sale or rent. Don't forget your public library and local college libraries. They lend tapes at no cost!

Troubleshooting Chart

Problem	Cause	Solution
VCR is not recording television program.	Connection is loose between VCR and television; tab on cassette case has been removed.	Check all connections and tighten if necessary; check cassette case. If tab is gone, cover space with adhesive tape.
There is no playback picture or picture is streaky.	VCR/TV selector not set correctly; channel 3 or 4 not properly tuned in.	Set selector to VCR; check that channel is tuned in without interference.
Videocassette ejects when record buttons are pressed.	Cassette cannot be recorded on.	If tab on cassette case is gone, cover space with adhesive tape.

(continued)

Troubleshooting Chart—Continued

Problem	*Cause*	*Solution*
Television channels don't tune in.	VCR/TV selector not set correctly.	Set selector to TV.

Cleaning, Maintenance, and Storage

Cleaning the Heads

Your VCR will not normally require head cleaning. It is possible, however, that the heads may become clogged by playing a damaged tape. If this happens, many manufacturers recommend that head cleaning be done by a qualified service technician.

You can also use a head cleaning cassette. Make sure that you read the instructions carefully, however, and don't use it often. Excessive use can easily damage the heads.

Wipe the Cabinet

Most manufacturers recommend that you clean the cabinet of your VCR with a slightly damp cloth or paper towel. Do not use cleaning fluids or aerosols that could soak or drip into the unit and cause electrical shock. Also stay away from any substance containing wax, which could harm the cabinet's surface.

Treat Tapes with Care

Treat video cassettes even more carefully than audio tapes:

- Shelve your library of cassettes as if they were books: standing up.
- Make sure that the take-up spool that holds the tape is on the bottom.
- Either rewind tape all the way before storing it or put it away with the tape wound to the end instead of the beginning. Strangely enough, rewinding the entire tape just before play-

ing it may improve the precision with which it feeds through your machine. All tapes stored for long periods require occasional rewinding as a kind of "exercise" to keep them in good shape. They shouldn't go much longer than six months without this workout.

- Store your cassettes in their original cartons. Better yet, buy special airtight plastic containers for longterm storage to keep them free from dust and moisture. Avoid smoking in the room where you keep your tapes.
- Video cassettes should be stored at a temperature of about 70°F with 50 percent humidity. If you've had a tape outside on a cold day, don't play it until it reaches room temperature. And if you have taken your VCR out of the house in cold weather, don't use it to play tapes until the machine has warmed up.

W

Waffle Irons	Water Filters
Wallpaper	Water Heaters
Washing Machines	Woks, Electric

WAFFLE IRONS

Waffle Iron Precautions

- Always make sure the waffle iron is off and unplugged after you make your last batch of waffles.
- Make sure the unit has cooled off considerably—to barely lukewarm—before cleaning.
- Never immerse your waffle iron in water.

Getting the Most from Your Product

Don't Rush the Waffles

When your stomach's growling in the morning, it's tempting to rush the waffles to the table. But if the waffles stick when you lift the lid to take a peek, they need a minute or two more to cook.

Waffles for People on the Go

If you're a waffle-lover but you just can't take the time in the morning to make them—not to mention cleaning a burnt iron— there is a solution. Cook up an extra big batch on the weekend. Cool them on a wire rack, wrap them in plastic wrap, and then freeze them. On workday mornings when time is short, take the waffles out of the freezer and defrost them as soon as you get up. When you're ready for breakfast, simply pop them in the toaster and *voilà*—instant breakfast.

Troubleshooting Chart

Problem	Cause	Solution
Waffle iron doesn't heat.	Electrical outlet defective; fuse blown or circuit breaker tripped.	Plug a lamp into outlet to test; replace fuse or reset circuit.

Troubleshooting Chart—Continued

Problem	Cause	Solution
Waffles stick to grids.	Grids are not seasoned properly.	Apply thin coat of vegetable oil to grids and heat iron briefly.
	Not enough vegetable oil in batter.	Add more vegetable oil to batter.
	Griddle is opened too soon.	Cook waffles a bit longer.

Cleaning and Maintenance

Season the Waffle Iron

A waffle iron must be seasoned the first time it is used. Simply apply a thin coat of vegetable oil to the grids and let the waffle iron operate, without batter, for a short period of time. No further conditioning should be necessary.

Wash It from Time to Time

There is no need to wash your waffle iron after each use. However, if you must remove burned-on batter, wash the grids in mild soapy water. Never use harsh abrasives. Before using the iron again, you must remember to re-season it.

WALLPAPER

Getting the Most from Your Product

A Tropical Environment

A bathroom has its own moist climate, and it can be murder on wallpaper. To make sure your wallpaper doesn't curl off the wall after the first few showers, brush every joint with clear varnish.

Allow the varnish to dry completely before taking a shower. Another problem brought on by bathroom humidity is mold. If your wallpaper gets moldy, you can kill the mold with a strong solution of chlorine bleach, but as long as the paper continues to get wet, the mold will come back. To prevent this, make sure your bathroom is well ventilated. You can also try wiping down the walls with a towel after a steamy shower or bath.

If you're thinking about papering a bathroom, the best kind of wallpaper to use is a waterproof vinyl-coated paper or fabric wallcovering, applied with an adhesive that contains a fungicide.

One Layer at a Time

As convenient as it may seem to simply paper over old wallpaper, your walls should never have more than one wallpaper layer on them at any given time. No matter how well preserved the old paper may look, you will soon be dismayed to see old seams and bubbles showing through your newly papered walls. So take the extra time to strip the walls before papering again. It's also not a good idea to paint over old paper for the same reasons.

Strip It

To remove wallpaper without a mess, wet it with a roller saturated with vinegar and hot water. Apply several coats of this mixture with the roller. (Vinyl wallcoverings will have to be scored with a fork or penknife to allow the water to seep behind it.) The paper should then be easy to scrape from the wall.

Cleaning and Maintenance

Use Care When Washing

Just because a wallpaper is labeled "washable" doesn't mean you can scrub it. Sponge the paper lightly with warm water, and if that doesn't do the trick, add a bit of mild dishwashing detergent. But be sure to use a light touch—if the paper gets soaked or is scrubbed hard, it may tear.

To clean nonwashable paper, try gently rubbing the soiled area with an artist's gum eraser.

Use Cornstarch for Grease Stains

Luckily there is an easy way to remove ugly grease stains from even delicate wall paper. First mix a paste of cornstarch and water (or a cleaning solvent). Apply the mixture to the grease stain with your fingers or a spatula and let it dry. Then gently wipe off the dry paste. You may have to do this more than once, but it should get the job done.

For light grease stains, try cleaning the paper with a mixture of ammonia, liquid dish soap, and warm water (test a small spot first to be sure it won't discolor the paper). If you're repapering, paint shellac over grease stains to keep them from showing through on the new wallpaper.

Don't Cut Patches

If you must patch your wallpaper, don't cut out the damaged area. Instead, *tear* it out. The thin, torn edges will blend in better on the wall than neatly cut edges.

WASHING MACHINES

Getting the Most from Your Product

The Hard Water Tipoff

Often, the harder the water, the harder it is for your washing machine to get your clothes clean. If you get any of the poor results listed below, you should consider changing your detergent to one specially made for hard water or adding a water softener:

- Dark-colored clothes emerge from the wash with a white residue.
- Whites turn gray.
- Towels have a rough, stiff texture.
- Garments look more worn than they should and seem to have grown old before their time.
- Permanent-press clothes acquire new wrinkles.
- Colors fade and lose their brightness or fade in spots where the detergent has touched them.

Use the Right Amount of Detergent

Wouldn't it be great if you could just use the amount of detergent suggested on the package and not have to give it any more thought? Unfortunately, it's not quite so simple. There are several factors that help to determine the right amount:

- If you don't already know the hardness level of the water in your area, you probably can get that information from your local water department. If not, you may want to hire a private company to check it for you. If the hardness level tops seven grains per gallon, you'll probably need more than the manufacturer's recommended amount of detergent for a clean wash.
- The size of your wash and how dirty it is are also factors to consider. If you know you're doing a load that's especially soiled, or if you're packing more than usual into the machine, increase the amount of detergent.
- You should also keep the temperature of the water in mind. Here's a good rule of thumb: the more delicate the wash and the cooler the water, the more detergent you may need. In cold water, you may need as much as twice the amount you would use at the hottest setting. Experiment to see how much detergent is right for your loads.

When to Add More Detergent

If your clothes simply don't look clean, you've been using too little detergent. Here are two signs that should tip you off:

- Since "ring-around-the-collar" is one of the toughest soil marks to remove, you'll know you've used an adequate amount of detergent when those stubborn rings finally do disappear. But if you can't rid your shirts of those rings no matter how much detergent you add, try a different tack. Shampoo is a soap made specifically to deal with hair oil, the source of much of the grime on your collars. Put some shampoo on the stain, rub the fabric together to work in the shampoo, and then launder.

• If your laundry still looks linty after a wash, you may not have added enough detergent. You must add enough so that the detergent is able to retain lint in the wash water long enough to dispose of it in the rinse. An insufficient amount of detergent permits the lint to adhere to your wash.

Sort the Wash

As you already know, items that are not colorfast don't mix well with light-colored fabrics in the washing machine. But do you also know that:

• Throwing in delicates and knits with clothes containing zippers or buckles can lead to extensive pilling. If you insist on combining these types of clothing, close all zippers and Velcro-type fasteners before they go in the machine. In addition, fasten all hooks and tie all loose strings on your garments. Remove anything sharp, such as decorative pins, from clothes before washing them. Also remember to check pockets twice to be sure they're empty.

• Washing really dirty clothes with those that are only slightly dirty can cause the transference of soil from one to the other. This can result in an overall graying of your wash. For best results, wash small loads of heavily soiled items separately.

Get Rid of Lint

You have to give lint credit for persistence. It seems to be able to stick to everything. But that means that you have to be just as persistent in thwarting it. To keep lint off your clothes:

• Separate clothes that shed lint from those that pick it up. Flannel garments and towels are examples of items that con-

tribute lint to the wash water, while permanent press fabrics and corduroy are prime victims for all that loose lint.
- Separate light and dark colors. Otherwise, dark, sticky lint could adhere to light clothing.
- Don't overload your machine. Lint consists of threads that come off fabrics, mainly through abrasion. When you overload the machine, you increase the amount of abrasion caused by clothes rubbing against each other. Maintaining the right clothing level in the washing machine also gives your appliance the chance it needs to hold the lint in the water instead of depositing it back on your clothes.
- Add enough detergent so that lint will remain in the wash water until it is rinsed away.
- Keep the wash time to a minimum if you've got a small or not very dirty load.
- Clean the machine's lint filter regularly, making it part of your post-wash routine. You'll find that taking care of this task while the filter is still wet is the most effective—and easiest—way of doing it.
- When you wash clothes that you know to be sources of lint, shake them out before doing the laundry to get rid of any loose lint.
- Empty all pockets and brush lint from inside cuffs before you do the wash. It's amazing how much lint will deposit on your entire washload from one little tissue left in a pants pocket.

The Good and Bad about Chlorine Bleach

Want to get your wash really white and maximize your machine's ability to get out stains? If you do, you should choose chlorine bleach over oxygen bleach. However, such a strong substance should be used cautiously. How do you know if you're using it correctly? You will know that you're overdoing the chlorine bleach when:

- Holes and rips, often circled by a yellowish stain, appear without an apparent cause. The garment will also tear easily when worn.
- The fluffy cotton finish on your towels disappears, exposing the weave below.
- The colors of your garments fade or disappear completely.

• You notice red or brown stains on your clothes after washing.

If you experience any of these problems, except the last, you're probably using too much bleach, soaking clothes in the bleach for too long, or accidentally permitting garments to come in contact with undiluted bleach. Red or brown stains, on the other hand, indicate that the chlorine is drawing iron out of your water. If this is the case, switch to an oxygen bleach.

Balanced Bleaching

If used too often, chlorine bleach will wear down just about any fabric, even when the label indicates it can be bleached. The key to getting the most from your chlorine bleach is to use it periodically; between applications, use oxygen bleach to keep away the "grays." You can, incidentally, boost the whitening power of the oxygen bleach if you double the dose.

Oxygen Bleach Blues

Yes, oxygen bleach is safer for use with more fabrics than chlorine bleach, and it is less likely to damage garments. But, not only does it lack some of the power of chlorine bleach, it has no deodorizing or disinfecting action and requires a longer soaking time. Oxygen bleach, like chlorine bleach, *can* run the color of some fabrics. If you have any doubts about a particular fabric, soak a hidden part of the garment—such as an inside seam—in a solution of 1 teaspoon of bleach dissolved in 1 cup of hot water. After about half an hour (less time if the manufacturer suggests it on the package), you will know if the color will run.

A Colorful Problem

Some garments are so brimming with bright colors that they want to share them with the rest of your laundry. This happens most often with sparkling blacks, blues, greens, pinks, purples, and reds. One way you can head off such color exchanges is to buy only colorfast clothes. But to stay on the safe side, launder any colorful piece of clothing separately the first time you wash it. Take special care not to overload the washing machine, and avoid leaving the wash in the machine for a long time after it's finished. Should you find yourself with dye transfer stains, try a bleach—preferably chlorine—or a color remover.

Cleaning Fabric Softener Stains

If you accidentally got some liquid fabric softener on a garment and it's already formed an ugly stain, don't worry—it's not difficult to remove. Wet the stain and scrape it with a bar of soap. Then put the garment back in the washing machine for another go around.

Presoak Limitations

Presoaking your clothes in a solution containing enzymes breaks up the protein in the stain and makes it easier for your washer to finish the job. These presoaks are most successful with blood, certain fruits, gravy, vegetables, milk, and grass. Unfortunately, they won't help rid your clothes of cooking oil, dyes, ink, rust, or motor oil.

Speed Is Essential

Your washing machine is only your second line of defense against stains. If you haven't done preliminary work to loosen those stains before tossing your clothes into the machine, all the washing in the world will probably do you no good. And keep in mind that the fresher the stain is, the easier it is to wash it out. Speed is essential.

If you are in doubt about which temperature setting to use for that initial emergency treatment, *try cold water first*. If you use hot water and the stain turns out to be protein—blood, for example—the spot will set.

A Stitch in Time

Do you have mending to do? Do it before you wash the garments, because the machine's action could further rip and tear the fabric.

Don't Let Your Washing Machine Take You to the Cleaners

Doing the laundry takes a small but noticeable slice out of the family budget. But you can minimize even that with these energy-conserving, money-saving tips:

- Most of the cost of running your washing machine comes from the use of hot water; the cost of the electricity needed to run the machine through one complete cycle is relatively small. So choose warm or cold water for your everyday laundry needs and save the hot water for heavy-duty cleaning.
- Always use cold water to rinse; for this cycle, it is just as effective as warm or hot water.
- Since there's a good chance you will re-launder clothes that don't come out clean, it makes sense to do the wash right the first time. One factor that many people overlook is the proper balancing of the load, particularly with heavy items such as towels and denim. It's worth the 30 seconds or so it takes to distribute the clothes evenly in the tub. This enables your machine to work at peak efficiency, saving you time and money in the long run.

When You *Want* to Be in Hot Water

Doing more than one wash that will require hot water? If you do two such loads in a row, your water heater may not be able to handle the extra demand. Either pause between them or, if you can, alternate hot washes with cold or warm ones.

Troubleshooting Chart

Problem	Cause	Solution
Water won't drain after rinse cycle.	Drain hose has kinks.	Check hose and straighten out kinks, if necessary.
Water leaks from machine.	Hose connections are loose.	Make sure hoses are tightly connected to faucets.

(continued)

Troubleshooting Chart—Continued

Problem	*Cause*	*Solution*
Water leaks from machine.	Drain hose incorrectly inserted in drain pipe.	Insert hose correctly.
Washer is excessively noisy and moves across the floor.	Washer not level; rubber pads not in place.	Adjust leveling feet; place rubber pads underneath.
	Wash load is unbalanced.	Stop machine and rearrange load.
Washer doesn't start.	Electrical outlet defective; fuse blown or circuit breaker tripped.	Plug a lamp into outlet to test; replace fuse or reset breaker.
	Cycle selector not set correctly.	Reset cycle selector.
	Door or lid not shut securely.	Shut door or lid.
Water doesn't enter the washer during the wash cycle.	Hot and cold water faucets not turned on completely.	Open faucets fully.
	Water is being used elsewhere in house.	Wait until other water use has ceased before starting the wash cycle.
	Water inlet hoses are kinked.	Check hoses and remove kinks.
Wash and rinse water temperatures do not match settings.	Hot and cold water hoses are connected to the wrong faucets.	Switch the connections.
Water doesn't drain or drains slowly.	Drain hose is blocked or kinked.	Check hose and remove blockage or kink.
Too many suds in wash cycle.	Too much detergent was used.	Use less detergent.
	Detergent used isn't correct for your area's water.	Change detergents.

Troubleshooting Chart—Continued

Problem	Cause	Solution
	Oxygen bleach is used.	Switch to chlorine bleach.

Cleaning, Maintenance, and Storage

Everyday Cleaning and Maintenance

After you've finished your laundry, always be sure to turn the water faucets off to prevent a buildup of pressure inside the hoses, and leave the door or lid of your washing machine *open* to allow all moisture inside to evaporate. Excess moisture can cause rust and mildew. Then clean the outside of the machine with mild soap and water.

Occasionally, you may want to give the inside of your machine a thorough cleaning. To do this, simply fill your empty machine with hot water and add a gallon of vinegar. Then run it through its full cycle.

Winterize Your Washer

If you have a washing machine at a summer home, follow these tips for winter storage:

1. Make sure there is no water in any part of the machine. Just run the appliance on spin dry for a few minutes to remove all the water.
2. Disconnect the water supply hose.
3. Unplug the machine.
4. Disconnect the drain hose from the pump and drain both the drain hose and the pump.
5. Reconnect the drain hose to the pump.

After not using your washing machine for a long time, you may find that the door is stiff. Don't worry, once you've used the machine a few times, the natural lubrication of the detergent and water will make the door easier to open.

WATER FILTERS

Getting the Most from Your Product

Faucet Filters

Follow these suggestions to get the most from your activated-carbon faucet filter:

- Change the filter frequently.
- Avoid powdered activated carbon—it can release particles of carbon into the water and introduce contaminants. Use granulated or solid block activated carbon filters.
- When you replace the filter, regardless of which type it is, let the water run for about 2 minutes to get rid of any loose carbon particles.
- Run the water for a few seconds before drawing some for drinking or cooking.
- Avoid using the filter with hot water, which impedes its operation.

For the Whole House

If you've decided to install a water filter to serve the whole house, bear in mind that:

- The filter is made only for cold water lines, with a maximum temperature of 100°F.
- Freezing will damage the filter. If you turn off the water to prevent pipes from bursting while you're away, use the water shutoff valve, not the filter's on/off selector.
- You will have to ground your home's electrical system with a jumper wire if it is already grounded through your water pipes.

Keep an Eye on the Pressure

If you have a reverse osmosis system, keep in mind that these units operate properly only when the water pressure is correct.

They will not perform if the pressure is below 35 pounds per square inch (psi). And if the pressure is more than 200 psi, it will compress the filter membranes and reduce the efficiency. It could even cause complete failure. If you have low water pressure, you can install a small pump along with your reverse osmosis system. You can relieve high pressure with a regulator valve.

Cleaning and Maintenance

Replace the Filter Regularly

Because bacteria will grow in wet carbon, it is very important that you replace the filter in your activated carbon unit regularly. Failure to do so will result in bacterial contamination of your water, which could lead to illness. In addition, you should clean the entire unit whenever you change the filter. Wipe the cover and filter body with a solution of one tablespoon of bleach in one quart of water. Then rinse with fresh water.

What Your Product Won't Do

Activated carbon filters will only remove *chemical* impurities from water—they do not remove or kill bacteria. If you have chlorinated municipal water, it is safe to use an activated carbon filter, but if you have a private well, have it tested annually for bacterial contamination. To remove bacteria in water, you must use a reverse osmosis system.

WATER HEATERS

Safety Notes

Lower the Thermostat

If you own a gas water heater and you often draw small amounts of hot water for short cleaning tasks, the water in the upper part of your tank—which is what comes out of your faucet first—will get exceptionally hot. Lower your thermostat setting to avoid drawing scalding water.

Getting the Most from Your Product

Economize on Heat

Just how hot should your hot water be? If you have a dishwasher and it doesn't have a preheater, your water heater should be set at 140°F. If the dishwasher has a preheater, keep the temperature of the hot water heater at 120°. Many people have their water heaters set way too high—around 150° or 160°—which can cause scalding. A cooler water temperature is not only safer but also more economical; for every increase of 10° above 140°F, the cost goes up 3 percent.

Save Money with Insulation

Some water heaters come with insulated tubing—heat traps—on the first few feet of pipe leading from the heater. Hot water naturally rises from the heater into the pipes, even when you're not running the tap. The heat traps prevent hot water from losing its heat via radiation through the pipes. If your unit doesn't have insulated tubing, ask your dealer where you can get it. But don't stop after the first few feet—insulate all hot water pipes between the tank and the faucet. And save even more money by enclosing your tank in an extra layer of fiberglass insulation. The older your unit, the more insulation will save you in fuel bills. Water heater wraps are available at home improvement stores.

Not Enough Hot Water?

If your household regularly runs out of hot water and your tank and pipes are insulated, and you've been cleaning out sediment in your tank (see cleaning tips, below), the problem most likely is one of size or recovery rate. The average family of four uses 70 gallons of hot water a day. If you have a 40-gallon tank, there are about 30 gallons of hot water at the top of the tank ready to be drawn out. You can easily use 30 gallons in one hot bath. The amount of time it takes your heater to produce another 30 gallons of hot water is called the recovery rate. If it takes your heater 45 minutes to do this, that's how long the next person must wait to take a shower or bath. If this is causing problems in your house, consider buying a new heater.

Heat on Demand

A tankless water heater will save you money because it does not store hot water. Instead, it heats water only as you need it. But this type of water heater costs more than twice as much as tank models and it has more limited heating capacities. For example, with these heaters, you could not do the laundry while a member of your family was taking a shower.

Troubleshooting Chart

Problem	Cause	Solution
Burner will not ignite in gas water heater.	Thermostat set too low.	Turn up thermostat.
	Burner is clogged.	Have serviceperson clean burner ports.
Burner flame too high.	Vent is blocked.	Check for blocked vent by placing hand near draft hood. An outflow of air indicates blockage. Check flue outlet for blockage and remove it.

(continued)

Troubleshooting Chart—Continued

Problem	*Cause*	*Solution*
Gas pilot won't remain lit.	Low gas pressure.	Make sure gas shutoff valve and gas cock are turned fully on.
	Flue is clogged.	Check for obstruction and remove it.
	Water heater is exposed to cold drafts.	Check for drafts and eliminate them.
Insufficient hot water.	Low gas pressure.	See above.
	Flue is clogged.	See above.
	Thermostat set too low.	See above.
	Sediment or lime deposit in tanks.	Drain tank completely. (First turn off power at fuse/circuit box for electric heaters; turn off gas for gas heaters.)

Cleaning and Maintenance

Keep It up to Par

Since water heaters use a substantial amount of fuel, it pays to do these maintenance checks every few months:

- Drain the unit until the water runs clear to avoid sediment buildup—as often as once a month if you have hard water in your area; three or four times a year for soft water.
- Inspect the venting systems (on the top of your heater) and the temperature and pressure relief valves (near the top of your unit) to make sure they are operating correctly.
- Observe the burner to see that the gas lights quickly and burns evenly.

WOKS, ELECTRIC

Safety Notes

Wok Precautions

When using your electric wok, keep in mind the following:

• Watch out for hot oil spatters when deep-frying.
• Make sure you turn the wok off after you finish cooking.
• Allow the wok to cool completely before cleaning.

Getting the Most from Your Product

Start with the Right Angle

You'll improve the flavor, texture, and appearance of foods you cook in your electric wok by cutting vegetables diagonally and thinly slicing meat across the grain. Cutting vegetables diagonally not only makes them look more attractive, it also allows them to cook quickly because more surface area is exposed. Thinly slicing meat across the grain allows for maximum tenderness and quicker cooking. And remember to cut your ingredients in uniform shapes and sizes for even cooking.

Peanut Oil Is Best

You can cook with soybean or corn oil in your wok, but peanut oil is the oil of choice because:

• Peanut oil does not overpower the flavor of the food.
• Peanut oil can be heated to the high temperatures required in wok cooking without smoking.

Faster Food

You can cook quickly with an electric wok. The trick, however, is in preparing all ingredients in advance. Slice, chop, mince, or dice vegetables, meat, and fish before you start cooking. Stir-fry cooking is fast cooking, so there is no time to hunt for an item, and then pare and chop it once the process is under way.

Check Oil Temperature When Deep Frying

For best results when deep frying in an electric wok, fill the wok no more than half full with oil and use a deep-frying thermometer to make sure the oil is the temperature called for in the recipe. Clip the thermometer to the edge of your unit, making sure it does not touch the bottom of the wok.

If you don't have a thermometer, you can do a simple test to see if the oil is hot enough. Gently drop a piece of food into the oil. If the food rises to the top and begins to turn brown, your oil is ready for frying. If the food browns instantly, however, the oil is too hot; if the food sinks to the bottom and stays there, the oil isn't hot enough.

Cleaning, Maintenance, and Storage

Caring for Your Electric Wok

To clean your electric wok, remember to always remove the heat control first. Then simply wash the wok with mild soap and water. Most electric woks are made with nonstick surfaces, so nothing further is required. However, if you own an aluminum one, you must recondition the surface with a light coating of oil after washing with soap and water, rinsing, and drying thoroughly.

Rodale Press, Inc., publishes PREVENTION, America's leading health magazine.
For information on how to order your subscription,
write to PREVENTION, Emmaus, PA 18098.